Puritanism and historical controversy

Puritanism and historical controversy

William Lamont
University of Sussex

UCL
PRESS

First published in 1996 by UCL Press

UCL Press Limited
University College London
Gower Street
London WC1E 6BT

The name of University College London (UCL) is a registered
trade mark used by UCL Press with the consent of the owner.

British Library Cataloguing in Publication Data
A catalogue record for this book is available from the British Library.

ISBNs: 1-85728-285-X HB
       1-85728-286-8 PB

Typeset in Classical Garamond.
Printed and bound by
Biddles Ltd, Guildford & King's Lynn, England.

To Lara, Oliver, Ciaran

"I am perswaded there was never poor persecuted Word since malice against God first seized on the damned Angels, and the graces of Heaven dwelt in the hearts of men, that passed through the mouths of all sorts of unregenerate men, with more distastefulness and gnashing of teeth, than the name of Puritanism doth at this day: which notwithstanding as it is now commonly meant, and ordinarily proceeds from the spleen and spirit of prophaneness and good fellowship, is an honourable nickname, that I may so speak, of Christianity and grace." Richard Baxter, *A Christian directory* (London, 1673): quoting a puritan predecessor, Robert Bolton.

Contents

Preface

When I began teaching at the University of Sussex in 1966, all history undergraduate students spent their first term studying why historians disagree with one another. That course was called "Historical Controversy", and it is still running thirty years later. It seemed to me then, as it does now, as good a way as any for students to learn about history. This book is a product of that course, and I hope it will be equally helpful in introducing students to the nature of historical debate. A recurring theme in the chapters that follow is how "puritanism" has often been misunderstood, because American historians in particular have been over-reverential in their approach to those whom they saw as their Founding Fathers. Perhaps there is displaced envy at work here that should be taken into account? The Sussex Founding Fathers placed those who came after them in their debt, not only for devising "Historical Controversy", but for a commitment to interdisciplinarity and small-group teaching that are not at present politically fashionable but that seem to me nevertheless to be what higher education is about. Nobody was rude enough to say that the rot set in with the 1966 faculty intake, but one could still feel crushed as a newcomer by the recognition of what had gone before. What better compensation for such feelings then than a whiff of parricide? Hence, perhaps, an excessive zeal may have been taken in the chapters that follow to demonstrate that Founding Fathers are not always what they are cracked up to be. My secretary, Anne Woodbridge, however, is everything that she is cracked up to be: she has once more grappled with my handwriting to produce a superbly professional typescript. My greatest debt remains to the successive generations of students who have taught me about "Historical Controversy", and much else besides.

Chapter One

Introduction

Thomas Fuller had wanted to banish the word "puritan" because of its imprecision. He said so in *The church history of Britain*, published in 1655.[1] Even earlier, in 1641, Henry Parker in his *A discourse concerning puritans* related the linguistic confusions of the term to the political convulsions that were about to occur.[2] So Fuller and Parker could be counted among the first of the abolitionists. They would not be the last. But the inadequacies of the word have not ensured its extinction. Raphael Samuel has shown in the last 200 years how its meaning has shifted in time and space (he notes how the term "changes colour and complexion when it crosses or recrosses the Atlantic", for instance), and his prolific range of examples of the use of "puritan" stretch from Islam fundamentalism to Laura Ashley and Habitat.[3] His essay begins with the unassailably modest assertion that "'Puritan' is an unstable term";[4] a holiday tourist might make a similar observation of Mount Vesuvius. No abolitionist has put the case against the use of the word with more eloquence than the historian C. H. George in 1968:

> much of the literature on puritanism has since Weber concentrated on determining the relationship of the undefined abstract "puritanism" to such undefined or non-historical abstracts as "capitalism", "the spirit of capitalism", "democracy", "individualism", "liberty", "revolution", "science", "Anglicanism", "progress" – even "modernity"....[5]

This is no bad description of the book that now follows. True, the relationship between "puritanism" and George's shopping-list of abstractions is not followed to the letter; some fall by the wayside,

1

fresh ones are taken up. But how can such an enterprise be possibly justified in the teeth of George's critique of what he was to call "manic abstractionism"?

This book offers three justifications for embarking on this risky venture. First, to satisfy historical curiosity. There can be all sorts of reasons why the student of history is drawn to England in the seventeenth century, but at least one of them (and a legitimate one) is the belief that this was the time when major changes took place that shaped our future development as a nation. Many of these perceived changes are contestable: was this indeed the time when magic was expelled from the universe, the scientific revolution began, capitalism drove out feudalism, liberty was enthroned, and so on? If any of these assumptions are correct, are any of them interconnected, and if so is the common denominator to be found in the activities of a group (how large?) of particularly fervent Protestants, however we choose to label them? No book – and certainly not such a short one as this one – can provide the conclusive *answers*; but more modestly it can try to show how historical research is currently changing our perception of these *questions*.

Secondly, we can try to give the term "puritan" a little more stability. Why not go further, and junk it? George tried himself to do just that – "the Protestant mind" became his substitute for "puritan".[6] Yet it didn't do the job. It was too wide. All puritans were Protestants certainly, but not all Protestants were puritans. Another historian, Michael Finlayson, wrestling with the same problem, argued that the essence of "puritanism" was simply anti-Catholicism.[7] This was, however, a necessary, but not sufficient, condition. Just how necessary will become clear in the chapters that follow: if there is one thing that historians of a previous generation have got wrong more consistently than anything else, it is in underrating the force of anti-Catholicism in the seventeenth century, and to that extent Finlayson's contribution is helpful. But it is still too negative: it defines the Antichrist, not the New Jerusalem. We can say the same even of the most subtle recent suggestion of an alternative: Professor Davis's "antiformalism".[8] There are rich possibilities that Davis milks from examining the term, but it can't – which he recognizes – any more than "puritan" make for greater precision: if in the old sloppy dispensation unlikely candidates such as Henrietta Maria and Bishop Joseph Hall could be claimed for "puritan", in the new disposition, "anti-formalists" (many of them, at least) would see Oliver Cromwell as *the* "formalist" *par excellence!*[9]

But if we can't come up with a better word, and if (as Raphael Samuel shows) we will go on incorrigibly using it anyway, we can adopt a different strategy, and this is in fact the one to be adopted in the rest of this book. George's lament was not *just* about that "undefined abstract, 'puritanism'". That too, but his complaint was wider in scope, striking at the process of "reification" itself, whereby concepts (whether well- or ill-defined) are separated from the experience of the living persons associated with them. In a word, too much puritanism, not enough puritans. Scott Fitzgerald had been there first: "Begin with an individual and before you know it you find that you have created a type; begin with a type, and you find that you have created – nothing."[10] Perhaps it was because controversialists, from Weber onwards, began with the type that nothing, at least in George's view, was in the end created? This book will begin with individuals in the first section, and only in the second section will it try to relate their experiences to the big questions that students will continue to want to ask.

Thirdly, there are three individuals who can be offered as case studies. The present writer has made detailed studies of them elsewhere. But, in the next three chapters, the readers can quickly familiarize themselves with the outlines of three extraordinary lives, and then in the rest of the book try to relate their experiences to the abstract questions (or some of them) that C. H. George had identified in his jeremiad. But here's the rub: these are (it has just been conceded) *extraordinary* stories, and so in what sense can they then be held to be representative of "puritanism" as a whole? To break with a "type" is one thing, but it is a poor exchange if we only end up with three "atypical" individuals.

There are three puritans at the centre of this book. One is William Prynne, a lawyer who lost his ears twice. Another is Lodowicke Muggleton, the tailor who founded a sect that only died out in 1979. The third is Richard Baxter, a divine who suffered at the hands of Judge Jeffreys. We will see striking differences between all three, but nothing of the sort to make the application of the epithet "puritan" to any one of them seem perverse. The problem runs the other way. The only definition of the word that will be aired here is that of H. L. Mencken who described "puritanism" as "the haunting fear that someone, somewhere, may be happy". This is witty, but surely well over the top? But then, as if on cue, step forward William Prynne. When listing "the universall overspreading still-increasing evills" of his England of 1633, he added to stage plays (the subject of his pamphlet *Histriomastix*) "Dancing, Musicke, Apparel, Effeminacy, lascivious Songs" and – yes – "Laughter". But then we have Richard Baxter and a fellow "grave divine" stuffing themselves into the bottom of their pew so that the rest of the congregation wouldn't see them giggling helplessly at the anecdotes of a particular crowd-pleasing preacher.[11] We also have Oliver Cromwell, in the last year of his life, celebrating his daughter's wedding by daubing the stools, on which the women guests were to sit, with "wet sweet-meates".[12] These episodes don't throw up "puritan" Prynne against "anti-puritan" Baxter and Cromwell; rather, what they do is expose the myth of one monolithic "puritanism". This was the problem that Martin Butler confronted when he tried to make sense of puritan attitudes to the stage in the 1630s. So powerful a shadow had been cast over the project by Prynne's formidable presence that – despite all the evidence to the contrary of skilled puritan use of "opposition" drama – it was assumed by many historians that *a* puritan response to theatre (Prynne's) was *the* puritan response to theatre.[13] A safeguard against such stereotyping in what follows is the very diversity of our three puritans. But that diversity has not encouraged even the most ambitious of revisionist historians (yet) to go so far as to deny that any one of the three is a "puritan" (however loosely defined that term is).

If the reader then is asked to take on trust that they *are* "puritans", he or she should not go on to take on trust anything else: neither the sources that were used to reconstruct their lives, nor the way this particular historian, or any other, has gone about the task of reconstructing from them. First, on the sources. The three puritans were not even-handed in what they left behind. William Prynne left behind a voluminous collection of published writings. The present writer's claim to have read them all, given their turgid, repetitive quality, is therefore less a scholarly boast than the claim for an entry in the Guinness Book of Records. What did not survive were personal papers on his death in 1669. We know that Archbishop Sheldon's agent, Jonas Moore, dined with Prynne's brother-in-law, George Clarke, in October of that year and sought access to surviving papers.[14] A few months later, two antiquarians, – Anthony Wood (who we shall see later on was introduced to the world of historical manuscripts by Prynne) and

Sir Thomas Dugdale – were lamenting the disappearance of that personal archive, which has never in fact been recovered.[15] This skews our reading of Prynne: we know him only through the public record. Lodowicke Muggleton, on the other hand, left behind a number of printed works (though nothing like Prynne's output), as well as a posthumous autobiography and a mass of private correspondence. The posthumous autobiography was largely ignored, however, until the Unitarian historian A. P. Gordon used it as the basis of a lecture on the Prophet and his sect in 1869.[16] The sympathy he displayed to the group on that occasion earned him an invitation to their annual dinner and subsequently, crucially, a week's access to their private archive. Two of the sect's leading members, the Frost brothers, had already printed some of the archive letters and other publications in the nineteenth century, but it was not until the twentieth century that the whole archive itself would be opened up to general scholarly scrutiny.

Richard Baxter seems privileged in comparison to the other two. He wrote a lot (like Prynne), he corresponded a lot (like Muggleton), and his private papers were accessible, along with his printed pamphlets. Like Muggleton, he even left behind a posthumous autobiography, but far from its being ignored, it has become a much-loved, and ransacked, source for historians. The problems Baxter posed were different, then, but no less formidable, as it turned out. The private papers were there, but were hardly ever consulted. One of the best of his twentieth-century biographers, F. J. Powicke, disarmingly confessed to a perfunctory consultation because of the illegibility of Baxter's hand, and the fact that much of the material was concerned with things "utterly dead and done with".[17] In a similar spirit, another early twentieth-century historian, E. Hockcliffe, would justify a truncated edition of another puritan minister's diary (Ralph Josselin's) in 1908 on the grounds that "many entries were of no interest whatsoever . . . trivial details of everyday life". With pardonable exaggeration, a later Josselin biographer, Alan Macfarlane, would say that "it is precisely such 'trivial details' which interest many historians most of all". He then went on to prove his point by writing a masterpiece (which even so – for other reasons – did not draw on the "full" Josselin).[18] Gordon made his mark on Muggletonian historiography by the respect he gave to Muggleton's posthumous memoirs; conversely, it was the respect given by historians to Baxter's posthumous memoirs that stood in the way of their seeing him whole. One historian went so far as to speak of "the almost religious reliance" historians had placed on them – and she wasn't intending this as a criticism.[19] But this was to ignore why he wrote them (retrospective special pleading), when he wrote them (under the constraints of Restoration censorship), and editorial tampering with what he wrote (Sylvester and Calamy, his first two editors, selected material for party advantage). What got lost in all this was the proper recognition of the centrality of Baxter's anti-Catholicism. This is particularly easy to do when the reader is consulting not even the Sylvester or Calamy editions of *Reliquiae Baxterianae*, but the more generally accessible *Everyman* edition compiled by the Reverend J. M. Lloyd Thomas in 1925. The new *Everyman* edition of 1974 has a good introduction by N. H. Keeble, but the text is still Lloyd Thomas's abridgement. New light has recently been thrown upon Lloyd Thomas's criteria for selection by a communication from one Margaret Phelan.[20] Her late husband had been interested in the stir created in Roman Catholic circles by a break-away movement among Unitarians at the beginning of the century, called *The Free Catholic Movement*. Lloyd Thomas was its leader, then minister at High Pavement Chapel, Nottingham, and from 1912 minister at the Old Meeting in Bristol Street, Birmingham. He admired Baxter's ecumenism, and his publication in 1907 of *A Free Catholic Church* acknowledged Baxter's influence as its central inspiration. By 1916 the group was publishing its own monthly magazine, *The Free Catholic*. The defection of a key member to Roman Catholicism in 1932 was a severe blow, and though Lloyd Thomas did not follow suit (despite speculation that he would), and remained uneasily within the Unitarian fold until the Old Meeting was destroyed by enemy bombs in 1941, his editorship of Baxter's memoirs is to be seen as part and parcel of a life-long commitment on his part to closer relations with Rome.

Later nonconformity has had problems coming to terms with seventeenth-century puritanism. Lloyd Thomas may be an extreme case of mistaken empathy; in a more venial form, Gladstone as prime minister would sit down of an evening for a perusal of Muggletonian hymns. But Caroline Hibbard, in her study of Popish Plots, showed how embarrassed S. R. Gardiner – our greatest of all puritan historians – became, when he encountered the force of anti-Catholicism in his forebears.[21] Hockliffe's deodorized Josselin would honour his evangelical piety, but not his interest in witches, the millennium and his own suppurating navel.

We seem then to be reverting after all to Finlayson's argument that "anti-Catholicism" would be a good substitute for this cloudy thing called "puritanism". There would be less chance then of the Hockliffes and Lloyd Thomases deluding themselves, as well as their readers, into the fantasy that seventeenth-century Protestants spoke the language of *their* contemporaries. But then, in putting anti-Catholicism back at the centre of the stage (which is where it belongs, as we shall see in all the subsequent controversies about puritanism discussed later), we may, in our turn, perpetrate a further distortion. We may import our own value judgements and then make Baxter appear as some sort of Paisleyite *avant la lettre*. And then we will be confounded by the fact that the instrument of Baxter's conversion would be a Jesuit book (even if one amended by a Protestant[22]), that he went wholly against the Protestant grain in denying that the Pope was Antichrist, and that his great mentor was Hugo Grotius (whose Dutch hand he nevertheless saw behind most Popish Plots of the seventeenth century).[23] Moreover, if Lloyd Thomas's maverick brand of Unitarianism made him the wrong man to interpret Baxter for us, Gordon's Unitarianism made him the *right* man to interpret Muggleton. When Gordon came to London he came under the influence of Robert Brook Aspland, editor for many years of the most influential Victorian Unitarian journals.[24] Aspland's cousin, J. D. Aspland, was a leading Muggletonian, and the man who invited Gordon to the sect's dinner. We know now from the recovered archive how important Unitarian (even Deist) influences were on later Muggletonians, and it was these shared beliefs that were to provide the entry for the historian into the life of the sect.

How far, in this introduction, have we now met C. H. George's objections to historical controversies about puritanism? We have accepted that the term itself is hopeless; we have only argued that no alternative is better. We have accepted that abstractionism, in his words, can be "manic"; we have tried to avoid this by focusing on three individuals – who will be the points of reference for all subsequent discussions in this book. We cannot prove the "puritanism" of all three, but no serious historian has ever argued the opposite. Though the next three chapters give their life stories in straightforward narratives, we have not concealed in this immediate discussion the treacheries of the sources at the historian's disposal (and these all have their own implications for the debates that follow). And what of the treacheries in the historian's *use* of these sources? Baxter's various editors (Sylvester, Calamy, Lloyd Thomas), as we have shown, raise that problem in an acute form. But not acute enough for C. H. George. His worry about controversies on puritanism relates not simply to the religious partisanship of those who wrote on that subject, although he worries about that too. He sees the theme as particularly seductive, however, to what R. G. Collingwood called "pigeon-holers": historians anxious to iron out complexities by fitting their facts into some preconceived pattern. Weber-and-puritanism was a particularly lethal cocktail in the eyes of C. H. George.

Some support for this gloom is provided, indirectly but revealingly, in the recent howler perpetrated by a fellow scholar. Alister McGrath has provided an excellent scholarly introduction to Reformation thought, already now deservedly into its second edition. He strays outside his own specialist field only to offer brief thoughts near the end of the book on the rise of capitalism. He says that Weber "associated this new attitude with the rise of Protestantism" and goes on: "It was particularly well illustrated by a number of seventeenth-century Calvinist writers such as Benjamin Franklin".[25] Wrong century, wrong religion. But if we turn to Weber himself, we can see why that wrong inference was made:

> If we thus ask, *why* should "money be made out of men", Benjamin Franklin himself, although he was a colourless deist, answers in his autobiography with a quotation from the Bible, which his strict Calvinistic father drummed into him again and again in his youth: Seest thou a man diligent in his business? He shall stand before kings (Prov. xxii 29).[26]

There are three points of interest about this passage. First, the wonderful parenthetical concession – "although he was a colourless deist" – makes the *defiance* of his father's theology seem to be less important than the *fact* of his father's theology. Secondly, the biblical text becomes a metaphor for the standing of the "man diligent in his business" in Weber's text. In *Franklin's* text, however, it becomes something different: a self-congratulatory itemizing of the five Kings he would eventually stand before (and one of whom he would even sit down to dinner with).[27] Prometheus becomes Pooter. Thirdly, Franklin's father becomes the guarantor of his "puritanism". Another controversy, another "puritan". Christopher Hill – more truly perhaps the pupil of Weber than Marx? – sees links between puritanism and science, as well as between puritanism and capitalism. Bacon is as important to the one thesis as Franklin to the other. But similar problems arise: what sort of puritan was Bacon? Not much to go on here, but he does have a devoutly Calvinistic mother.[28] Which prompts thoughts of the marriage made in heaven – Bacon's Mum and Franklin's Dad – and what would be their progeny? Why, the perfect puritan/capitalist/scientist. Similar thoughts are raised by Christopher Hill's essay on "William Perkins and the poor". Perkins, the great Elizabethan puritan casuist, had much to say on the poor. Hill draws up a formidable list of statements, culled from his sermons, to show how the puritan equated justification with material success. It is what any reader of Weber would expect to encounter. Then, however, comes a confession: "I am selecting unfairly", and then follows a three-line (undocumented) statement of the opposite view to be found in Perkins' sermons. Thus we would seem to be back to square one, but that is not how Hill resolves it:

> But I suspect that many good bourgeois in the congregations of Perkins and his followers would follow the same principles of selection as I have done: the new concessions would be noted, the traditional qualifications would be forgotten, as with Calvin's shift of emphasis in dealing with usury.

Perkins is thus in the end convicted, not on the balance of the evidence cited, but on a twentieth-century historian's hunch that he and the seventeenth-century "good bourgeois" were on the same wavelength.[29]

No historian is neutral. We all carry with us some ideological baggage. Edward Thompson called himself "a Muggletonian Marxist"[30]; I'm not even "a Muggletonian non-Marxist" (though students have sometimes suggested as much). To these puritan controversies at least I can say that I don't bring with me either a Weber master-plan or a Lloyd Thomas secret religious commitment. But I do have a sympathy with the puritans: why else would I have spent a lifetime writing about them? The reader should keep that bias in mind, when I try to sort out puritan contributions to such abstractions as "revolution" or "liberty" later. David Underdown best encapsulated the puritan appeal for me in the introduction to his recent study of seventeenth-century Dorchester:

> I also grew up in a time – the 1940s – when to many people it seemed possible that we might be able to build a better world, and that there was something else to life beyond the mere pursuit of our own self-interest. Once again, the differences between seventeenth-century Puritans and twentieth-century democratic Socialists are too obvious to be worth mentioning. But having shared something of that vision of a better society makes it more possible for me to appreciate how others with a very different vision may have been motivated.[31]

Underdown is too good a historian to let his sympathy with John White's efforts to make Dorchester into a Geneva blind him to the downside of that rigour, or to withhold sympathy in turn from White's appalling (but appealing) unregenerate enemies and victims, the Pouncey family. Similarly, I hope that I have not been too indulgent to my own puritans. Finding myself next to Prynne at the dinner table, I would have reacted with the same irritation as Pepys did, on being regaled with stories of naughty nuns. I would have responded, as Coleridge did, to Baxter's revelations about the "Popish Plot" to kill Charles I: "The Pope in his Conclave had about the same influence in Charles's fate as the Pope's eye in a leg of mutton."[32] And I would not have found attractive Muggleton's path to serenity: a daily bout of cursing enemies to damnation (a sort of spiritual jogging). But I am impressed when Prynne, ears dangling after a botched mutilation, responds with these lines: "the more I am beat down, the more am I lift up". Baxter's vision of a primitive Christianity "when the Spirit of Love made the Christians sell all that they had and live in common" seems, to me, a noble one.[33] When Muggleton breaks a lifetime of trembling before a vengeful God to embrace the proposition that "if there were no God yet could I not doe any otherwise than I do", his words seem to me impressively liberating.[34]

All of which is only to say that I, as much as Underdown, am a child of the 1940s. I have argued elsewhere for recognition of affinity of mood between the 1650s and the 1940s. For the Common Wealth movement of the 1940s read the "Commonwealth" commitment in writers as diverse as Baxter, Muggleton, Harrington and Winstanley; for Beveridge and Tawney, read Comenius, Durie and Hartlib.[35] It was an affinity that the 1940s themselves recognized. Whom does L. S. Amery turn to but Cromwell, in May 1940, to speak for the nation: "You have sat too long here for any good you have been doing. Depart, I say, and let us have done with you. In the name of God, go." But less well known is the fact that advertisements in wartime for shoe polish were adorned with a portrait of Cromwell, under the reassuring title, "The Great Protector". Good shoes, the copy ran, "*deserve* PURITAN leather shoe" protection, while "others *need* them": thus making a profound theological distinction on how "godly rule" served elect and reprobate alike. Protection was also very much in the mind of those who compiled the Army Officers' Manual in 1941.[36] Officers were told that it was important to have men under them who "know what they fight for and love what they know". The famous phrase is not attributed here to Cromwell; it doesn't have to be – itself a remarkable comment on shared cultural assumptions. It is more remarkable still when one reads Paul Fussell's account of World War Two morale and propaganda, and learns how extreme was the backlash against the high-flown rhetoric of the previous world war. He calls his tenth chapter simply "The ideological vacuum",[37] but it is clear even from these examples we have given that there were some, at least, around at the time who knew where to turn to, in order to fill it. And, we might say, if "puritanism" saw off Hitler, what hope had C. H. George?

Part I

Puritans

Chapter Two

William Prynne (1600–1669)[1]

By permission of the British Library.

William Prynne was born in Swainswick, outside Bath. He came from a well-to-do family. He was the grandson of an Elizabethan Mayor of Bath; a fact that he dragged into many of his pamphlets (though not by the ears). He went to Bath Grammar School in 1612, and from 1616 to 1621 attended Oriel College, Oxford. There is no evidence that he was a firebrand at university: a mitigating point urged in his petition to his great enemy, Archbishop Laud, in 1634. In 1621 he went to Lincoln's Inn to read law. In 1628 he was called to the Bar, and had begun his flood of pamphlets.

Prynne in his career would write more than 200 pamphlets. "Pamphlet" is a very loose term: it could mean a few pages, or, as in the case of *Histriomastix*, a thousand pages plus. We know how he worked, from the description given by John Aubrey. He had a set routine. He wore a long quilt cap, two or three inches over his eyes, to protect them from the light. A servant would bring him a roll and pot of ale every three hours, to revive his spirits, and he would study and drink into the early hours. Prynne was solemn, prolix, and packed with footnotes: perhaps the first modern historian. His style was distinctive. The pages of text were supplemented by copious marginal annotations; this was true even of his verse, and earned him his nickname "Marginal" Prynne. Milton said of Prynne, "I will expect other arguments to be persuaded of the good health of a sound answer than the gout and dropsy of a big margent, litter'd and overlaid with crude and huddl'd quotations". But from Prynne he didn't get it.

Why did he write so much? An anonymous critic shrewdly noted the obsessional nature of his writings: "as necessary as meat and drink – a thing without which he cannot live". What was he obsessed about? Chiefly the innocence of England in the 1630s, which slept while Popery advanced. Prynne's task was to rouse Protestant England from its slumbers, and he had formidable gifts to offer in that direction. One critic spoke of his having "the Countenance of a Witch". Another spoke of "his long meager face . . . ears cropt close to his head, which is stuft with Plots". Prynne believed that the Jesuits were everywhere and could "metamorphose themselves into any shape". In the world of magic, which historians like Sir Keith Thomas have opened up for us, these statements are not rhetorical, and represent stone sober conviction.

Prynne saw Papist activity behind England's moral decline. That decline was catalogued in a number of pamphlets in the 1630s. First, there was the length of Englishmen's hair. *The unloveliness of love locks* – (Prynne was good on punning titles, but he tended to use up his humour on them) – became a diatribe against Caroline Teddy Boys:

> Alas! may I not truly say of too many, the Barber is their Chaplain; his Shop, their Chapel; the Looking Glass their Bible; and their Hair and Locks their God. Would they not rather have the Common-Wealth disturbed, than their Haire disordered?

One of the many ironies of Prynne's career was that, as a result of the mutilation of his ears, he would have to wear *his* hair long for the rest of his life to conceal the disfigurement; a fact noted with pleasure by opponents.

Drink prompted another Prynne pamphlet, and another punning title: *Healthes sickness*. He attacked the custom of loyal toasts, by which you were obliged to honour the entire members of the royal family. If you didn't, you were disloyal; if you did, you were horizontal. He went on, in other writings, to attack ostentation in Church ceremonies (like bowing at the name of Jesus), the profanation of the Sabbath with sports, and the retreat from Calvinist doctrines of predestination. On the latter point he commented that, to question Calvin on Grace, was like questioning that the Sun went round the Earth just because "one brainesicke Copernicus out of the Sublimitie of his quintessential transcendental speculations hath more senselessly than metaphysically, more ridiculously than singularly, averred it". Heliocentrism is thus dragged into a doctrinal argument by this puritan as a *reductio ad absurdum*: so much for the natural convergence of the Puritan and Scientific Revolutions.

Now Prynne believed that all these evils of the age were not merely coincidentally happening when William Laud dominated the religious scene. For Laud was a Jesuit in disguise. The barbs got home: read the correspondence of two of Laud's intimates, Montague and Cosin. Nevertheless it was not until 1633 that Prynne gave his enemies the chance to strike. His weighty hostage to fortune, *Histriomastix*, was the most ambitious writing he had attempted at this stage: nothing less than an attack on all plays that had ever been written. This was not quite true. Bale, Chaucer and Skelton were exempted from his strictures: "their subjects being al serious, sacred, divine, not scurrilous, Wanton or prophane, as al modern plays, po-

17

ems are". Here is the authentic "Indignant, Tunbridge Wells" note, sounded no less resonantly in the pamphlet against long hair five years earlier: "Strange it is to see, and Lamentable to consider, how farre our Nation is of late degenerated from what it was in former Ages". Indeed Prynne was no more curmudgeonly in 1633 than he had been in 1628: he had shifted the location of his attack, that is all. And the target he aimed at was one that had tempted puritans of Elizabethan times too. So there was nothing novel about the tract. What he said had been said before. He said it at greater length, of course, but he wasn't the only seventeenth-century person to lament that people were more familiar with Shakespeare than with the Bible. And it is true that he did inject a prurient note of particular nastiness, when he suggested that the motive in theatre-going was, for the most part, the lascivious thrill at seeing boys embrace one another on stage. He sailed close to the wind, perhaps, in his description of the sticky fate that inevitably befell rulers who let stage plays take place. Was he, as the prosecution alleged, inviting his subjects to remove Charles I by comparing him to Nero? In fact it is difficult to see misanthropy, on so generalized a scale as is evident in *Histriomastix*, having this *specific* seditious implication. As one contemporary had the wit to see: it was "fitter to be called ANTHROPOMASTIX than HISTRIOMASTIX; the scourge of mankind rather than the Kings sacred person". As for the tendency to read history in retributive terms this was too platitudinous to be sinister. In 1631 there had appeared the third edition of Thomas Beard's *Theatre of Gods judgments*, which told the whole of history (not just of stage plays) in terms of God's retributive justice. Prynne quotes from it profusely, and ransacks Beard's history for much of his work. But again there is nothing novel, or indeed specially puritan, about Beard's exercise; the fact that he was schoolmaster to Cromwell has invested him with greater significance (Dr Morrill has suggested) than his actual influence warrants. Archbishop Laud used to keep fit by swinging on rafters. He overdid it on one occasion and ruptured himself. In his meticulous way he recorded this fact in his diary. A puritan, reading it, noted how *he* also indulged in gymnastics and never ruptured himself – the ways of the Lord are strange. It wasn't this trite providentialism that did for Prynne; it was circumstantial evidence. His attack on female actors coincided with Henrietta Maria's appearance in a court masque. Prynne's defence was that the work had been long in preparation; he could not have known that the Queen's performance would coincide with publication of his treatise. This defence would have been a little more impressive if the onslaught on female actors had not been inserted in an Appendix to the work – written while Henrietta Maria was rehearsing for the part.

In the event he was fined £5,000, sentenced to life imprisonment, and had his ears cut off. He wrote an indignant protest in prison that, one gathers, went much further than his printed works to date in his denunciation of Laud. The story goes that Laud – delighted at this gift – took the paper to Prynne in his cell, and confronted him with its authorship. Prynne then seized the paper from Laud (which we must imagine was of less bulk than the thousand-pages-plus of *Histriomastix*), swallowed it in front of the bemused Archbishop, and boasted that this was one piece of evidence that would not be used against him.

Between 1634 and 1637 Prynne, in imprisonment but with a friendly gaoler, went on producing papers against the Laudian regime. He was joined in this enterprise by two fellow puritans, Henry Burton (a divine) and John Bastwick (a doctor). This led in 1637 to the prosecution of all three, and to another conviction. Indeed, Prynne was sentenced to having his ears cut off a second time, as well as having his nose slit, and the initials "S. L." burnt into his cheeks (standing for "Seditious Libeller", but in Prynne's eyes for "Stigma of Laud"). How can ears be cut off twice? The reader has to steer between two interpretations here. Prynne's version is that his ears were cut off on the first occasion, and God by a miracle made them grow again. This is not how his opponents saw it. According to them, his ears were only lightly cropped the first time, but Prynne gave the executioner not the customary ten shillings' tip, but only five shillings: proof positive – to anticipate a later controversy to be discussed – of the correlation between puritanism and the rise of capitalism. Alas, the *same* executioner was on call in 1637; as a contemporary noted, "now the hangman was quit with him".

In a pamphlet of 1641 Prynne described – in the third person and retrospectively – his sufferings of 1637. The executioner, he said, had heated the iron very hot and burnt one of his cheeks twice. After this, he cut one of his ears so close that he cut off a piece of his cheek too and cut him deep in the neck near the jugular vein. Then, hacking the other ear until it was almost off, he kept it hanging and went down from the

19

scaffold. He was called back by the surgeon, who made him perform a complete amputation. This was Prynne's description of his anguish:

> At which exquisite torture he never moved with his body, or so much as changed his countenance, but still looked up as well as he could towards Heaven, with a smiling countenance, even to the astonishment of all the beholders. And uttered (as soon as the Executioner had done) this heavenly sentence – "The more I am beat down, the more am I lift up."

In that one sentence is encapsulated the whole resilient magnificence of puritanism: "The more I am beat down, the more am I lift up." It was a sentence that would have a resonance for its audience, in a way that his earlier sufferings had not. In 1633, Prynne was generally seen as a maverick figure who had fallen foul of the law. But in 1637 the prosecution of Prynne, Bastwick and Burton was a show trial, not in the sense intended by their accusers: it became, in the perception of many, a trial *of the regime*. It was not the brutality of the punishment that touched a public nerve; punishments *were* brutal in those days. Think of what the radical young Lilburne was to suffer – but he was an apprentice. Prynne, Bastwick and Burton represented the great professions – Law, Medicine and Gospel – and there was a social undercurrent in the resentment many felt at *their* punishments. Perhaps there is no more telling indictment of the isolation of the regime than the fact that it had estranged representatives of the three professions that should have been its natural allies. And would be so again. The whirligig of time would see Nicholas Culpepper in 1649 declaring that the liberty of the Commonwealth was infringed by three monopolies – priest, physician and lawyer. The monopolists of 1649 were the martyrs of 1637.

In 1637 a generation reared on Foxe's Book of Martyrs could draw the instructive parallels between two periods of history. For Cranmer, Latimer and Ridley, read Prynne, Bastwick and Burton; one crop of martyrs had suffered at the hands of Papists, the later crop at the hands of crypto-Papists. A contemporary recorded his reactions to the scene: "at the cutting of each ear there was such a roaring as if every one of them had at the same instant lost an ear." The Catholic, Kenelm Digby, noting sardonically the scramble for flappets of ear at the executions, made a good Catholic point: "You may see how

Nature leads men to respect relics of martyrs." There was a crazy woman who had three cats. She called them Prynne, Bastwick and Burton, and cut off their ears. This was a psychotic response, too extreme to be typical, but which tells something of the cult status the three martyrs had acquired. In Paul Seaver's re-creation of the world of Nehemiah Wallington, a London artisan, an incident from February 1640 is particularly revealing. Wallington records how two men were talking together "in Mr Munday's house in Little Britain just east of St Bartholomew's Hospital". The first one referred to the pitiful plight of the three puritan martyrs.

> "Push", quoth the other, swearing a bloody oath, "it were no matter if they had been hanged, base schismatical jacks to trouble the whole kingdom with their base opinions". After uttering this fierce and passionate condemnation, he fell to "bloody and fearfull curses", whereupon he suddenly began to sweat and faint "and taking out of his pocket a handkerchief to wipe his face and head, his ears fell a bleeding", which needless to say "wrought a strong amazement to all that stood by".

To call the English Civil War the War of Prynne's Ears would be to overstate its importance by a huge margin, but as a powerful emotional focus for the discontent of the times the sufferings of Prynne and his fellows should not be discounted. The martyrs' exile to the Channel Islands became one triumphal procession, with thousands thronging to catch a glimpse of the heroes. The return to London in November 1640, with the summoning of the Long Parliament, was another rapturous reception, as glimpsed in the diary of Robert Woodford:

> Oh blessed be the Lord for this day! This day those holy living Martyrs Mr. Burton and Mr. Prynne came to town and the Lords providence brought me out of the temple to see them. My heart rejoiceth in the Lord for this day; its even like the return of the captivity from Babylon. There went to meet them about 1500 or 2000 horsemen, and about 100 coaches, and the streets were all thronged with people, and there was very great rejoicing.

Prynne became the official apologist for Parliament in the Civil War.

His *Soveraigne powers of parliaments* is a disappointing contribution to political theory, being much more an *ad hoc* justification of actions already taken by Parliament than a discourse on sovereignty itself. But it reflects the embarrassment of many of his co-religionists in fighting a limited war of self-preservation against the evil Papist counsellors who had infiltrated the Church and had poisoned the mind of the King. One of these counsellors was Laud, and to Prynne fell the task of prosecuting his old enemy, and writing up the proceedings subsequently. Though the Archbishop would be executed in 1645 – after a shameful period of imprisonment without trial – it is clear, from independent accounts, that Prynne's official version is not to be trusted (reflecting more the way he wished the trial to have gone – as an indictment of the Archbishop's *undermining* of the Royal Supremacy, rather than – as the trial developed – of his *inflating* it). He served on the Committee of Accounts during the war and became MP for Newport (Cornwall) in 1648.

The death of Laud had not meant the death of the Catholic threat. Rather, it had forced a significant change of tactics. The Jesuits now sought to infiltrate the Army as they had tried to infiltrate the Church of England. Prynne saw Army Levellers as Jesuit agents, a theme developed in a number of pamphlets in the late 1640s. What was the evidence for what seems at first a preposterous charge? First, the Jesuits pleaded necessity to justify their actions, as the Levellers would too. Secondly, *The agreement of the people* – the ark of the Leveller covenant – had been presented, not in October or December 1647, but November: the month of the Guy Fawkes Plot. Third, the Pope, who seems to have been uncommonly free with his opinions, had told a Jesuit of his secret plan who had, said Prynne, affirmed it "lately to a friend of mine". Fourth, the Jesuit founder, Ignatius Loyola, had been a soldier. Fifth, the details of the Jesuit conspiracy to work through the Army had been related to Prynne by "a grave, Protestant Gentleman of the Temple".

So now the Army had to be stopped, and peace made with the King. Prynne, as a leading advocate of a deal with the King at the Isle of Wight, was among the MPs expelled in Pride's Purge. He bitterly excoriated the unconstitutionality of that action and opposed the trial, and execution, of the King. The Jesuits' part in the regicide, under the mask of army radicals, was proved when the indiscreet Henrietta Maria's confessor was alleged to have been seen to wave his sword in

22

triumph as the King's head was cut off. Charles I had expiated all his former sins by martyrdom at the hands of Catholics. In the 1650s there was no more eloquent Royalist than Prynne; it was a Royalist admirer who now called him "the Cato of his Age". His attacks on Cromwell ("Richard the Third revived") led to his imprisonment in several castles between 1650 and 1653. In February 1660 the Long Parliament was recalled, not merely as a result of Prynne's strenuous pamphleteering on its behalf, but certainly there was no braver or more tenacious a champion of its cause. Triumph, as always with Prynne, however, was tinged with farce. As Prynne swaggered in, with a ceremonial long sword, it got caught in the short, fat legs of Sir William Waller, and both men rolled to the floor which, said the parliamentary diarist, caused much laughter.

Charles II expressed his gratitude to Prynne at the Restoration by making him Keeper of the Records in the Tower of London. No task could have been more congenial to Prynne. Our greatest of all historians, F. W. Maitland, would call Prynne in this role a "heroic" figure, burrowing among the records of antiquity. It was a task, said Prynne, "so filthy and unpleasant that Mr Riley and others would not soil their hands, or clothes, nor endanger their healths to assist me in it". Prynne had domesticated his craving for martyrdom.

Post-Restoration Prynne seems altogether a more mellow figure, destined to die in the odour of sanctity. He is even a little more balanced about sex, compared to the days of *Histriomastix* repressions. In November 1660 a bill was introduced to prevent wives, living apart from their husbands, from incurring debts in their husbands' name. The parliamentary diarist said that "Mr Knightley moved to lay the bill aside, but Mr Prynne humorously saying, That if they did, those that had ill wives would call it again within a day or two, the question was put." A few days later, a bill was introduced against women who refused to cohabit with their husbands, and the diarist noted that "Mr Prynne said he was for the bill, though he never had a good or bad wife in his life". Seven years later, the young historian Anthony Wood, armed with letters of commendation from Oriel, Prynne's old College, called upon Prynne to learn from him how to study records. Wood recalls what happened, in the third person:

Mr Prynne received him with old fashion compliments, such as were used in the reign of King James I, and he told him he should see what he desired, and seemed to be glad that such a young man as he was (for so he called him) should have inclinations towards venerable antiquity. He told him then that if he would call upon him the next morning at 8 of the clock, he would conduct him to the Tower, for he had business then to do there, being about to print another book.

Wood continues that

he went precisely at the time appointed, and found Mr Prynne in his black and taffety-cloak, edged with black lace at the bottom. They went to the Tower directly through the City, then lying in ruins (occasion'd by the grand conflagration that happened in 1666); but by his meeting with several citizens and prating with them, it was about 10 of the clock before they could come to the same place.

Here is an irresistible vignette: Prynne, black and taffety-cloak and all, conducting his young pupil through the smoking ruins of London after the Great Fire, and unable to resist the chance of a yarn with acquaintances before getting down to the documents. But the reference to the Great Fire should be a warning against our sentimentalizing the later Prynne. The Great Fire, *he knew*, was the product of Papist deception. He remained implacably hostile to Catholics. But he was no less hostile to Quakers, since they were Catholics in disguise (a pretty hard proposition to swallow, though Professor Bossy, the modern historian of Catholicism, has suggested affinities between Catholics and Quakers that others have failed to find). He was, more disturbing to us, vindictive to the Jews. He bitterly opposed their readmission into England and justified this to an Independent minister, Philip Nye, on the grounds of the Blood Accusation: the belief that Jews seized the Christian boy martyr, to drink his blood in a parody of the Eucharist, to rid themselves of their atrocious smell. Nye laughed this off as codswallop, though the same legend would be revived effectively by Julius Streicher in the 1930s. Prynne admired Clarendon for his *gravitas*; an admiration that was not reciprocated. When Clarendon faced banishment, Prynne protested: "I pray God this be not a foreigner's plot." Samuel Pepys, not the most fastidious of men, found himself at the dinner table with Prynne, and was repelled by his boorishness. He had secreted on his person some documents filched from the Tower of London, revealing how nuns had been evicted from their nunneries in the medieval period on account of their debauchery. At the time of the Great Fire of London, a public servant complained of receiving a long and tiresome letter from one William Prynne, "a stranger to him, speaking of fears and jealousies, of plots and designs of Jesuits and Romanists against the Church and Religion". He was afraid that it would "stir up hornets". Prynne would go on stirring up hornets until his death in 1669.

The last word should be with Anthony Wood. Beware the smiling research assistant! This was how Wood repaid the aged scholar's kindness to him, with this obituary in verse:

Hear earless William Prynne doth lie
And so will eternally
For when the last trump sounds to appear
He that hath ears then let *him* heare.

Chapter Three

Lodowicke Muggleton (1609–1698)[1]

Courtesy of the author.

The story begins with an article by Christopher Hill in *The Times Literary Supplement* in 1974. Hill was arguing the case – later expanded into a book – that Milton was a radical. Since on Hill's calculation, under Parliament's Blasphemy Ordinance of 1648, Milton's views would have rendered him liable to five death sentences and eight life imprisonments, he had a case. But he went further:

> I tried once to list those sects and radical groups, like Levellers, Diggers, Fifth Monarchists, General Baptists, Socinians, Quakers, Ranters, Muggletonians, which shared any of Milton's characteristic radical views – anti-clericalism, millenarianism, anti-trinitarianism, mortalism, materialism, hell internal. I was a little startled by the result – the group closest to Milton was the Muggletonians, followers of John Reeve and Lodowicke Muggleton, who in 1652 were commissioned by God as the Two Last Witnesses foretold in Revelation XI.

If Hill was a little startled, his readers were even more so. In the following few weeks the correspondence pages would express the outrage of literary scholars at a comparison of Milton with religious loonies of his day. Then came a significant contribution on the other side from E. P. Thompson, expressing his outrage at a comparison of Muggletonians with religious loonies. Thompson, like Hill, was interested in Muggletonian affinities with a literary giant; but it was Blake, not Milton, who had been his point of entry. His interest had been further stimulated by two remarkable lectures by a Unitarian historian, A. P. Gordon, on the sect in 1869 and 1870 in Liverpool. The leading Unitarian minister Robert Aspland had a cousin, J. D. Aspland, who was a Muggletonian; through Aspland, the non-believer Gordon was allowed to attend a dinner of the sect and to gain access to their private archive. The 1869 lecture was sympathetic but derivative upon Muggleton's posthumous memoirs; however, a year later, Gordon was to be able to write in an informed way, drawing upon the private archive. This was the archive that Thompson now drew attention to in his letter. The letter was seen by the son-in-law of the person whom we now call the Last Muggletonian, Philip Noakes. Noakes made this material – carefully hoarded in apple boxes on his Kent farm, as a haven from the Blitz, for over 30 years – available to Thompson. Subsequently, in 88 volumes, the archive was transferred to the British

Library. Though Noakes died in 1979 his widow had private documents, to which the present writer was given access, and presented a portrait of Muggleton and a plaque commemorating the opening of the Muggletonian Reading Room in 1869 (referred to in Gordon's 1870 lecture) to the University of Sussex. Both are now to be found in the Quiet Room of the Meeting House of the University, whose motto is "Be Still and Know". It is a good final resting place for the man whose repeated desire was "to be quiet and still".

To be "quiet and still" doesn't sound like the radical sect that Hill described; it sounds more like modern-day Quakers. Here is one aspect of the intellectual challenge posed by puritanism. To recover what it meant in its own day, we must not allow our knowledge of later developments to distort. In David Cannadine's fine recent biography of G. M. Trevelyan (*A life in history*, London, 1992, p. 100) he says that the seventeenth-century puritan squires were "not wholly unlike the Evangelical cliques of the early nineteenth century". Perhaps, but they were not wholly like them either, and that should have weighed with Trevelyan more than it did. Both Quakers and Muggletonians evolved in a spectacular way from their origins. Both found the leaders (George Fox and Lodowicke Muggleton respectively) who would take a rowdy, confrontational, cursing, miracle-working group and map a quietist future that would ensure for each its survival.

But the Quakers are a success story in the way that the Muggletonians are not. They were, above all else, evangelical, whereas the Muggletonians were not proselytizers. Their failure to recruit members on the Quaker scale is hardly surprising therefore; the surprise is that they survived as long as they did. Common belief was that the movement had petered out some time in the nineteenth century; *The Chambers Encyclopaedia* of 1881, for instance, pronounced the sect as extinct. How big was the sect? Muggleton's funeral in 1698 was attended by 248 followers; from then on, the archive shows a continual decline. There are over 100 names in a paper of 1803; 46 present at a Clerkenwell pub in 1850; 17 in a monthly meeting in 1906; 8 at a meeting in 1927. The archive is studded with believers' worries about this decline, but their beliefs stood in the way of doing anything to arrest it. Muggleton explained in 1682 how he only opened the gate of Heaven to those who knocked first; he noted, with no sense of shame, his poor harvest of converts (actually one, cousin Roger). The Last Muggletonian (like the First) never tried to convert within the family, although he swapped texts with enthusiasm when Jehovah's Witnesses made a Sunday call. There are touching glimpses in the archive of Muggletonians hanging around Bible classes in the nineteenth century in the hope that somebody would approach *them*. Why were they so coy? They did not believe that only Muggletonians would be saved. There is an appealing lack of elitism about the group. Muggleton reckoned that something like half the world would be saved. Of those fortunate many (which would include all children) there was an even more fortunate few (the Muggletonians) who had the *assurance* of salvation, which came from a belief in the Prophets. But salvation and assurance were not conterminous. Many could be saved without that assurance. What of those, however, who consciously rejected doctrines to which they had been innocently exposed? They were as much damned as those who had blasphemed against the Prophets. Sir Walter Scott came into the latter category. He had described them roughly in *Woodstock* (he'd actually confused them with Familists). Robert Wallis, a Muggletonian, cursed Scott to all eternity. From that point Scott's fortunes went into decline.[2] This information was passed on by the present writer to an English literature colleague, who was a Scott specialist, with a sense of urgency: (British Library) Additional MSS 60169, it was now clear, held the key to Scott. The communication was received courteously but unexcitedly: what a phlegmatic lot one's English literature colleagues are! Scott was a scoffer, but, less dramatically, relatives could be imperilled by being subjected to the full majesty of Muggletonian doctrine, and choosing not to accept it. Better then to stay unconquerably ignorant and be saved *without* assurance: the lesson that the young Mary McCarthy, in her memoirs of Catholic girlhood, learnt when she was dissuaded from leaving Catholic tracts in the lavatory for her beloved Protestant grandparents to read.

What were the doctrines that the convert to Muggletonianism would adopt? The starting point was to accept that, on three successive mornings in February 1652, God spoke to John Reeve, a London tailor, and told him that he and his cousin, Lodowicke Muggleton, were the Two Last Witnesses promised in Revelation. This is the foundation of the movement, although it does not figure much in the later archive correspondence. A believer, John Frost, responds testily to the sceptical Reverend John Willis in 1858: "Now he says what proof have we that God spoke to John Reeve? It is very easy to ask questions." The encounter, however, conferred authenticity on all the subsequent blessing and cursing, which was the most distinctive badge of the Muggletonians in the 1650s. Reeve had gone round to Muggleton's house in 1652 with the momentous news that God had spoken personally to him. "Cousin Lodowicke now, saith he, I know what Revelation of Scripture is, as well as Thee" – and who could gainsay him? There was one accidental witness. Sarah, Muggleton's 14-year-old daughter, was coming down the stairs when Reeve was speaking to her father. Her initial reaction was one of dread. She thought that Reeve would curse her (he had always preferred her younger sister). Instead he blessed her, not from affection, but "as the Revelation moved him".

This was the prelude to some frenetic blessing and cursing. A few examples will give the flavour. A rival Prophet, Thomas Tany (a London goldsmith who had circumcised himself in fulfilment of the Mosaic Law) was cursed. He would perish in 1655 on a boat, on the way to Jerusalem to convert the Jews. A man called Penson smote blows on Muggleton's head; ten days later he was dead. At a Ranter tavern in the Minories, Reeve placed his head on the ground for an enemy to trample upon. The infidel's foot was arrested in flight: he could not go through with it. Muggleton noted, "the people all marvelled at this thing". The cynical Captain Stasy arranged a dinner for the Prophets with a divine called Goffin. The dinner ended predictably enough with a curse on the clergyman, which may have been the Captain's intention since, according to Muggleton, "he was a great Enemy to the Clergy". For Reeve and Muggleton the outcome was less satisfactory: six months in Bridewell. They were released in 1654, four years before Reeve's death.

From 1658 to 1698 Muggleton ruled alone; and a very different pattern emerged. The man who believed in being "quiet and still" imposed his character on the movement. He saw off two efforts to depose him: the first, in 1660, by Lawrence Clarkson; the second – a more serious one – in 1671 by Buchanan and Medgate. Many of the doctrines, put forward earlier in the names of the two Prophets jointly, were now elaborated on, and in some cases altered, by Muggleton. Many of them were unoriginal, and were to be found in other contemporary groupings. Muggletonians believed that the soul was mortal. Hell was in the person's own mind. Public worship and services were forbidden. John Gratton, a Quaker, joined the Muggletonians in the

1670s, and attended a meeting at Mrs Dorothy Carter's house. To his disgust, *nothing happened*. That is to say, there was no Church service that could be recognized; just meditations on letters from the Prophets. When the mother of Thomas Tomkinson (who himself was to become a key figure in the movement) became a Muggletonian, she found that all she was asked to do was to give up her old Presbyterian habit of praying to God. Dreams were demystified as products of anxiety. Witches, likewise, were the projection of people's fears: a remarkable contribution this, to be discussed in Chapter 9. Two rival seeds – Faith and Reason – were implanted in all men and women. There was thus no clear-cut elect/reprobate distinction on Calvinist lines. One of Muggleton's children had been melancholic and died early. But no witchcraft was involved, Muggleton reassured a correspondent: it was simply that the seed of Reason had been uppermost in Muggleton's wife when the child was conceived. In 1870, a paper in the archive boasts that the Muggletonians had been as successful in seeing off the Victorian fad of spiritualism as their predecessors in the seventeenth century had routed witchcraft beliefs. The Muggletonians were Unitarians – the secret heretical belief of Milton, Locke and Newton; as recently as 1612 a Unitarian had been executed for that belief, the last Protestant to be put to death for heresy. Muggletonians taught that God *was* the Man Jesus, five feet tall, who had come down on Earth to share in the experiences of Mankind. While the Man Jesus was on Earth, Moses and Elias had watched over the shop in Heaven. The Muggletonians, in the twelfth-century Joachimite tradition, believed in three stages of history. The First Age was that of Law, the text was the Old Testament, the Prophet was Moses. The Second Age was that of Gospel, the text was the New Testament, the Prophet was Jesus. The year 1652 marked the Third Age, that of the Spirit, the text was the Prophets' writings, and the Prophets were Reeve and Muggleton. Muggletonians therefore often described themselves as believers in the Third Commission. How long would that last? In a letter of 1656, Reeve spoke in terms of months. That sense of an imminent transformation of society disappeared with his death. An eighteenth-century rival Prophet, James Birch, claimed to be recapturing that lost Reeve urgency when he spoke witheringly of "Literal wandering Muggletonians that will wander in the dead Letter to the World's End".

The public image of Muggletonianism had been set in the rowdy years of tavern confrontations: the routing of rival Prophets (Robins and Tany) and the damning of clergymen. Under Muggleton's able leadership, the sect moved in a different direction, however. Because members did not have regular meetings they avoided prosecution under the 1664 Conventicle Act; unlike the Quakers, they avoided head-on confrontation. Occasionally members came up before the church courts for refusing to attend services, though Muggleton was indulgent to the practice of occasional conformity by his followers, particularly those who were well off. Most members were drawn from the artisan class, just under half of them women, at the sect's peak period in the late seventeenth century. Their concentration was mainly in the south and the Midlands; London and Derbyshire were the most important centres. The areas were not linked by the tireless activities of their leader. Muggleton once asked rhetorically if there had ever been a leader who had travelled up and down the country *less* than he had. 1672 was a bad summer. His wife was off to Kent to visit relatives. Muggleton was "loath to leave the House with no body in it" (from the same motives, the Man Jesus had delegated responsibilities to Moses and Elias, while He was on the Earth). This isn't the stuff of travellers, let alone martyrs. Travelling repelled him: "I am a free born Englishman, and a free man of London by birth and borne there and never was out of England in all my life." As for his fellow puritans who risked the Atlantic crossing:

> So you say William Newcombe is intended to goo to Virginia and take two of his children along with him. I wonder what is in men's minds to run amongst the Heathen that are without God in the World besides the Climate doth not agree with the English Nature to live there contentedly.

In a highly fanciful essay Lytton Strachey wrote of Muggleton's gathering of disciples around him "in ever-thickening crowds". This wasn't how he worked. He wasn't a Wesley or a George Fox. The influence he had over his followers (which was considerable) was not made by personal contact; as we shall see, it was letters that would be his medium.

Only once did Muggleton clash publicly with the Law in the Restoration, when he was imprisoned in Newgate in 1677 for blasphemy. Even then his retrospective comments were couched with gratitude for the strict observance of legal processes that had saved his life. When his head was thrust in a pillory, he would be rescued by head keeper Captain Richardson: "God Damn you what makes you put the Mans Head in, for it is contrary to his sentence." A shopkeeper who had assaulted Muggleton in the pillory with an orange was struck to the ground by a believer, who got away with it because he was assumed to be a sheriff's clerk. So respectful of the Law was Muggleton that a rumour that he had recanted his beliefs at his trial was accepted for a time even by his own followers. George Borrow's *Lavengro* shows how these principles were no less binding on nineteenth-century successors. He purchased a Bible from an antinomian bookseller in Norwich, and recorded the following conversation:

> "... know that those who call us Antinomians call us so despitefully, we do not acknowledge the designation." "Then you do not set all laws at nought?" said I. "Far be it for us," said the old man, "we only hope that, being sanctified by the Spirit from above, we have no need of the law to keep us in order. Did you ever hear tell of Lodowick Muggleton?" "Not I" "That is strange; know then that he was the founder of our poor society, and after him were frequently, though opprobriously termed Muggletonians, for we are Christians."[3]

The "poor society" of Muggletonians had established their rhythm of behaviour by the time of the Prophet's death in 1698. There would be monthly meetings in pubs, singing of "Divine Songs", and exchanges of spiritual greetings between believers. The songs were important – tributes to the Prophets, sung to the tune of hymns and popular ballads of the day. This is a characteristic verse of 1736:

> My father is a true believer
> My mother is the same
> And they that despise the Commission
> I think they are much to blame.

(One believes that Christopher Hill did not intend the Milton–Muggletonian link to be pressed too hard.) The group would hire a room in a pub to honour covertly the Prophets. Other pub attenders would only hear patriotic or devout songs billowing out from an adjacent room. It was, incidentally, this association with pubs that led Macaulay into the erroneous belief that Muggleton was a tippler. As late as 1930, the Last Muggletonian's parents had an appreciative letter from an American correspondent: "the Divine Songs, they are delightful, and my poor old Dad could sing them so nice, he would sit down at the piano and play and sing the Divine Songs like an angel." When Gladstone was prime minister, he spent the evening of 13 December 1881 reading "Muggletonian Hymns!!"[4]

Two anniversaries were regularly celebrated (February, when God spoke to Reeve, and July, when Muggleton was released from prison). One Anniversary Dinner, at the Green Man in 1692, has left behind memorable accounts. All the guests paid five shillings "except the Prophet and his wife". And another item records: "paid for the prophetts coach – 3/6". We have records of debates at the monthly meetings, on such arcane subjects as whether Adam's prick stood in Paradise, and whether beasts were capable of reflection. More serious controversies divided the sect in the latter part of the eighteenth century, as James Birch challenged Muggletonian orthodoxy in the name of Reeve. He and his followers were seen off with curses. But many Muggletonians were now becoming uneasy with the practice of cursing. "I was not of the Damning Order" was Gibbs's excuse for refusing to cast his opponent into eternal damnation. There was even a Muggletonian revisionist, in the eighteenth century, to argue that not everybody whom the Prophets had cursed would necessarily be damned.

The shrinking number of members continued to meet in pubs. The dinginess of the surroundings repelled the Victorian believer J. D. Aspland. He said to an older member that he had heard that a move was imminent: "Ah, she replied with some warmth, they have been talking about that ever since I have been here, I shall believe it when I see it." The move to central premises in Bishopsgate did take place eventually in 1869: the plaque commemorating the opening is the one that A. P. Gordon saw when he obtained access to the sect, and which is now to be found in the University of Sussex. There would be another move later, in May 1918, when the group moved its headquarters to 74 Worship Street.

There were divisions in the nineteenth century too. At an 1850 meeting in the Coach and Horses, Clerkenwell, John Cates was found guilty of having used language like "Witchcraft mania". His actions were condemned as "very sinful and without parallel since the commission was first given". The sentence comes as something of an anticlimax: "the Church for Peace and Unity sake will decline any further correspondence with Mr John Cates on the subject in question". The great age of cursing was on its way out. Significantly it wasn't invoked even when a serious intellectual division erupted in the 1850s, and divided the movement into "Old Believers" and "a party which called themselves Reevonians". The latter stuck to the 1656 text of *A divine looking glass*; "Old Believers" preferred Muggleton's amendments of 1661.

To focus on the divisions may be to distort the history. A lot of correspondence consists simply of loving greetings between believers. There is no sense of election. "What a happy and peculiar people are we and moreover a chosen people out of this world" – this from one 1864 letter strikes an unusual, vainglorious note. But closer scrutiny shows only an over-flowery thanks for a welcome cup of tea from Muggletonian strangers in Faversham. As a Muggletonian pointed out, the exclusiveness of the sect was not willed by it but imposed from outside: he instanced the refusal of *The Times* in 1871 to take advertisements for Muggleton's writings "because as they said they were contrary to the received opinion of the Age".

What the correspondence reveals is a low-key generosity and toleration. An Uxbridge correspondent, who traced Muggletonians in her family tree, commented: "from the contents of their letters I think they must have been very nice people".[5] A letter from a Dalston Muggletonian in 1905 conveys the flavour of many:

> Sorry to say Katie her husband and child are neither well. her husband has fell down a hole in the garden and shook himself very much. Katie has those horrid spots out again change of the weather I expect, what sort of weather have you there, it is bright here but bitter cold – Mr Frost asked me what office Elijah holds in Heaven what do you think.

Or there is Mr T. Brown's deposition in 1909:

> Some of his ancestors, he said, formed the Reeve and Muggleton Society – his father's mother, I think, and two of his father's

brothers. Asked what sort of religion it was he said he thought it was not a bad sort. They went in for both body and soul at the same time. Whilst at their devotions in one room there was plenty of eating and drinking being prepared in the kitchen. Everything was very pleasant, and those who could not get home at night would stay till the small hours of the morning.

Two world wars, and the continued shrinking of the sect, cast a shadow over twentieth-century Muggletonians. Believers only found comfort in the thought that they might portend the end of the world. Meetings between the remaining believers became less frequent, but topics did not change. In 1927 a meeting agreed that horses, dogs, bears and lions would be found in heaven, "but not such as come by cross-breeding", and in 1933 believers were still divided about whether to follow the 1656 or 1661 edition of *A divine looking glass*. One of the last of Muggletonian letters records Philip Noakes's distress at developments in modern biological warfare.

Muggleton has had a wretched press. He was Macaulay's "Mad Tailor". One historian called him "an unstable and deeply troubled neurotic who sought release from his anxieties by acting the wild-eyed prophet". Another snobbishly saw him as the "product of the religious culture of the London slums". Another way of seeing him is as the product of a different culture, the great puritan casuist tradition of Bolton, Preston, Sibbes, Gouge, Perkins – and Baxter.

What is impressive in reading Muggleton's correspondence is the ability to empathize, the refusal to make judgements. He, it is true, could be brusque at times. Tomkinson wrote to him in the 1660s, with a lovingly tormented analysis of the state of his soul. Muggleton was economic in his reply: "Nothing venture, nothing have". Tomkinson would afterwards make frequent admiring reference to the patience that the Prophet had displayed towards him. Muggleton summed it up differently to a third person: "what a deale of paine to please the unsatisfied fancy of one particular man". A correspondent asks: should he remain a pacifist in Antigua? Muggleton replies: "As the old proverb saith, if you will live at Rome you must doo as Rome doth". This was not the language of an Ayatollah. Mrs Dorothy Carter worries in 1670 whether she should feel responsible for her young lodger, Sarah Hatter, who has an improvident father. Muggleton says she shouldn't: "take no thought for her what she will do when you are gone; leave that to providence". Her unsatisfactory son-in-law wanted to marry his maid, though her daughter had only recently died, and they had two young children. Muggleton wouldn't censure him, however: "you know that is a common thing with young men". But this wasn't indifference. He teased out legal problems with the estate, and didn't duck the challenge of emotional ties: "how to persuade you to doo to a daughter in law as you did by your owne [the joint running of a school between them] I cannot presse you to do it, for I could not doo it if I were in your Condition". Muggleton had indicated to Elizabeth Atkinson the perils of her proposed love-match. She went ahead with it, and her mother cursed her for it. Muggleton had been on the mother's side at first, but he now championed the daughter. He warned the mother against words spoken in the heat of the moment: "they bring nothing but hell into the mind". But this quarrel was put in a wider philosophical perspective: the relations between parents and children. Drawing on personal experience, he asked her: "what hath Parents to do with children that are free as themselves, but to forgive them their Offences – the Love of God and the Law of Nature doth bind parents to have a Love of their Children – but Children are not bound to have a Love of Parents". Filmer's patriarch joins Bodin's witch and Luther's devil on the Muggletonian hit list.

Mary Gamble worried in 1681 about a sister troubled with melancholia. Muggleton knew what she shouldn't be prescribed: giving physic and letting blood "makes the Spirit of the person so weak that they can never get strength in the brain more to the day at their death". Kitchen broth, on the other hand, would provide her with the strength "to reason out these Melancholly thoughts". In 1941 a Muggletonian reminded her ailing aunt of "the Prophets good advice about Kitchen broths". Earlier, in 1928, the same woman had written, "We are now reading the Letter Book and are continually delighted not only with the Prophet's explanation of heavenly matters, but also with his understanding of human nature and human frailties." The "Letter Book" referred to, sometimes also called "the Great Book", was the compilation of Muggleton's letters into one volume in 1682, now more prosaically known as (British Library) Additional MS 60171. As Muggleton neared the end of his life, followers wanted his oral blessings written into that volume. They seemed to think that, otherwise, they would not count. Muggleton tried to disabuse them of this belief, but then was prepared to humour them (just as he permitted his followers to pray, even if he doubted its efficacy).

The 1928 letter writer had connected Muggleton's humanity to his "explanation of heavenly matters". She was right to do so. The Prophets had an internal disagreement over doctrine before Reeve's death in 1658. Muggleton put it about – though we only have his word for it – that Reeve had been won over to Muggleton's point of view. Muggleton had argued against Reeve that God took no "immediate notice" of His creatures. Thus praying was pointless, martyrdom unnecessary, and a forgiving God an illusion. This doctrine was stark enough to provoke opposition throughout the history of the sect, from the Buchanan/Medgate schism of 1671, the Birchite rebellion in the late eighteenth century, right down to the "Reevonian" challenge to "Old Believers" in Victorian England. It subverted the providentialist framework of Beard's *Theatre of God's judgments* and Prynne's *Histriomastix*, and much else besides. When Muggleton tells rebel Buchanan that if no God existed to reward the virtuous, or to punish the vicious, "yet could I not doe any otherwise than I doe" he is anticipating the Kantian doctrine of the autonomy of ethics.

But he is doing something more: he is giving himself elbow-room in his counselling, which was denied to the puritan Richard Baxter, who is the subject of the next chapter. Baxter was, like Muggleton, a marvellously humane and feeling correspondent. He wrote over 1,200 letters, many of them to melancholic women (just as many of Muggleton's correspondents were). But Muggleton's rejection of "immediate notice" gave him the edge over his orthodox Christian contemporary. It is what the eighteenth-century Muggletonian Arden Bonell grasped when he claimed that, with the abolition of God's "immediate notice", men could now be ruled by love, not fear. The same emancipation is evident in the scorn of the nineteenth-century Muggletonian Thomas Robinson for "the slavish worship of fear and trembling and awe towards God, the which giveth neither Love or Peace". It is not that Baxter did not want to comfort his tormented correspondents. When one woman wrote to him about her fear of the dark, he responded that he too had once been terrified of the dark; one simply outgrew these fears. The tone is absolutely right, but the weakness in his position is that his theology ensured that he himself would continue to be terrified by ghosts, witches and hobgoblins. He trembled at the significance of dreams. Eternal hell-fire, he said, would "cause the worm of conscience never to die". Disbelieve in witches and spirits, and you end up disbelieving in God. The soul was immortal – otherwise, how could you trust your wife or servant? When one correspondent wrote to him of her fear of the Devil, Baxter had this homely anecdote for comfort:

> Mr White of Dorchester, living in a house at Lambeth that was wont to be haunted, the Devil one night appeared to be standing at his beds foot. When he had stood there a while, saith Mr White to him, If thou hast nothing else to do, stand there still and so settled himself to sleepe, and the Devil vanished, as ashamed of the contempt.

Admirable, and yet contrived! Contrast this with the simple observations of Muggleton to correspondents that: the Devil is the figment of men's imaginations; the soul is mortal; witches and ghosts, like dreams, are the product of fear. Baxter (like Prynne) wanted Adultery Acts and capital punishment for offenders. Muggleton (perhaps anticipating Groucho Marx's comment that he was a teetotaller until Prohibition) noted that the one sure consequence of an Adultery Act was a higher incidence of adultery.

So nothing could be wider of the mark than the nineteenth-century description of the sect as "fanatics, whose inordinate conceit prompts them to believe that the Deity must be more engrossed with the affairs of an obscure Muggletonian in Ebenezer Alley, Shoreditch, than with the general and immutable laws of the universe". What gave the charge such plausibility as it had was the continuation of Muggletonian cursing and blessing, which sits uneasily with the austere precept that God takes no "immediate notice" of His creatures. The cursing didn't die out until the mid-nineteenth century (a Swedenborgian may have been the last victim) but we have seen that, much earlier, the steam had gone out of it. The idea that God took no "immediate notice" of His creatures explained its appeal to eighteenth-century Deists, and why Muggletonians then would want to annotate Hobbes. When Sir Keith Thomas describes that great intellectual mutation in seventeenth-century England, which saw the displacement of magic and Providence, Macaulay's "Mad Tailor" is perhaps worth more than a glancing footnote.

Chapter Four

Richard Baxter (1615–1691)[1]

Courtesy of Dr Williams's library.

Richard Baxter was born in a village five miles from Shrewsbury in Shropshire. He describes the appalling level of preaching the Gospel there in his famous memoirs, published after his death and written over a period of time after the Restoration. What made him and his father "puritans", on his account, was no commitment to a theological position, but simply being called such by the "vulgar rabble", because puritans were men who preferred "constant competent preachers" to the tipplers and gamblers who were "the schoolmasters of my youth". There weren't too many of those "constant competent preachers" on the ground – Baxter remembers three or four at most near him – but of these, interestingly enough, only one was *not* conformable. For Baxter, as for Prynne, "puritan" was then a label foist upon them by enemies in the first place, but inasmuch as it stood for concern at moral laxity one not to be repudiated. What both men repudiated – and would do so for the rest of their lives – was the assumption that such concern was incompatible with membership of the Church of England; rather, they would see it as a prerequisite of conformity to the sort of Church they believed in (as three out of his four admired preachers had done).

Baxter was a bad lad, that is to say he was "much addicted to the excessive gluttonous eating of apples and pears" and was too fond of teachers' praise of his learning. At the age of 15, he was rescued from this condition by reading *Bunny's resolution* (a Jesuit tract by Parsons, amended by the puritan Edmund Bunny). This is all desperately low-key: the sins so footling, the redemption so undramatic. Think of the agonized yo-yoing of John Bunyan's conversion experiences in *Grace abounding*! Or of the Quaker, Francis Howgill, who replays the Book of Revelation in his own soul – "the Ark of the Testament was opened, and there was thunder, and lightning and great haile . . . and the Sun was darkened, and the Moon turned into blood, and the Stars did fall", and so on for more than 20 lines of description. Baxter actually did see this low-keyness as a personal deficiency. He was troubled that he could not date a time or place of conversion with the precision, say, of John Wesley a century later. The nearest he could come to this, we shall see, is related to an experience of his in the Civil War. Looking back on his younger self before he took up the ministry, he was conscious of physical, as much as spiritual, disabilities. Lawrence Stone once remarked that the seventeenth century was an age that seemed to live on its nerves. Baxter was not unique in his hypochondria then, but few men were more solicitous of their bodily movements. Baxter's first published work, *Aphorismes of justification,* was called his "dying thoughts" in 1649; he lived on until 1691. "Oh my Head, Oh my Stomach, Oh my Sides, or Oh my bowels" is not so much a cry from the heart in his *The saints everlasting rest,* as from every other organ of his body. Perhaps his aches and pains made him bad tempered. One who suffered at his hands suggested an alternative title for his great work, *The saints everlasting contention.* Certainly he could mix it with the best of them in print. An Anglican enemy, Stillingfleet, noted that peace and concord usually figured prominently on the title pages of a Baxter publication, while inside there was nothing but war and disharmony. This wasn't altogether fair. Baxter had genuine ecumenical leanings, a gentler side comes out in his vast correspondence with those who sought guidance from him (he was particularly good with women), but print, it must be said, brought out a combative side in him. He borrowed from Prynne the language, as well as the arguments, that were used against Papists and Quakers (who, both men knew, were Papists in disguise). That is not so surprising. Perhaps the level of his invective against Baptists, on the other hand, does surprise. He had once shared the Baptists' premises. His celebrated ministry at Kidderminster had indeed got off to a terrible start with outraged women of that parish almost stoning him to death for having asserted that "hell was paved with infants' skulls". Hazlitt thought little of the resolution of that particular quarrel: "by the force of argument, and of learned quotations from the Fathers, the reverend preacher at length prevailed over the scruples of his congregation, and over reason, and humanity". Later Baxter would recant, and joining up with the scruples of the mothers, and reason and humanity, by then would have no time for Baptist neighbours like the minister John Tombes. Adult baptism appealed to Tombes, alleged Baxter, because his ambition was to baptize naked "all the maids in Bewdley" (echoing here the prurience of Prynne, in telling us why it is thought we go to see plays). An even more ingenious suggestion – one that earned him the epithet, of "Mountebanck" from an opponent – was that shopkeepers in London, especially women, "that take but little of the cold air", would die in their thousands from dipping in cold water. Covetous landlords, therefore, would encourage Baptist conversions as good for trade.

Baxter's war of words with the Baptists was one that was to be fought in the 1650s. When the Civil War broke out in 1642, however, he had written none of his 140 pamphlets. He was then aged 27 (it was a year earlier that he became lecturer at Kidderminster in Worcestershire). He sided with Parliament, retiring for safety, first to Gloucester and then to Coventry. In 1645 he became an army chaplain in the regiment of his friend Edward Whalley. Without the experience of Civil War, would he have remained an obscure puritan of Baptist leanings, a minister with ecumenical longings and Billingsgate language?

We shall never know, but at least we know that it was the Civil War that propelled him from obscurity, and which governed his thinking for the rest of his life. This might seem a platitudinous point to make, but enjoyable re-creations of battles by organizations like the Sealed Knot Society, allied to the (correct) perception that the English Civil War lacked the intensity and barbarity of the European experience, have combined to make the years between 1642 and 1649 seem less traumatic in retrospect than they were for many of those who lived through them. A recent informed guess has it that something like 180,000 people died in the conflict. This seems small beer until we think these figures proportionately, in a population of some 5,000,000, and then they outscore World War Two and even, more surprisingly, World War One in their military losses. True, there were fewer Magdeburg atrocities in the English Civil War, but those that did occur usually involved the Irish (one historian has noted how the Cornish, no less alien to many Englishmen, failed to ignite the religious and racial fires evoked by the Irish in military engagements). Dr Ian Roy showed how the siege of Gloucester politicized an uninvolved population, through plunder and rape, in a way that we understand in relation to Vietnam.

What effect all this had on Baxter is evident in his later writings, as a random few instances, and they are a few from many, testify. Like most of his contemporaries Baxter believed in witches and ghosts, and the real presence of the Devil. One of the last works he wrote was a defence of these views. When, drawing upon his Civil War experiences, he would later call soldiers "Devils", this is therefore not a piece of rhetoric. Indeed he would argue that the supernatural kind of Devil is more innocuous:

Devils that haunt houses seldom hurt or much impoverish any

but only affright them by noises of apparitions. But soldiers (men Devills) rage, blaspheme, domineere, wound and kill and take away all that they can carry.

In another passage he named the ultimate losers of civil wars: the poor. He says of the military:

They keep the poore in terror night and day, and when they have burnt their houses and taken all their goods and cattell, leave them to seeke as beggars, to some other County for entertainment, if they do not kill them to prevent that distresse.

On another occasion Baxter referred to Germany "after the warre in 1632 when men were faine to watch the graves in the church yards, lest the famished people should dig up the dead to eate". But Baxter knew, from his own experience, that England could match Germany in this regard, and used that knowledge in a sermon against pride in his Restoration work, *A Christian directory*:

He that had seen what the late doleful Wars did often show us, that the fields were strewed with the carkasses of men, and when they lay by heaps among the rubbish of the Ditches of Towns and Castles that had been assaulted, would think such loathsome lumpes of flesh, should never have been proud.

Baxter projected that horror into the domestic sphere. He married late (1661). Margaret Charlton was 21 years his junior but she predeceased him by ten years (1681). Theirs was a happy marriage, but Baxter knew how much she (like many of his parishioners) was disabled by "melancholy" and how much of that in turn could be attributed to experiences of the Civil War. For her mother's house had been used as a garrison, it was stormed while she was in it and houses were burnt all around, and she saw before her very eyes men "being killed, threatened, and stripped of their clothes". When, in later life, Baxter would say, and mean it, that bad government was preferable to no government, it was the anarchy of civil war that was etched into his soul. Sentimentally he could applaud the Huguenot resisters of La Rochelle, and yet wonder in the end whether the price they had paid for that resistance was too high, "the description of whose case cannot

45

be read without horror".

What were the political and religious lessons that Baxter learnt from the Civil War, apart from these emotional ones? We should here distinguish two phases of the Civil War, as Baxter himself did. The first was its origins. About this Baxter had much to say in his memoirs, and they have been much used subsequently by historians. They are misleading, however, for a number of reasons. They were composed a long time after the events described; they were edited by a friend, Matthew Sylvester, after Baxter's death (the Everyman edition of his autobiography – the source most commonly used by the general reader – is itself an abridgement of Sylvester's work); they were written in secret with an eye on the Stuart censor. Baxter's real thoughts (though also retrospective) are confined to letters and private papers, though they surface to some extent in his embarrassingly frank *A holy commonwealth* of 1659. To summarize them baldly: the Civil War was a just defence by Parliamentarians against Irish Catholic rebels, who had killed 200,000 Protestants in their own Rebellion of October 1641 as the first stage of a planned take-over of the three Kingdoms (remember this mythical, but widely touted, figure was in excess of the estimated total casualties of the entire war); the King was heavily implicated in this, through the dealings of his Catholic wife Henrietta Maria, and through his own secret agreement with the Earl of Antrim, one of the leaders of the Irish Rebellion. Up until about 1643 Parliament's war was defensive and legitimate; its resolution would be the return of the deluded Charles I to his senses, and then to his rightful throne. Baxter's analysis is here at one with Prynne's. So too there is a common perception that the war changed its nature in the middle: the "good old cause" became debased. Baxter puts it like this: the war became one for religion, as it had not been before. This has often put historians on the wrong scent. Baxter didn't mean that until 1643 it had been simply about the constitution. Rather, his argument was that a Protestant self-preservative war became prostituted by religious zealots for their sectarian ends.

Up to a point Prynne agreed with him. Rome changed its direction, gave up working through Laudian fellow-travellers (whose game had been rumbled) and now worked through army radicals. That was why Henrietta Maria's chaplain had waved his sword in triumph when the King's head was cut off! Baxter found none of this too far-fetched. He indeed depended upon Prynne for much of his evidence about Popish

Plots. He disseminated the smear against Henrietta Maria's chaplain without embarrassment. But in two respects Prynne and Baxter now diverged. Prynne became the Royalists' "Cato", doing his notable bit for the Cult of the Royal Martyr. Baxter was less forgiving of Charles I. He didn't approve of the regicide, of course, and he wouldn't subsequently take the Engagement to the Commonwealth, but he couldn't also forget the role that Charles I had played in precipitating the crisis in the first place. That was one difference. Another was that, while sharing Prynne's readiness to see Rome's sinister hand in the rise of democracy, he could not leave it there. The wildness of the zealots may have been encouraged by Rome, but their bad behaviour was related to *bad doctrine*. It was his exposure as a chaplain to the ultra-Calvinist views of men like Saltmarsh, Dell and Peter that made him rethink Calvinism. Was the world being turned upside down because of an over-zealous derogation of works? He (like other puritans) had called the clergy who opposed them before the Civil War "Arminians", without knowing what the term meant. Was the time ripe for a reconsideration of Arminianism?

Baxter's health (or lack of it) would be the stimulus for this reappraisal of theology. In February 1647 he had to give up his chaplaincy with the loss of "a Gallon of Blood by the Nose". While convalescing at Rous-Lench, and writing what was intended to be his first published work, *The saints everlasting rest*, he reached page 68 of the manuscript. This was his watershed – "I discovered more in one weeke than in 17 years reading, hearing and wrangling" – and he reaches out for the language of religious conversion (for the only time in his life) to describe his excitement. He had reached a point in the argument – discussing in what sense men could be called righteous – where he was blessed with a "clear apprehension". That apprehension billowed out into a book, his first, *The aphorismes of justification*, originally intended as an appendix to *The saints everlasting rest*. His was not the first puritan *defence* of Arminianism: John Goodwin was there earlier, so too was John Milton, so too later would be George Fox and the Quakers (a link that Baxter would not acknowledge), and so too, earlier, in their opponents' perception, had been the New England ministers who had put the antinomian Anne Hutchinson on trial between 1636 and 1638. It may, though, have been the most telling and most divisive of all these defences; it would prove to be the rock on which negotiations between Baxterian Presbyterians and John

Owen's Independents after the Restoration would founder. All this passed by Prynne, whose Calvinist faith remained undimmed. For him Arminians were just, as they had always been, new-fangled "Copernicans".

The Commonwealth years were the best years of Baxter's life: again a fact that would not be evident from the printed record of Baxter's memoirs. They were the best years, because they were the ones in which he developed a ministry at Kidderminster, after his return from the wars, which became a by-word for pastoral discipline. The key to that discipline lay in catechizing. Mondays and Tuesdays from morning to night were spent in catechizing, taking in 15 or 16 families in a week, and throughout the period about 800 a year. No family *refused* to come. Only a few persons made excuses for not coming. At the delivery of catechisms, Baxter took a catalogue of all understanding persons in the parish. A week before, the clerk would send to every family to tell them when to come, and at what hour. He would normally see them *as a family*; only rarely would outsiders be present. Baxter rejoiced at the results: "I bless God for the change that I see in the Countrey; and among the people, even in my own charge."

But its significance was not confined to the boundaries of Kidderminster. It was a model for export, first within Worcestershire and then to other counties at large. The Worcestershire Association of Ministers was launched in September 1652, and 72 ministers joined in the first three years of its existence. The ministers conferred on discipline and controversy; there were monthly meetings in five major towns, and quarterly meetings at Worcester. The ministers came from Presbyterians, Independents, Baptists (despite those prurient exchanges with Tombes) and Episcopalians – it has been said that "for a mixed organisation of this kind" there was "no previous precedent in England", although Baxter himself acknowledged his debt to Grindal's "prophesyings" in Elizabeth's reign. By the end of 1655 six counties had formed Associations on the Worcestershire model; another seven would be added by 1659.

The Kidderminster catechizings, the Ministerial Associations – these were only possible in a regime that allowed such developments to take place. Was no honour due to the magistrate responsible? There was, and Baxter gave it fully and generously in letters to his friend, John Howe, who was now a chaplain to Oliver Cromwell. None of this comes out in the memoirs written after the Restoration; it wasn't safe to do so. Baxter's *A holy commonwealth* was published at a wretchedly inappropriate time. This notable tribute to Cromwellian rule came out just as Richard Cromwell's Protectorate was tumbling. Baxter had to write a formal retraction in 1670, just as Muggleton had to rewrite *A divine looking glass* in 1661. The effect, in both cases, has been to obscure both men's very real commitment to Cromwell in the earlier period.

The Earl of Lauderdale feared prophetically, in a letter to Baxter in March 1660, that Baxter would lose his chance of playing a decisive role in the restoration of the monarchy precisely because of the wide perception of his Cromwellian commitment. Lauderdale had no time for sentimentalism about Baxter's lost leader: "And as for poore R. P. alas he was but one appendix of his fathers unjust violence." Nevertheless Baxter was offered a bishopric in November 1660, declined it, but gave Lord Chancellor Hyde 17 alternative names to fill the vacant see! Suspicions on the Royalist side nevertheless ran deep. After 1660 he was accused of having killed a man in cold blood in the Civil War. His reply was that the worst he had ever done was to wrestle with a friend in his youth and accidentally break his leg. Roger L'Estrange, the Cavalier propagandist, claimed that Baxter had stolen a medal from his Civil War victim – a canard still operating against Baxter as late as 1704. It had not helped his cause that Pym and Hampden were among the saints whom he had looked forward to meeting in Heaven in his *The saints everlasting rest*.

Many Royalists and Anglicans did not trust him. There were at least two different sorts of Royalists and Anglicans; the real question for Baxter was which one was in the ascendancy. The offer of a bishopric could mean that the right sort were in charge; or that they were only in charge temporarily; or that the wrong sort were making an insincere offer. Both the similarities and dissimilarities between Baxter and Prynne are evident here. Prynne, too, knew there were two sorts of Royalists and Anglicans. There is a sense in which both Baxter and Prynne were themselves one sort of Royalist and Anglican. Both were sentimentally attached to the Elizabethan Church of Foxe and Jewel. Both honoured the perpetuation of that tradition in bishops like Hall, Morton and, above all, Archbishop Usher of Armagh. Usher's model of a "reduced episcopacy" – seemingly a real option in 1660 – was what Baxter sought at the Restoration, because it seemed one way of preserving the pastoral discipline of Kidderminster. When these hopes were dashed, Baxter lost interest in the vacant bishopric of Hereford. Even after the traumatic shock of the Clarendon Code, and expulsion from Kidderminster, Baxter would go on working at negotiations with like-minded divines of the Church such as Wilkins and Tillotson to keep the Usher flame burning. Tillotson – a future Archbishop of Canterbury – was a hero to both Prynne and Baxter. It was to Tillotson, in his will, that Prynne bequeathed one of his turgid volumes. It was Tillotson who encouraged Baxter's executor, Matthew Sylvester, to get on with the posthumous edition of his memoirs.

In what way then did Baxter and Prynne differ? In two important respects: in their assessment of the roles of Charles I and Laud. For Prynne, the King had been blameworthy in listening to false counsel. That false counsel needed to be removed, and the King would then be restored to his senses. This was the basis of his official defence of Parliament in the Civil War. He only strayed briefly from that line in 1643 when his *Popish royall favourite* makes the accusation of active, not passive, complicity against Charles I (and this was a pamphlet to be much drawn upon by Baxter). As we saw, by the time of the trial and regicide, Charles I had become for Prynne the spotless Protestant martyr (though unkind opponents did draw attention to differences of portraiture between 1643 and 1649). Laud, on the other hand, was for Prynne a Papist agent. Prynne tried to rig his trial on these lines, and the misleading account he wrote up later of the trial represents the way it *should* have gone, not how it did. True, a raid on Laud's study yielded no incriminating evidence, but this was "not credible"; he had had time to get rid of the material. And the Popish Plot he did uncover (the Habernfeld Plot) had one great weakness. It was a Popish Plot, but it was one *against* Laud. This forced even Prynne to the concession that Laud was not a straight Catholic, but a "middle man between an absolute Papist and a reall Protestant".

Baxter's analysis was more sophisticated. Charles I and Laud were not straight Papists, it is true. Their culpability lay at a deeper level. They both subscribed to the thesis of the great Dutchman, Hugo Grotius, that there could be a reconciliation between Rome and the Church of England, the "French" way (local autonomy and conciliar power) rather than the "Italian" way (submission to the sovereignty of the Pope). Baxter agreed that Charles I had been done to death by Papists, but this was not because of his fidelity to Protestantism, but because "Italian" Catholics wanted to do down "French" Catholics.

Hence Baxter's repudiation of the regicide is lukewarm compared to Prynne's; hence, too, he could countenance (as Prynne never could) working with regicides in the Commonwealth. *A key for Catholicks*, written in the same year (1659) as his *A holy commonwealth*, was to prove equally embarrassing to Baxter later, because of the candour there with which he exposed the "Grotian" Plot and Charles I's complicity in it. The 1674 edition of that same work is as much a radical reworking of material as Muggleton's 1661 version of the 1656 *A divine looking glass*, and for the same reasons. Baxter would claim (though this with hindsight, in manuscript) that it was secret negotiations with Peter Gunning (later to be bishop of Chichester, and then Ely) in 1659 and 1660 that convinced him that the Church had not abandoned its "Grotian" designs, and therefore he could not accept a bishopric. Again, in manuscript and with hindsight, Baxter alleged that as early as 1660 most of the bishops knew that Charles II was a secret Papist.

There are roughly three distinct phases in Baxter's attitude to the Church of England after the Restoration. Between 1660 and 1676 – outed by the Clarendon Code – Baxter preaches submission. This is the period when he writes off *A holy commonwealth* as a folly; urges fellow Protestant victims not to become separatists; invests in the Wilkinses and Tillotsons of the Church, not the Heylyns and L'Estranges; and abandons clerical attempts to control the State in his massive treatise, *A Christian directory*, of 1673. Between 1676 and 1684 he moves in a more sectarian direction. Like Andrew Marvell, he gives up on the bishops: "Grotianism" has triumphed. And the Treaty of Dover (secret and non-secret) confirms the worst suspicions about Charles II. In 1682 he would argue that the "world turned upside down" zealotry in the Roundhead Army (which had propelled him in reaction into Arminianism in 1647) was tame stuff after the revelations of Titus Oates: "whats the absurd Speeches of a few ignorant Souldiers, that are dead with them, to the Heresies and Schisms that these 1000 or 1200 years continue in all the Roman Communion". Retaliation would follow swiftly. In June 1682 his goods were seized. In 1683 the Oxford Convocation organized a notorious bookburning, in which Baxter's *A holy commonwealth* went up in flames with Hobbes's *Leviathan* and Milton's writings. And in 1684 his *Paraphrase of the New Testament* was interpreted as seditious, and brought him before Judge Jeffreys. Before the inevitable guilty verdict by a packed jury, this exchange was recorded:

> Now Dr Oates being whipped a little before, and my lord and the government being in a whipping mood . . . the people, especially the ladies, of whom there were some of good quality, burst out a-weeping, and amongst the rest a Conformist in his gown and scarf, one Dr Ford, a comely, grave man, who stood near my lord upon his left hand, who seemed not at all to like these things. But Jeffreys, turning his wall-eyes hither and thither, and seeing all the persons upon the bench almost (except himself) in tears, he calls out to Mr Baxter, saying to this effect:
> *Lord Chief Justice* Come you, what do you say for yourself, you old knave! Come, speak up: what doth he say? I am not afraid of you for all the snivelling calves that are got about you.
> *Mr Baxter* Your lordship need not, for I will not hurt you. But these things will surely be understood one day, what tools one sort of Protestants are made to persecute and vex the other.

Baxter had spent a lifetime unravelling the "Grotian" conspiracy, which ensured that "one sort of Protestants" persecuted and vexed the other. But he had failed; his enemies had triumphed. He was to languish in prison between 1684 and 1686. By the end of his sentence, an open Catholic, James II, sat on the English throne. No time would have seemed less propitious for Baxter to rediscover the virtues of "National Churches" and the power of Christian Magistracy and to turn his back upon separatism. But, in this third and final phase of his Restoration thinking, this is precisely what he did. Secret investigations into the Apocalypse led him back to its greatest English interpreter, John Foxe, and to the role of the Christian emperor. But there was the rub: Foxe had his Elizabeth; Baxter on the other hand had James II. He was released from prison in 1686, but two years later the providential turn of events gave England an unambiguous Protestant sovereign at last – the first since Richard Cromwell and Oliver Cromwell, and before them Elizabeth herself. The result was a flood of pamphlets in his last two years of life in praise of "National Churches", and a posthumous tract called *The poor husbandman's advocate*, which would not be published until 1926, but which contains the most savage critique of the Protestant Ethic, from the man commonly seen as its supreme exponent.

Part II

Historical controversy

Chapter Five

Puritanism and revolution

The circumstantial case for linking puritanism to revolution seems at first sight overwhelming. It was puritans who debated the ends of government at Putney in 1647: these were no chinless wonders from Sandhurst but men like Nasser's colonels from Egypt, impregnated with revolutionary ideas. Puritans subscribed to a political theory of resistance: the great names here were Calvin himself, Beza, Buchanan, Knox, du Plessis Mornay and Hotman. They had a determinist faith ("God made them as stubble to our swords", was Cromwell's chilling verdict on the enemy at Marston Moor) that a latter-day Lenin, Hitler, or Mao, could recognize. They knew how to organize revolutions: John Field's "classical system" for English Presbyterians in the 1570s and 1580s could have been the model for the Algerian Revolution of the twentieth century. Indeed in Pontecorvo's great film *The battle of Algiers*, the revolutionary cellular system – in one scene sketched out on a blackboard – could have been lifted straight from Cartwright, Travers and the Presbyterian Book of Discipline.

Our three puritan case studies only serve, it would seem, to reinforce that connection. To the American historian of puritanism, William Haller, Prynne stood for all the cranky nihilism of "root and branch" puritanism. Muggleton's was only one of many radical groupings thrown up by the "world turned upside down" upheavals of the 1650s. And as for Baxter, he was the man who justified rebellion in 1659, repudiated these sentiments to save his skin in 1670, but lived long enough to see his writings publicly burnt in 1683 for their seditious content.

When we probe a little further, the case, however, becomes more complex. Not all puritans fought for Parliament; not all anti-puritans fought for the King. Baxter drew up lists of names to support both points, though it must be said that they were not gargantuan in size.[1] More important is the fact that he and Prynne never fought against the King (they said), only against his advisers. Leveller activities at Putney they both abhorred, not admired. If they both had revolutionary theories available to use, what is impressive is the fact that they didn't use them. Nor did most of their English co-religionists until well into the Civil War. Calvinist determinism actually put Baxter off when he met it in face-to-face encounters with army chaplains in 1645 and 1646. Neither Prynne nor Baxter was the least bit interested in a Presbyterian remodelling of the Church; indeed from August 1645 it was what Prynne fought strenuously to avoid happening. We shall see that Haller's Prynne is a caricature, that Muggleton broke irrevocably with his origins in 1661, and that the Oxford Convocation of 1683 condemned Baxter's *A holy commonwealth* for most of the same principles which that book itself condemns. Baxter protested at being lumped with Hobbes in the book-burning at Oxford. But he didn't object to book-burning *per se*: it was, after all, the medicine that he was ready, with the Master of Trinity College, Cambridge, to prescribe for *Leviathan*, as early as March 1652.[2] For Baxter, *A holy commonwealth* is therefore the wrong book in the right bonfire.

All three puritans were (we shall see) legatees, not of a continuous revolutionary tradition, but of a continuous *counter-revolutionary* one. They were, in other words, Protestant imperialists, brought up on a diet of Foxe and Jewel to recognize the authority of the sovereign. A common hero was Thomas Bilson, bishop of Winchester, who in 1585 had established the general rules for debate: "Christian Subjection" for Protestants, "Unchristian Rebellion" for Papists. No limits, it would seem, could be set to the obligations of "Christian Subjection" on a Protestant – even a Nero must be endured. Except one limit, that is, although that was a hypothetical one: if a Protestant king sold out to Popery, then the case was altered. Bilson was reassuring here: "none but a madman will doe it". But still that is what a madman did try to do in 1688. And earlier? Andrew Marvell's searing essay *An account of the growth of Popery* applies conspiracy theories to James II's brother in the 1670s, and we know that by that date Baxter shared Marvell's view of the man who had negotiated the secret Treaty of Dover.[3] And earlier still – what of their father? For Baxter and Prynne, the Ulster rebellion of October 1641 was the supreme justification for the later English Civil War: in Baxter's words, "and when the Irish murdered two hundred thousand, it's like they would have destroyed a protestant nation if they could".[4]

What Bilson had offered in 1585 as the wildest of conceits – a madman/ruler on the English throne in thrall to Popery – was what Protestants were actually to experience in the successive reigns of Charles I, Charles II and James II in varying degrees. That becomes the imperial case for disobedience that Baxter made in 1691 at the end of his long life. Before we dismiss it out of hand as special pleading let us play for a moment the counter-factual game: suppose all three sovereigns to be wholly untainted with Popery, would puritans then ever have been so plausibly linked with the concept of revolution? Turn to their successors. Certainly Dutch and Hanoverian successors seemed to have been given the benefit of very large doubts as they extended the royal prerogative, but *in a Protestant direction.*[5] Turn back to their predecessors. Seventeenth-century puritans vied with Professor J. E. Neale in their love of Elizabeth I. A cynic might object that it is easier to love a memory than an actuality, and that it was all very well for the London "root and branchers", Stephen Marshall and Cornelius Burges, to open the Long Parliament on the anniversary of her accession day with fulsome tributes to her reign but what of the puritans *of her time*? Were the two Wentworths, Stricklands, Nortons, Fields, Cartwrights and company remarkable for their loyalty then? But this is a trap about "puritanism" we mustn't fall into. It is not a monolith. The puritans of one century can't be made to speak for the puritans of the next. The Presbyterianism of Elizabethan puritans left men like Prynne and Baxter cold. Prynne called Cartwright an "opposite" and even claimed Archbishop Whitgift as a "puritan".[6] For Cornelius Burges – Elizabethan "root and brancher" – to *decline* the Covenant in 1643 as a Scottish/Presbyterian imposition therefore necessitated no gymnastic somersaults.[7] If Burges, Baxter and Prynne sentimentalized the Elizabethan establishment, it was self-deception; that sentimentalism itself becomes part of the baggage they bring with them for the inspection of the twentieth-century historian.

The weak link in this puritan justificatory chain is Charles I. He seems to be just one madman (on the Bilson definition) too many. Two American historians have made us think again. Caroline Hibbard, without ever saying that Charles I *was* involved in a Popish Plot, shows how in the context of the age his actions could make such a belief plausible.[8] The identification is pressed more closely still in Jane Ohlmeyer's researches. For her it remains very much an open question whether Charles I had secretly commissioned his friend, the Earl of Antrim, to raise an army in 1641 to crush Protestantism in Ireland. The Antrim Commission is central in what has survived of Baxter's memoirs in manuscript form on the origins of the Civil War: a centrality not acknowledged in Sylvester's 1696 edition, still less in Lloyd Thomas's twentieth-century *Everyman* abridgement, but only fully recognized in published form in Calamy's 1702 abridgement of Sylvester. There is a real problem here with evidence. Antrim "revealed" the plot in a series of declarations in May 1650. These depositions have not survived in their original form; nor similarly has any correspondence between Charles I and Antrim. But Ohlmeyer is persuaded that "the balance of evidence indicates clearly enough that it was not just a figment of Antrim's imagination", and nobody is better qualified than Antrim's biographer to pronounce on the workings of the mind of that strange man.[9] All of which does not make Charles I himself guilty of having planned Popish Plots, but it does make contemporary fears to the contrary, just that little bit more understandable.

So far, we have stayed with the negative side of Protestant imperialism – how should a Protestant subject cope with a Popish king? But what of the positive side, what Bilson called "Christian Subjection", which he had wanted to differentiate so sharply from "Unchristian" (i.e. "Papist") Rebellion? And we begin that discussion with the first of our case studies, Prynne.

Until civil war broke out, Prynne was more royalist than the King. Parliament had its susceptibilities ruffled in the 1620s by court flatterers like Mainwaring, Dickinson and Sibthorpe.[10] Of this we get no intimation in any of Prynne's voluminous writings in the 1630s. Only when he was castigating "Parasites" at the court of Oliver Cromwell in 1656 would he permit himself a backward shocked reference to the excesses of Mainwaring.[11] Why not in 1627 when the shock could have made an impact? It was similarly not until he was producing his imaginative history of Laud's trial in the Civil War that he would refer back to Sibthorpe's controversial sermon – and then not for the absolutist doctrines that had caused offence when Sibthorpe delivered it, but for alleged anti-Catholic passages in it that had been expunged, from the printed sermon, by agents of Laud.[12] As a puritan his quarrel with the bishops was not with their absolutism but with their clericalism, which put their *iure divino* claims for their office above *iure humano* claims for the Royal Supremacy.

William Bradshaw in 1605 is arguably the first puritan to accept that he *was* one. And it is interesting that his litmus test for a "puritan" was fidelity to *iure humano* claims for episcopacy.[13] Prynne agreed, and that is why Whitgift, in not claiming more for his office (as his successors fatally would go on to do) was "in this very point ane arrant Puritane", according to Prynne. Foxe and Jewel were his heroes, earning between them in one pamphlet of 1637, (of over 300 pages), no less than 67 citations.[14] Prynne in his pamphlet *Histriomastix*, which cost him his first round of ears, followed John White of Dorchester in extolling Constantine, first Christian Emperor, for suppressing plays, in linking Constantine with "our famous Queen Elizabeth", and in comparing the depravities of the 1630s with those that faced Constantine when he began *his* reforms.[15] We know about White's Dorchester now through the researches of David Underdown, and it looks very much as if it were England's own Geneva.[16] And yet – as Underdown points out – White's is an evangelism *within the Church of England* and owes nothing to creeping Presbyterian sympathies. And it was not just Prynne who claimed for himself tenuous links with Archbishop Whitgift. His Presbyterian opponent, George Gillespie, would say as much from the opposite side in 1646 when he noted how Prynne's advocacy of Christian magistracy took up the themes of "Bishop Whitgift's plea against the ruling Elders".[17] Part of the case against Prynne in his first trial was that "he seems to vilifie the presente Parlms. and Counsell in comparison of Queene Eliz. and hers".[18] That old-fashioned Elizabethanism could be construed as new-fangled revolution was, to Henry Parker in 1641, a proof of the way in which the word "puritan" was becoming debased. And he saw in the authorities' equation of Prynne/Bastwick/Burton with Catholic regicides Garnet/Fawkes/Ravilliac a dangerous self-fulfilling prophecy.[19]

Even so, as late as mid-1641, it was not certain that the Elizabethan compromise now on offer would not prove acceptable to Prynne; it was what the Scot Robert Baillie feared, and what the anti-Laudian bishop John Williams hoped.[20] If he became in the end a "root and brancher", it was for the satisfaction of millenarian hopes and for the resolution of anti-Catholic fears, not as the result of hankerings after Scottish Presbyterianism. Nor did Scotland (or Geneva) provide for him the texts for rebellion. The first thing that Prynne ever wrote on the Civil War was an immediate justification of Sir John Hotham's refusal to yield Hull to the King on imperial grounds.[21] He turned not to Calvinist resistance theory then, but to the teachings of an *anti-Calvinist*, Hugo Grotius: "That a King who aliens and would actually deliver up possession of all or any part of his Realm to another forraign power without the peoples consent, may lawfully be resisted with force of arms by his Subjects."[22] And this is the interpretation that he would develop at length in the most bitter of all his works, *The Popish royall favourite* of 1643.[23] The argument of the book is set out in the preface. The Irish had rebelled because Parliament had threatened the Papists. The Queen left the country to help them. The King deserted Parliament and gathered malignants around him. And when in the same year Prynne produced the official case for Parliament, he wrote there of a grand conspiracy against the Protestant religion, "the very Embrio and primitive cause of the deplorable warre".[24] The King could not shelter behind his advisers: "Judge then whether the Kings departure from, and taking up Armes against the Parliament, be not only and wholly to maintaine his Roman Catholikes and their Religion . . . what ever he pretended, protesteth to the contrary."[25] As the war proceeded, Prynne was shaken by the cumulative documentary evidence that was thrown up of the traffic between Rome and the Stuart monarchy. The rot went back as far as James I, he now had to accept. When James Howell sought to exculpate James I from complicity with "evile counsellors" in the negotiations for the Spanish marriage, Prynne angrily rebuked him: "King James, and some of his great Ministers of State . . . have had overmuch commerce with Rome, which is now no time to palliate."[26] A rare Prynne manuscript has survived, in 1643, in the form of a letter that shows the importance to him of learning the details about the abortive Spanish match.[27] He noted too an exchange of letters between James I and Bishop Williams on the subject of dispensations for Catholics: two former heroes now had serious question marks against them. Even Archbishop Abbot's hostility to the match was put in a wider context of "divers Bishops" approving of it. Where did this leave James I? Prynne wondered indeed "whether King James were really so zealous a Protestant, and anti-Papist, as the ignorant world reputed him, especially in his declining age?" He described Buckingham as "the first Great Favorite . . . who laid the foundation of the Spanish and French Marriage-Treaties";[28] as early as 1628 Prynne had been on the scent of Buckingham's links with Papists.[29] And at the centre of all intrigues was the Queen: "all things are subject to the Command of Mary".[30]

There is a copy extant of *The Popish royall favourite* that Prynne had presented to the Abbey Library, Bath. A contemporary had scribbled across the margin of page 58 (which lists royal intrigues with Catholics against Protestants) the words: "note Mr. Pryns Loyalty". As another noted at the time: "he would not put his Majestie in an Open Shame; he doth but onely implie that our King is guiltie of Common Breach of Oaths and Promises; and that he is in his Dotage, not able to governe his Kingdome, nor Himselfe".[31]

Historians have been disappointed with Prynne's official defence of the sovereignty of Parliament in 1643. He knew what "sovereignty" was; he had read (and quoted) Bodin. But the result is a confused mish-mash. Historians would have been less disappointed if they had paid attention to the *full title* of his work: *The treachery and disloyalty of Papists to their soveraignes, in doctrine and practise, together with the first part of the soveraigne power of parliaments and kingdomes.* Prynne's priorities could not be more clearly set out there: *first* an exposé of Papist treachery; and *only then* the defence of parliamentary sovereignty. Similarly when he came to write up Archbishop Laud's trial, he turned it into an indictment of Laud's "Popery", not of his encouragement of royal absolutism. And, as we saw, Laud is blamed by Prynne not for encouraging Sibthorpe to cry up the royal prerogative but for editing anti-Catholic excerpts out of the published sermon. His apologia for inserting, into the narrative of the trial, material that hadn't come out during it, is revealing: "no indifferent persons can justly taxe me with partiality or injustice for inserting them into the History, for the fuller discovery of his Popish intentions in this kinde".[32] In 1647 he wrote his most systematic treatise on magistracy. He there drew upon the lessons from Laud's trial: "the late Archbishops familiarity, correspondence and confederacy with Priests and Jesuites to introduce Popish Superstitions, and subvert the established Protestant Religion, was charged against him by the whole House of Commons, as a Treasonable and Capitall Offence".[33] This is a fair summary, not of the proceedings, but of Prynne's account of those proceedings. The rest of the pamphlet spelled out what Christian magistracy *should* be. Prynne wanted *Leviathan*, not Geneva. Like Hobbes, Prynne believed that Charles I had failed, not through being too absolutist (hence his indifference to the court sermons of a

Mainwaring or a Sibthorpe) but through not being absolutist enough. From the Old Testament, Prynne derived his concept of what Christian magistracy should be. His ideal ruler would punish without hesitation even his nearest relatives or friends if they propagated false doctrine: "he SHAL SURELY KILL THEM (without mercy) and his own hand shal be first upon them to put them to death; and afterwards the hands of all the people, and they shal stone them with stones that they dye."[34]

But does this not postulate blind obedience in the subject to the sovereign? Yes, but what is wrong with "blind obedience"?: "it is most evident, that there alwayes hath been, and ever will be much blind obedience in the Church of God, arising principally from the Ignorance, Idlenesse, want of love to the truth and inconstancy of man."[35] There have been in history, one suspects, more ringing advocacies than this of the puritan commitment to "revolution", and indeed (with reference to the next chapter) to "liberty", for that matter.

What is odd about this hymn to "blind obedience", given what we now understand about his philosophy, is not what he said but when he said it. From his earliest writings until 1643 we can see that "blind obedience" to the ruler was no crime in this particular puritan's book; the reverse rather, that the clerics' refusal to give such "blind obedience" to the magistrate (in pursuit of their dubious Papist games) was precisely *their* crime. From "The Popish royall favourite" of 1643 onward, however, the Bilson nightmare had come to pass, and the madness of Charles I may even have had its origins, given fresh dirt on James I in manuscripts discovered by Prynne, in his genes. For this puritan his "revolutionary" period (in his entire life) was some four years, during which his continued desire for "blind obedience" to magistracy had no focus, not even when he was writing his apologia for it in 1647. He would find again that focus ultimately only in a rehabilitated Charles I. The Papists switched their tactics; they no longer tried to work *through* the monarchy by a fifth column in the Church, but *against* the monarchy by Leveller radicalism in the Army. Prynne was thus won back to a royalism from which he would never again depart, although as we shall see the Restoration would test that faith to the limits. Hence the important symbolism for Prynne, at the time of the execution of Charles I, of Henrietta Maria's Jesuit confessor allegedly waving his sword in exaltation as the Royal Martyr's head was severed from its body.[36]

Prynne had left some hostages to fortune in those four years of "revolutionary" writing. In 1648 John Goodwin flatly accused him of "melting down" the "mountain" he had first set up in 1643.[37] Six articles in the Army's impeachment of the King were "collected out of *Romes master-peece*, and will be more fully asserted and maintained from the severall Writings and labours of Mr. Wil Pryn, Esquire".[38] One nice line in sarcasm at the time (*Mr. Prinns charge against the King*) purported to be written in order to scotch rumours in the mouths of the "over-credulous vulgar" that Prynne had now become the King's advocate, and quoted with glee the opposite case that Prynne had mounted in *The Popish royall favourite*.[39] A bogus pamphlet in 1649 even had Prynne defending stage plays: "it is no disparagement for any man to alter his judgement upon better information, besides it was done long ago, and when the King (whose virtues I did not then so perfectly understand) governed without control".[40] It was gibes like these that stung Prynne to a vindication of his "wounded reputation against all imputation of inconstancy and mutability" in his principles or actions. His Calvinistic regard for constancy was expressed in the words "It is Gods own glory to be unchangeable, unvariable, and without shadow of turning . . . So I trust to manifest my selfe . . . to be still the same I am heretofore."[41] He went on to stress in another pamphlet of that time that Parliament, in all its legislation, had professed not to be against the Crown; that Jewish kings, however sinful, had never been judicially deposed; that the depositions of English kings were "only by Popish parliaments in time of ignorance"; and that Charles I was "a protestant King" and "of a temperate and sober life".[42]

Royalists were, not surprisingly perhaps, equivocal about their new champion. A Cavalier news-journal asked: "who would ever have thought, that William should have become a Creature of the contrary Faction?"[43] Another noted that the vices of the "Saints" were now "acknowledged by those of their own gang".[44] Somebody like Matthew Rowe, who deeply abhorred the Army's actions in January 1649, could still say complacently of Prynne's imprisonment for *attacking* them: "so that thus you see, all transgressors must suffer".[45] Only William Sancroft, writing to his father on 11 January 1649, when Royalist hopes were at their nadir, was prophetic in hailing the new convert to their cause:

> You see, the army could never ruine the King, till they null'd the
> Lords and enslaved the Commons, and soe ruined the Parlia-
> ment, that lent the first hand to the setting of them up, and pulling
> down the King. And what shall wee say if Wm. Prinne (Utter barr.
> of Linc. Inne) who was the first incendiary and sowed the first
> seeds of sedition, suffer at last in the Kings quarrell? You will see
> by the papers I send you, he is engag'd: so you neither know him
> and his pertinacity, if you thinke he will retreat.[46]

Other papers have come to light that show how far Prynne indeed was
now committed to royalism: in one episode Milton had been given a
search warrant of Prynne's chambers for papers *belonging to* the
Commonwealth, as well as those written *against it*. Thus *Comus*
would be avenged on *Histriomastix*; moreover, it would seem that
Prynne's amiable practice, as Keeper of the Records in the Tower of
London ten years later, of purloining documents that took his fancy
was already in evidence.[47] His "engagement", as Sancroft called it,
brought him spells of imprisonment in three different castles between
1650 and 1653, but, as Sancroft prophesied, there would be no
"retreat". But if there would be no retreat from royalist principles,
there would be a significant de-escalation of the claims that Prynne
had made for magistracy in 1647. This is clear in a remarkable face-
to-face encounter with Bradshaw at Gray's Inn in December 1654
after his release. Bradshaw defended the Army's actions – even if they
were illegal – on the self-preservative grounds that Prynne had himself
invoked in his defence of parliamentary sovereignty earlier. This led
Prynne to muse on the licence to tyranny, given to men like Cromwell
and Bradshaw, by cant terms like "liberty" (on this, see Chapter 6).
But he went further and, in (I think) a unique piece of self-examina-
tion, questioned his own earlier beliefs. Magistrates, it is true, *should*
be like Gods, whose deputies they were, but there was "a strange cor-
rupting transfusing venom . . . in Soveragne power and dignities".
Therefore (and this is not remarkable) he would not censure earlier
actions of Charles I and his predecessors, since whatever errors they
had committed were surpassed by their reformers. But another moral
(and this *is* remarkable) that he drew was "not greedily or arbitrarily
to seek after Empire, Sovereignty, Power, Majesty". The most valuable trait in a ruler was a compassionate heart:

to listen with a willing ear and thankfull heart to the infirmities, admonitions, oppositions, reprehensions of their reallest Christian friends, and eminentest sincerest Patrons of the Countries Laws, Rights, Liberties, in all cases of publick concernment; rather than to meer creatures and dependents of their own, or to suggestions of projecting selfseekers.[48]

What Prynne wanted now was not a vengeful Constantine but a listening Charles II. There can be no question of the enduring nature of his royalism in the 1650s: Clarendon's papers abound with testimonies to his contribution;[49] they were fully recognized by Charles II himself.[50] But what would happen after 1660 if Charles II listened not to his "reallest Christian friends" but to "meer creatures and dependents of their own"?

There were signs that were not favourable. Sir Thomas Bridges wrote to Secretary Nicholas on 20 March 1661 to suggest that at all costs Prynne must be prevented from continuing as MP in the Cavalier Parliament.[51] The lengths to which some opponents would go is vividly illustrated in the minutes of Bath Council. In September of that same year Prynne's supporters were actually kidnapped in a mayoral election to prevent them from voting.[52] At Archbishop Juxon's funeral in 1663, Robert South delivered a gratuitous swipe at the "famous and scurrilous" Prynne.[53] As late as 18 March 1668, when Prynne pressed for the exemption of an opponent from the royal pardon, Sir Thomas Littleton pointed out that "if Prynne had not had his, he might have been in the same predicament".[54]

Unforgiving royalism was one problem; another surely was the gap between puritan Prynne and the very unpuritan court of Charles II? One historian has scolded Prynne for not being more outspoken about that gap: why not attack the Corporation Act and other Restoration excrescences?[55] The criticism is misplaced. He would go on attacking duels, taverns and drinking of healths:[56] he even reprinted his *Healthes sicknesse* after the Restoration. Yet always these criticisms went in tandem with professions of loyalty to the monarchy. They were aimed, in other words, at a listening king. When the Baptist Henry Jessey, on the other hand, lifted Prynne's criticisms, he dropped their royalist accompaniment.[57] But Prynne did attack the Corporation Act, not only legally if futilely in the Commons,[58] but by an extra-constitutional anonymous printed plea to the Lords.[59] On 12

July 1661 the Commons Committee investigated the authorship of the paper which was described as "seditious". On 15 July the Committee reported that Prynne had confessed to the authorship, and the House proceeded to consider the offence.[60]

The sequel was astonishing. Prynne made a full recantation. According to one news-journal, "he spoke with a great sense of his own offence and the Houses goodness, not offering to justifie the least line of his Paper, which his conscience told him he could not".[61] The House was satisfied with his statement and remitted his offence. Some of Prynne's enemies were even more satisfied. Lord Herbert wrote to his wife:

> Mr. Prinne, contrary to what everybody expected from his temper, very humbly and penitently begg'd pardon of the House, named the judgment they had given to be just and that he did concurre with us in it, and shoulde receive the pardon he askt from us as a meere mercy and not at all pretended to by any merit of his. This we esteem I assure you a conquest worthy to be bragged of, and therefore I cannot forbeare letting you kno it.[62]

Was 1661 the "conquest" Herbert bragged of? That judgement needs qualifying. After 1661 Prynne would continue to attack manifestations of the new "Laudianism" where he found it. But he drew comfort in contrary tendencies, exemplified by men like Tillotson (the future Archbishop of Canterbury) to whom he would leave one of his tomes in his will. In any case Prynne saw the Corporation Act not, as Shaftesbury would later, as the first step in "the State Master-Piece",[63] but as another round in the Commons-versus-Lord struggle. His partisanship of the Lords would lead him into further trouble after 1661,[64] and he would be censured again by the Commons for breach of privilege.[65] Nor does it seem that the skirmish affected his standing in the Commons, since a fortnight later he would find himself managing a conference with the Lords on restraining unlicensed printing (on which he was now presumably something of an expert).[66] In March 1662 he would be on a committee appointed to investigate a seditious libel by George Wither.[67]

The "conquest" was more personal than political, but on that level it was a traumatic one for Prynne. Lord Herbert understood as much: "Mr Prinne . . . did that to us hee never could bee brought to do before to any persons breathing by any meanes imaginable. Hee owned himself very submissively to have committed an offence, and askt our pardon with teares in his eyes".[68] Why allow the Lord Herberts their triumph? In February 1661 he called himself "quite tyred out".[69] Is this the explanation, understandable enough, although it is one not supported by the zeal with which he would continue to hound Jesuits, Jews and Quakers in the 1660s? There is another explanation. A news-journal noted that, in his recantation, Prynne "spake largely, setting forth what service he had done for the King formerly, how kind and civil the King had been to him etc."[70] Prynne was no placeman. He was the last man to be swayed by considerations of "how kind and civil the King had been to him". Prynne saw it the other way round. The King had been kind and civil to him *because* of the service that Prynne had done for him. Modesty was not Prynne's strong suit: he had given Charles II back his throne; that was his perception. In recognition of this fact Charles had made him Keeper of the Records in the Tower of London. Psychologically this made the bond tighter: Prynne felt for Charles the gratitude of a patron for his protégé. Stephen Charleton had noted in May 1661 that "Parliament have voted it a *Premunire* to say that His Majesty is popishly affected".[71] In 1691 Baxter would say that he himself was "past doubt" as early as 1660 that Charles II was a Papist.[72] There is no evidence that Prynne shared this insight, if true. He was certainly no Byzantinist (and could therefore oppose Excise and the impeachment of Clarendon after the Restoration). What he was, though, was an imperialist, but one with scaled-down aspirations. He used the records in the Tower of London that Charles II had entrusted him with, to advance Charles's imperial role. Thus he would call his *Aurum reginae* of 1668 a minor contribution to the defence and assistance of "all Jurisdiction, Priviledges, Preheminences and Authorities granted to or belonging to the IMPERIAL CROWN of the REALM".[73] The major contribution was the four volumes entitled *An exact chronologicall vindication . . . of our Kings supreme ecclesiastical jurisdiction*. In the introduction to the fourth volume he would argue: that the King embodied the patriarchal authority of Adam; that he was God's viceroy to implement His rule upon earth; that the distinction between civil and ecclesiastical is an artful invention of the Papists; that clerical power has no authority underived from the Crown.[74] These were the four principles, not of his dotage, but of his lifetime. And they were *anti-revolutionary* principles: it was his misfortune (and that of fellow puritans?) that there was a period between 1642 and 1647 when, in fidelity to these same anti-revolutionary principles, paradoxically he would have to oppose the Crown. But he found his way back to royalism by 1647 – not always, as we have seen, convincing his new allies – and never thereafter departed from it.

And why didn't Richard Baxter do the same? In the Baxter archive there exists an anonymous, undated letter to him. It shrewdly points out the contradictions between Prynne's attacks on "The Popish royall favourite" in 1642 and 1643 and his royalism in 1647, 1648 and 1649, and then asks why Baxter doesn't simply recant, like Prynne did, his misinformed views of earlier times?[75]

The writer could simply have been on the wrong tack. The two men might have been called "puritans", but their political views might still have been poles apart. But that is not the case. Baxter would have subscribed wholeheartedly to Prynne's four imperial principles. Like Prynne he was blown off a royalist course in 1642 by a shared perception that the Crown itself was not to be trusted as the custodian of these four imperial principles. Crucial to this perception was belief in a "Popish Plot", and Baxter reveals in all his subsequent writings his indebtedness to Prynne for the revelations provided by Prynne's researches.[76] Nothing was more telling than the link both men made between the Irish Rebellion of October 1641 and the English Civil War, and the part played by Charles I in commissioning the Earl of Antrim to raise rebel forces.[77] In Prynne's *Romes master-piece* there are references to how the Papists "procured the Queene, by the Earle of Antrims and Dutchesse of Buckinghams mediation, to send amunition to the Irish Rebels"[78] and more direct still, in his *The Popish royall favourite*:

> the bloody slaughter, and butchery of above one hundred and forty thousand Innocent Protestants (whose blood must passe altogether unrevenged by the hands of Royall publick justice) and by Special Commissions (as we are most certainly informed), a very probable argument they had not only pretended but reall Commissions from the King at first for what they acted against the Protestants in Ireland.[79]

The importance that Baxter gave to the Irish Rebellion and the

Antrim Commission in the origins of the Civil War is evident, in profuse detail, in his private papers. That importance has been obscured by his memoirs, first by Baxter's own reticence in writing up his recollections of past events in Restoration England, but second (and even more deadly), by the selectivity of those who later edited them. Calamy, alone among his editors, emphasized the paramount importance of Irish rebellion and royal complicity: Sylvester (his first) and Lloyd Thomas (his last) were at pains, for different reasons, to play down these preoccupations. Unlike Prynne, Baxter was not a *contemporary* public commentator on the Civil War, but between 1658 and 1659 he did commit to print his reflections on what had brought about the conflict. These were written up in three pamphlets.

The first was *The Grotian religion discovered*. He acknowledged in this work his profound debt to Hugo Grotius, not least (as with Prynne) for his insight that obedience to the magistrate had its self-preservative limits. But he came to bury Grotius, not to praise him; or at least to bury the design, associated with Grotius, to bring about a reconciliation between English Protestants and French Catholics. Baxter called "the Grotian design" the "cause of all our wars and changes here in England". Charles I was not a Catholic (he did not need to be) but "while he as a Moderate Protestant took hands with the Queen a Moderate Papist, the Grotian design had great advantage in England, which he himself boasted of". The Pope and the Italians so feared it "that they might very probably have a considerable hand in raising our war, to break the plot". No doubt, said Baxter, the Pope thought himself unsafe when "Grotius and such as he" argued for a combination of "France, England and the (now Popish) Queen of Sweden". Like Prynne, Baxter saw the regicide as an *Italian* Papist manoeuvre: "it was by the Roman influence that the late King was put to death".[80]

The second was *A key for Catholicks*, published in 1659 but republished in 1674. The later edition drops the dedication to Richard Cromwell and replaces it with the Earl of Lauderdale's name. But equally revealing are the textual omissions. In the earlier edition the justification for fighting the Civil War – "offensive Armes only against Delinquents" – is replaced by a statement in 1674 of the opposite: an argument on the illegality of raising arms against the King.[81] Dropped from the 1674 edition is his concern for the life of the Protector, and his perception of the Army/Jesuit tie-up that constitutes the threat:

"And whence came it that Sexby, and others, that have been Soldiers in our Armies have confederated with Spain to murder the Lord Protector? And whence came their Jesuiticall Treasonable Pamphlets (such as Killing no Murder)?"[82] The regicide cannot be made a Protestant responsibility, but he goes further than in the previous pamphlet in arguing that "if the Body of a Common-wealth, or those that have part in the Legislative Power, and so in the Supremacy, should unwillingly be engaged in a war with the Prince, and after many years blood and desolations, judicially take away his life as guilty of all this blood, and not to be trusted any more with Government, and all this they do, not as private men, but as the remaining Sovereign Power, and say they do it according to the Laws", this then is a different kettle of fish from "the Powder-Plot or Papists murdering of Kings".[83] This passage too was dropped from the 1674 edition.

The third of his pamphlets, also published in 1659, was *A holy commonwealth*. This would have no reprinting in 1674; indeed by 1670 he had formally repudiated it, and in 1683 the Oxford Convocation cast it to the flames. Did he confess to having been a revolutionary in his recantation? Actually no – the wording of his recantation is exquisitely opaque.[84] It was the evasiveness of his response that tempered one correspondent's pleasure in his having made it.[85] And did the Oxford authorities make their "revolutionary" case against *him*? Baxter's reply is actually impressive. He notes the first of the 27 condemned propositions, "all civil authority is derived originally from the people", and shows how he had refuted it throughout the book – which was true – as the poisoned legacy of Hooker.[86] He then looks at the five "*de facto*" propositions attributed to him in turn. First, "if lawful persons become tyrants they forfeit right to government". This is answered, correctly, by Baxter's appeals to non-resistance of "even infidel, yea, and even atheist kings": Nero must be obeyed.[87] Secondly, Parliament has a part in legislation: here he invokes the King's own answer to the XIX Propositions of June 1642 and points out that he never said that the King "may be overruled by the other two" of the three Estates.[88] Thirdly, possession gives right to government: like popular sovereignty, a doctrine expressly repudiated by Baxter in his writings; he quotes, as his counter-authority, the works of Edward Gee.[89] Fourthly, new covenants cancel old: a doctrine deplored by Baxter as subversive of all government.[90] The fifth allegation is the only one to come near to Baxter: "*The Twenty-seventh Proposition*", that "*King Charles the first made war upon his Parliament, and in such a case, the King may not only be resisted, but he ceaseth to be King*". Baxter claimed that he had renounced the first point in 1670, that he "cannot find" that he ever said the second, but admits he cited Grotius "for somewhat like it". Nevertheless saying "somewhat like it" is not the same as "owning it"; all he said was that Natural Law allows for self-defence, that Grotius had said that *regere* and *perdere* were incompatible, and that Bilson had said of the possibility Grotius thereby raised, of a ruler selling out his own realm, "*None but a madman will do it.*" And its relevance to 1642? – "And when the Irish murdered two hundred thousand, it's like they would have destroyed a protestant nation if they could". And its relevance to Charles I? – "Whether the false pretending to the King's commission made it unlawful for the two hundred thousand murdered protestants to have defended themselves against the Irish, or whether they might have done had it been true, I meddle not with that."[91]

It is notable that Baxter's sure-footed responses to charges of sedition in 1683, and confident quoting of the supposedly incriminating texts in his defence, only breaks down on the question of whether Charles I *was* Bilson's "madman". The proposition, which in 1683 he would not meddle with, became the central thesis of one of the last works he ever wrote in 1691. "French" Catholics (seeking reconciliation with Protestants) are a *greater* menace than "Italian" Catholics. They seem different, and more acceptable than their "Italian" rivals, in not being for toleration, and in not being for the Pope but for conciliar supremacy. But these differences are illusory. It is not "the Mass and other Corruptions" they have in common that matters: "it is government that is the form of Popery" and "French" Catholics, as much as "Italian" Catholics, submit to a foreign jurisdiction. Baxter asks: "must we be Frenchified?" The worst that the Papists ever did was "by pretending his Commission for that most inhumane War and Massacre in Ireland".[92] It seems something of an irrelevancy that in a pamphlet justifying *two* revolutions – 1642 and 1688 – on Protestant imperialist grounds (*in both cases* Protestants had to take self-preservative action against a ruler hell-bent on selling out his realm to "French" Popery), Baxter should interpose this remark: "And though my Exposition of the Revelation have offended many, upon far close study of it since, I am not less but more persuaded" that John Foxe is "much to be regarded".[93]

But this is no irrelevancy: this is the proof of Baxter's good faith in invoking Protestant imperial principles. His "Exposition of the Revelation" *had* offended many Protestants by refusing to cast Rome as Antichrist,[94] but it is his further secret researches into the Apocalypse in prison in 1686 that led to this renewed regard for John Foxe.[95]

Foxe had got it right – unlike the millenarians of Baxter's days – in recognizing that the millennium was a past one, that the rule of the Christian emperor had brought a thousand years of felicity, and that the Papacy who denied this was "Antichrist", *not now in a scriptural sense*, but as the usurper of the King's royal prerogative. Because of their apocalyptic grounding it could be argued that Baxter's last writings are *even more* emphatic on the unlimited majesty of imperial rule than Prynne's had been.[96] And by 1691 they had a focus: William III was as worthy a Constantine to head the "National Church" as (fleetingly before him) Richard Cromwell and, further back still, Elizabeth I and Edward VI had been for *their* times.[97]

We have seen that Prynne was not welcomed unequivocally into the Royalist camp. But it is Baxter who has come down to us as the "revolutionary" puritan *par excellence*. What after all was Prynne's tiff with the Commons over a pamphlet addressed to the Lords, compared with the burning of Baxter's book in 1683 for sedition and his trial on the same charge before Judge Jeffreys, and imprisonment, in 1686? There was a reason for this imbalance. Charles I had wiped out all his past errors, in Prynne's reckoning, when he fell victim to the Papist/ Army plot and died as the Protestant Martyr. Baxter was no less impressed by the documentation in Prynne's works of this Papist/ Army plot. Even in 1691 he would seek to augment it with fresh bits of information. For instance, he had not known at the time

> of Archbishop Bramhall's Letter, printed by Dr. Parr in Archbishop Usher's Life, confidently assuring Archbishop Usher that, on his certain Information, the Papists in 1647 got into Cromwell's Army, and confederated with the Papists at Oxford in the King's Army and have the King put to death: And whether they went beyond Sea for Approbation, and obtained it.[98]

But Baxter had a wider perception than Prynne of the schism between "French" and "Italian" Popery, and on this view Charles I died, not as a Protestant Martyr, but as a "French" Catholic victim. Though initially anti-Cromwellian, and declining the Engagement, he was not committed (as Prynne was) to *Stuart* royalism, and by the end of the decade was looking to Richard Cromwell to introduce a "Holy Commonwealth". We know from Baxter's letters and private papers that he never lost this suspicion of the Stuart monarchy's attachment to "French" Popery, whether that monarch was Charles I, Charles II or James II.[99] He could formally repudiate *A holy commonwealth* in 1670, and rewrite passages in *A key for Catholicks* in 1674, but the authorities were not fooled. And when the loyal Sylvester came to edit his memoirs in 1696 he had to scotch (in his introduction) the persistent rumours that Baxter had it in for the Stuarts. The liberties that Sylvester took with Baxter's text were to clear him of the widespread perception that he was a King-hater.[100]

Which, in one sense, he never was. Prynne had prophesied in 1644 that, if the King failed to deliver, the Jesuits had "an Indian poysoned Nut reserved for him".[101] Now Prynne and Baxter had agreed that the regicide *was* the Jesuits' Indian poisoned nut. But this could not convert Baxter to a *King-lover* (as it did Prynne), because of his recognition of a civil war within the Civil War. Charles I was not a Protestant Martyr to (as Prynne now saw him), but a "French Catholic" victim of, what both men recognized to be an "Italian Catholic" plot in 1649. So Baxter was cooler about Charles I than Prynne was: uncertain whether he was more dupe or accomplice when it came to commissions that he gave to Irish rebels in 1641. This made possible Baxter's late conversion to Cromwellianism, but only when he saw it (in father and son) as an expression of *anti-revolutionary* beliefs. To be in favour of Oliver, then Richard, Cromwell was also in Baxter's eyes to be against democracy, against liberty (see Chapter 6), for "blind obedience" to magistracy, and for Protestantism. They were what both Prynne and Baxter had believed in during the 1630s and 1640s; in the 1650s they made one puritan a Cavalier, the other a Cromwellian, but neither of them a revolutionary.

The Muggletonians would seem at first sight to be outside this consensus: they stood, it appeared, for the ungovernability of the world turned upside down, alien to "mainstream" puritans like Baxter and Prynne. But this is false. Even in the very first of their pamphlets in 1652, Muggleton and Reeve asked a question very pertinent to Baxter and Prynne: "do you not allow of the civil magistrate to govern the rude people?" The answer is begged in the question – a "rude people" *needs* firm magisterial control – and is duly provided: "the magistrate is very needful in every inhabited land, for the government of the people in all civil things, to do equal justice between man and man". In 1652, however, the wrong assumption is that "if such a magistrate could be found, it would be a rare thing".[102] That rare thing *would* happen in 1656, and we shall see the implications of that discovery. After the Restoration, however, expectations would again be lowered, but the need to have an honoured magistrate, to keep the rude multitude in check, was as strong as ever. Muggleton's Pauline respect for magistracy was rooted in the treatment that he and Reeve had received at the hands of the people. Pulled out of his house by head and shoulders, beaten with fists, knocked down in the garden, pursued into fields, Muggleton was saved by the woman whose house he was eventually pulled out of. His assailants slunk off, "lest she should have the Law of them", for abuse perpetrated in her house. Muggleton drew his lesson from the fracas: "So that I am not unacquainted, nor ignorant of Paul's Words, for it hath been always my Desire ever since to be delivered from the rude Multitude, who doth not go by the Law of Reason, but doth act as Brute-Beasts, who have no Reason in them, therefore called unreasonable Men."[103]

Not only Muggleton but also his followers right through to the twentieth century were impressively consistent in applying that lesson. "The Law is good", said Muggleton: it doesn't allow any man to cheat his neighbour.[104] Quakers brought trouble on themselves after the Restoration by holding meetings contrary to the law.[105] Muggleton, it is true, had found himself on the wrong side of the law in 1677, but only because anti-Quaker writings of his, written 13 years earlier, had been dredged up illegitimately by the prosecution. With a better defence counsel, even so, he would have got off: "he made no mention of the Wardens breaking open four doors, contrary to the Laws of England, which was by the Law absolute Burglary."[106] The "thee-thou"-ing of Quakers, and their refusal to pay honour to magistrates, is an attempt to ape the Prophets of ancient times, and this practice results in "every silly man and woman" addressing "thee and thou to Kings and Magistrates of the Earth".[107] No good the chastened Quakers of later history boasting that they were the most peaceful people in the king's dominions – the Muggletonian of 1870 would claim that accolade for his faith: "it is not remembered that even one was ever charged before any tribunal with a breach of confidence".[108]

Perhaps Muggleton even went too far in compliance with the magistrate: he acknowledged the harm done in giving *carte blanche* to his follower, Powell,[109] and made clear to another, Thomas Tomkinson, his displeasure that Tomkinson's brother and sister evaded persecution in the political climate of 1680 by sheltering under the then *safe* label of "Papist"![110] Nevertheless to the scrupulous in 1671 he had pointed out the benefits of the commission that "hath given you Liberty to pay Tythes and to defend yourselves by Law to keep Our Selves from Imprisonment and Sufferings".[111] An unsettled political climate in 1672 was a good reason to Muggleton not to venture out of his house.[112] In another letter in that year he stressed another reason to be around; like Trotsky and Khrushchev, he would find that the Medgate/Buchanan rebellion against his leadership was hatched in his absence through flight "when the Kings Messengers sought after me when they took away the bookes".[113] He advises Tomkinson in 1675 to try putting off being church-warden that year: "who knows what the next year will produce?"[114] A year later in manuscript Tomkinson would go beyond this pragmatism to the most fulsome testament of obedience to magistracy, in terms that would be echoed by Prynne and Baxter:

> it is the law that gives proprietye a man could call nothing his owne if it where not for the law. The desperate distructive divels would cut one anothers throates they would act with the unmercyfull divell spoken of in the gospell take these felons by the throte saying pay mee what thou owest mee but give mee what thou hast or will bee thy death.[115]

If this sounds Hobbesian it is not surprising: in 1707 it is "learned Hobbes" that Tomkinson will invoke, though "opposed all most by all sects and opinions"[116] (though not by fellow Muggletonians in the eighteenth century, some of whom would even annotate *Leviathan*).[117] In 1692 Tomkinson could be candid about Charles II's failings (as Baxter also, a year earlier): "that dark prince sett up Bishops much what like himself to uphold debauchery" and to vindicate harlots.[118] That candour would not be so apparent while Charles II was actually on the throne, for all Muggleton's brave words (as in a letter to a follower in 1675) that "every true prophet cometh to bring a Sword upon the Earth to sett the Nearest Relations one against another".[119] Apart from cousin Roger as his one convert, Muggleton's track record does not support that boast.

The "dark prince's" failings would not set Muggletonians off on a revolutionary path; the danger lay elsewhere. Muggleton (and this is no less true of his followers after) was sincere in wanting to stamp out any actions that were against the law. He was no friend of practical antinomianism, and was aghast at the licence claimed by three followers who had been blessed by the now dead Reeve: "because they had the blessing they said they could not be damned to Eternity".[120] But Muggleton's letter to one particular sinner, William Cleve from Cambridge in 1665, seems almost pusillanimous. Cleve pleaded alcohol to excuse his adultery. Muggleton called both of these sins wicked, but his actual crime was worse still. He had slept with a whore and contracted the pox. The doctor who treated him did not fail to point out to Cleve's fellow-believers what light this behaviour threw on the morals of their sect. So there were to be no comforting words from Muggleton except the recognition that, appalling though his sins were, Cleve's was "not that unpardonable Sinne which can never be forgiven in the world to come".[121] The unpardonable sin, which earned the solemn curse, was of course denying the Prophets' commission. Cleve's sin carries the curse throughout his life, but a minister like John Cotton "may doo well enough in this Life but the Curse will follow hereafter". Muggleton is not meaning to let Cleve off lightly: the reverse. Yet his conclusion *seems* insouciant: "So I must leave your faith and the guilt of your Sin to strive together and which getteth the victory will be Lord." The Muggletonians made an important break with Calvinism when they abandoned the elect/reprobate distinction in favour of the recognition of the two seeds in every person, but they had not broken with the Calvinist insight that salvation and good works were not conterminous. In 1787 a Muggletonian would contrast two rivals: John Peat who, "though a corrupt Man in Nature", died a faithful believer and Joseph Buck, a follower of the schismatic Birch, who "being of the seed of Reason, yet more orderly in nature, but could not rely on that sovereign Balm aforesaid" and committed suicide.[122] Recognition of this paradoxical insight inhibited condemnation of those who transgressed *external* laws in the same round terms as those who challenged the authenticity of the commission. But they were still condemned: *a fortiori* if the rare just ruler solicited their obedience.

That was the scenario in 1656, and led to the most controversial Muggletonian work, *A divine looking glass*. The text would be reprinted in its entirety in 1719 and 1760; revised by Muggleton in 1661, it would be reprinted in that form in 1846. By then Joseph Frost would make acceptance of that edition (pressed upon the British Museum Trustees) as the litmus test for "Old Believers" against "Reevonian" rebels.[123] Controversy over the authentic text was still high among believers in 1933.[124]

Why should this have been so? On the surface it was a matter of dropping over-fulsome references to Cromwell after the Restoration, when the political climate made them embarrassing. It was on those grounds that Thomas Robinson argued, against Frost in 1857, that the original text could be restored once the reasons for political censorship had been removed.[125] The Muggletonians, on this view, had performed a sleight of hand similar to that performed by the Quakers at the Restoration. That was the charge made against the Quakers by Charles Leslie in 1696; ironically, in a pamphlet drawing parallels between Quakers and Muggletonians, he *misses* Muggleton's doctoring of the 1656 text.[126] Now it could be argued, on the basis of some of the omitted passages, that the 1656 text was only a pragmatic justification of obedience to the ruler who happened to be around at that time. Thus the Prophets in 1656 defend Cromwell from the charge of not having been chosen by a free Parliament; argue from Scripture the sanctity of non-resistance; attack populists who undermine magistracy; defend Cromwell's office of Protector; refuse to shed tears for the failure of John Lilburne's rebellion against him; believe that it is not worth setting "the Nation together by the Ears" for constitutional proprieties; see the particular mode of office, in the eyes of God, as a matter of indifference.[127] If Muggleton's omissions had only been of those points, Robinson would have been right. But what he cut out were much more damning passages than these. "Most Heroick Cromwell" is not merely a "rare" just ruler: he is "exalted unto Temporal Dignity beyond the Foreknowledge of Men or Angels in the most holy Name and Nature of our Lord Jesus Christ". It is Providence that has put Cromwell on the throne:

Who can tell for what End the Protector of Heaven and Earth hath so highly exalted him? Again, if thou hast but a little Patience, and shalt see the Lord Jehovah make use of Oliver

> Cromwell to be an Instrument of Acts of general good beyond thy
> Expectation.

They castigate "rational Atheism" or "spiritual Weakness" in those
subjects who were failing to be attuned to "the wonderful Transactions of the Most High God, in this present Age". It is "by full Assurance from the everlasting Emanuel" that Cromwell's expansionist
foreign policy and generous religious freedom is justified. The
"mighty God of Jacob" has brought to pass *both* Cromwell's rule and
the Prophets' commission – they are equated in this argument – and it
is not "Chance" or "deep Subtelty" that has exalted Cromwell, but
Providence.[128]

In 1661 Muggleton cancels Providence as well as Cromwell: they
rose and fell together. He constructs a theology against his co-
founder, Reeve, which denies the thesis that God takes "immediate
notice" of His creatures: a theology that sparks off rebellions
throughout the history of the movement (Medgate and Buchanan in
the seventeenth century; James Birch and Martha Collier in the eighteenth century; the "Reevonians" in the nineteenth century), in which
the authenticity of the particular text of *A divine looking glass*
becomes crucial in the discussion. No wonder that in 1791 a
Muggletonian could say of it that "both Scepticks and Deists approve
of it as the best system of Reveald Religion that they ever saw" – but
he could only have said that of the *amended* text of 1661.[129]

For a period in the 1650s Muggleton had shared with Baxter a
belief in Cromwell's providential destiny to rule. After the Restoration both men settled for less during Charles II's unholy Commonwealth. Unlike them, Prynne had rallied to Charles II but, as we have
seen, with greatly lowered expectations. For Baxter expectations
were raised once more with the turnabout of politics in 1688: William
III would fill the providential role once cast for Richard Cromwell.
For Muggleton providential expectations had gone forever with the
insight that God took no "immediate notice" of His subjects. But a
strange relic survived: the cursing to eternity of one's opponents.
Arden Bonell saw how incompatible this practice was with the new
theology (which he thoroughly approved of). His revision of 1739
makes two points. First, all believers who are not Prophets have only a
conditional power of cursing. Second, even the Prophets, armed with
unconditional powers, could find in the fullness of time that God

would not ratify their curses.[130] While no magistrate would ever again enjoy the status of Cromwell in 1656, for the future history of the movement it is perhaps more important that no magistrate, certainly after 1739, needed to fear the curse of his Muggletonian subjects.

Chapter Six

Puritanism and liberty

"Liberty" and "puritanism" seem as natural a pairing at first as "revolution" and "puritanism" had seemed in the previous chapter. In W. K. Jordan's massive investigation of the rise of religious toleration, puritans have a prominent place.[1] A. S. P. Woodhouse's edition of the Putney Debates is entitled *Puritanism and liberty*.[2] "Liberty" is on the title-page of two of William Haller's studies of puritanism, and is at the heart of all of them.[3] The sensitivity of American scholars in particular to this association may have something to do with ancestor worship. But how firmly based is this connection in reality?

Our three puritans seem at first to make convincing defence witnesses. Were not the three martyrs of 1637 sufferers in the cause of religious freedom? Was not Baxter both victim of Judge Jeffreys' bigotry and champion of ecumenism? Could not the Muggletonian apologist of 1870 with justice claim for his co-religionists a consistent devotion to the principle of toleration?[4] What they have in common in reality is the status of *victims*, and this unfortunately confers a spurious light on these subsequent claims made for them. The Leveller William Walwyn, who is one puritan who did put liberty consistently at the centre of his philosophy, was aware of the ambivalent attitude of some of his fair-weather friends. He applied this insight in turn to his own beliefs – "if we were in power, we would bear our selves as Tyrannically as others have done"[5] – and went on to work out constitutional arrangements to tame the beast in himself.

Prynne, Burton and Bastwick were not freedom fighters like Walwyn, but, in their various ways, they were, rather, disappointed disciplinarians. Their critique of pre-Civil War Laudianism was for its licence, not its rigidity. Bastwick was a late convert to Scottish Presby-

81

terianism – Prynne a transient one – because of the belief that it would effect a godly discipline. Prynne and Burton damned it in the end, because it didn't. Burton saw the autonomy of congregational worship, not as an asylum from tyranny, but as a better way of securing that discipline. The recognition of that common disciplinary aim would, for a period, fuel hopes of a reconciliation between Presbyterian and Independent: that was why Walwyn, in his *The compassionate Samaritane* of 1644, was so bitterly disappointed with the Independent ministers' document, *An apologeticall narration*. It stressed the nearness of position between them and their Presbyterian colleagues, but based on an intolerance of separatists, who were "left in the lurch".[6] Blair Worden correctly sees toleration as that "Victorian subject, a monument to Victorian liberalism".[7] It is the wrong term to apply to puritan efforts to minimize differences among the godly. These were the efforts that Baxter sought to advance through his Brotherly Association of Ministers, begun in Worcestershire and spreading in the 1650s across the English counties. But these were efforts to accelerate discipline, not to advance the cause of freedom. Toleration, on the other hand, meant to Baxter freedom for Papists, the abandonment of the distinction between precious and vile, the renunciation of unity. Spenser's "Una" was set in the puritan mind against the seventeenth-century (false) image of Machiavelli as the apologist for disunity.[8] That is why Haller's portrayal of Prynne as a man who has wandered into the seventeenth century from nineteenth-century anarchism wholly misses the mark.[9]

Prynne's opposition – to Laud in the 1630s, to the King in 1643, to Presbyterian ministers between 1645 and 1646, and to the Commons after 1647 – was not in pursuit of freedom, but in search of bodies who would be fit to carry out the duties of Christian magistracy. The volatile nature of that search, the readiness to pick up and discard instruments for that purpose, betrays a pathological restlessness. It is what Roger Williams – who would certainly prove to be as impressive a defender of religious freedom as Walwyn, but via a totally different route, as we shall see – detected as a psychological weakness in those who hungered for authoritarian solutions: a readiness to "cut off the skirts" when hopes were dashed.[10] Because Prynne does cut off skirts he is no "Byzantinist" (which would have put him at the opposite end of the spectrum from an advocate of "liberty"). To the argument, for instance, that the Clarendon Code rested on the historic rights of magistrates to punish non-attenders at worship, Prynne pointed out that the same logic would justify a Jewish or Turkish take-over of the courts after a successful invasion of this country – to him a *reductio ad absurdum*.[11] Indeed he would oppose not merely magistrates who established Judaism, but even those who would do no more than *tolerate* Jews – like the hapless King John.[12] These qualifications of Byzantinism are not the same thing, however, as an advocacy of liberty. There was one exceptional moment in time, in 1641, when Prynne even thought that an attraction of Presbyterianism was its *independence* of the magistrate.[13] That, and its discipline, made him a fellow-travelling "root and brancher" in 1641 as it also did Milton at the same time.[14] Both were unworried then by the prospective challenge to liberty of "a Pope in every parish". Milton saw this appeal to liberty as the specious cry of the *libertine*. Both had changed their minds in 1644 but for different reasons. Milton had discovered liberty by the time he wrote *Areopagitica*; by that date, Prynne had discovered only that the Presbyterians were not very good at the discipline. In 1641 he had cast sneaking admiring glances to the Continent, to France and Geneva, where the Reformed Churches were promoting godly disciplines. The contrast then was acute in 1641 with a Laudian Church, characterized by "commutates of penance, admission of prophane and scandalous persons to the sacrament, toleration of scandalous, superstitious, lasie, non-preaching and insufficient Ministers".[15] The anonymous writer of 1727, who saw Prynne as a gullible victim of Presbyterian propaganda at that time, had a point; the author of the work called himself a lover of "Christian (but not licentious) Liberty".[16]

The "licentious liberty" that Prynne attacked in the Laudians in the 1630s was to be found for him in the early 1640s in the rise of Independency. One victim of Prynne's broadsides, William Godfrey, protested at Prynne's gross caricature of the movement: "a title properly belonging to the hearde of papists and popish priests and Jesuites".[17] What Prynne had done, drawing upon Aristotle, was to claim Independency as an affront to man's *sociable* nature.[18] But, said the Independent John Goodwin, the discipline, that he and his fellow ministers sought, was that of the Reformed Churches at large.[19] Prynne called this an "improbable untrue surmise",[20] but by 1645 he could not ignore the common desire of Presbyterian, as well as Independent, ministers to suspend communicants from the Sacrament of the Lord's Supper. Since one plank of his anti-Laudian platform had been an attack on the willingness of the clerics then to admit the profane to the Sacrament, surely the suspending power was only the exercise of the very discipline that he was seeking? That is what those ministers said, who advocated suspension. But what they were doing, in Prynne's book, was *depriving* the people of their spiritual food. In other words, suspension was not discipline (with its real, or imagined, threats to liberty), but its opposite: the renunciation of discipline. The words that Prynne uses to deride respectively Presbyterian ministers' suspending powers, Independent ministers' pleas for toleration, and Laudian ministers' neglect of preaching – "a Soul-murthering tyranny", "a very uncharitable, arrogant, yea unchristian practice", "murthering the very soules of thousands of Gods people, by robbing them of their Spiritual food" – sound the same, because they are motivated by the same concern. That concern was not for liberty, but for discipline.[21]

For Prynne the Sacrament was a potential instrument of conversion. To debar sinners from it on dubious grounds was therefore a scandal. Prynne did not (even if he was caricatured as saying this) want admission for the notoriously scandalous, but he did argue that no person *professing penitence* should be denied communion. No wonder that the vaunted speedy reformation promised by "root and branch" ministers had not materialized! By 1645 he would say that "reall speedy reformation in our Church" *could* not come from that "strict discipline, which really reforms very few or none". No more sighs now for what they did on the Continent! On the contrary, "many of our English Congregations", unlike Anabaptists and Brownists "both abroad and at home", had achieved reform with "powerfull preaching without the practice of excommunication or suspension from the Sacrament".[22] The Commons, in the first Parliamentary Ordinance for Scandal of 20 October 1645, would ultimately uphold the *principle* of suspension, but deny the Westminster Assembly's claims to *iure divino* powers in the clergy who exercised it.[23] Six days earlier, Prynne himself was appointed one of the Triers of the Elders for the Classis at the Inns of Court. His subsequent writings would reveal a tortuous attempt to limit his attacks on suspension to the *iure divino* issue, but his fundamental objections to the whole exercise kept breaking through.[24]

The contemporary critique of his former ally Henry Burton is illuminating. Burton honoured Prynne's desire for "a speedy accomplishment of a Reformation", but England "cannot become a Mount Sion in one day".[25] But it was men like Burton who had persuaded Prynne in 1641 that it *could*; that was why he felt such a subsequent let-down. In 1645 Burton argued the virtues of slowness, to give time for people to be educated in the ways of a right reformation. At present, he pointed out, the bulk of the people were ignorant and incapable of playing an active part in the new order. This was no news to Prynne. As a Calvinist he accepted that that was what the reprobate majority *were* and would always be, and that is why they needed to be disciplined into external submission. The externality of the discipline was what bothered another Independent, William Dell: it did not touch the inner man.[26] Oh yes, it did, replied Prynne: "the very body and outward man infect the created soule infused into it".[27] Burton was worrying "that we may not goe blindfold" into reformation; that was just how we should go, thought Prynne. Burton is a puritan who, on this issue at least, sounds therefore distinctly friendlier than Prynne to the cause of liberty. But how sincere was he in asking for delays in order to educate the people? Elsewhere he would argue that all worthwhile disciplinary reform must be *anti-popular* in aim and narrow in structure: for Burton too was a Calvinist. The discipline to be sought was one that refused "indulgence to such manners, as cannot easily be brought to enter in at the strait gate, and narrow way, that leads into Christs Kingdome".[28]

Burton posed these alternatives. Either – ideally – have a national church organized around the principle of unmixed communion; or – if this can't be achieved – have a toleration, which would be liberal enough to permit individual congregations to exercise their own discipline.[29] Presbyterians like Ley and Gillespie were right to argue that, if they could deliver the national discipline, they would, at a stroke, destroy the Independents' case for toleration.[30] Hence the three very different perspectives of the three anti-Laudian martyrs in the 1640s. Prynne saw toleration and suspension as twin vices, which sprang from a common indifference to the fate of the ungodly. Burton saw them as twin virtues, which sprang from a common concern for the purity of congregations. Bastwick, following Ley and Gillespie, saw suspension as a virtue, which eliminated the case for toleration, which he saw as a vice.

The Presbyterian and Independent honeymoon did not last. Scottish Presbyterians like Robert Baillie egged on their English co-religionists, like Bastwick and Thomas Edwards, with his *Gangraena*, to write books against "Libertines" (and he picked out Burton's Independent colleague, Jeremiah Burroughs, as a likely target). That was on 17 June 1645.[31] But only three months later he was identifying a new enemy: "Mr. Prin and the Erastian lawyers".[32] There would be now a dramatic realignment of forces. Instead of Presbyterians and Independents converging on discipline, now it would *seem* that Independents and Erastians were converging on liberty. In October 1645 Burton would lament the "Pens and Tongues of blasphemy, lashing out, and running over all the bounds and banks, not only of Christianity, but even of common modesty and humanity". A marginal note referred to "those infamous books of Tho. Edwards and John Bastwick, too wel known to all".[33] In the same month the Draft of the Commons' Declaration on Church Government showed why Burton was right now to see Erastians as better potential friends for Independency than Presbyterians:

> To such as plead for a toleration of all religious opinions we shall not give an ear, but cannot deny the modest request and reasonable relief of tender consciences, in whose behalf we shall stretch out the line of charity as far as the word of God and the peace of the Kingdom will bear.[34]

This was admirably put: no to a universal toleration; yes to a relief of tender consciences. This would be Oliver Cromwell's formula – and Richard Baxter's. Burton, ever the opportunist, now quoted Henry Parker against the Presbyterian "trojan horse", attacked its religion for "the unreasonableness of it in State-policie" (hardly Burton's overriding aim during the rest of his life), and saw it as a system more suited actually to the Scottish genius than to the English.[35] Burton's behaviour was the sort of thing, as Walwyn saw, that gave advocates of liberty a bad name. For the Independents, "liberty" was in truth a second-best, only to be contemplated if discipline could not be found by any other way. For the Erastians like Prynne, "liberty" was simply a non-issue: discipline would come through the civil magistracy, and its consequence *would* be (no worries on that score) "blind obedience" in the subject.[36] For the Presbyterians, on the other hand, it was a smear word: "liberty" was identical with "libertinism".

The 1650s saw the revival of hopes for union between Presbyterian and Independent ministers, again founded on a common perception of the need for unmixed communion. It was an Independent minister, Anthony Palmer, who would voice these hopes. He would quote the "learned" Presbyterian George Gillespie and sneer at the Erastian tenet "of Church-power being in the Magistrate". He praised Cromwell for allowing Church fellowships to form "through common subjection to Christ, not through coercion by human power".[37] It might have been thought that Baxter's ecumenism would have made him sympathetic to Palmer's argument. Not so: the Ministerial Associations he formed were based, not on unmixed communion, but on the more modest requirements of "visible holiness" in the communicants. When the Independent ministers in the Savoy Declaration of 1658 insisted on "a deeper discoverie", Baxter saw his ecumenical hopes dashed.[38] And he didn't *want* passivity in Cromwell, as Palmer did; he lamented it.[39] Coleridge would think him wrong on this: "it was one among a thousand proofs of Cromwell's attachment to the best interests of human nature".[40] But a fellow puritan minister, John Pointer, sided with Baxter on this: "Take heed of that rotten principle that Magistrates have nothing to do with Religion – they are called in Scripture phrase Lords of restraint".[41] Later, in the 1650s, Baxter's access to Oliver (and then to Richard) Cromwell through the chaplain they shared, John Howe, went a long way to removing these doubts. His *A holy commonwealth* of 1659 expressed his vision of union between an *active* magistrate and a reforming ministry.[42] Reform was to be measured, however, not by how pure the communion was, but by how many souls were saved.

Prynne should have endorsed these aims. He believed in magistrates who should be "Lords of restraint" and in parishioners who should not be debarred from communion on finicky grounds. The trouble was, for Prynne, that Cromwell couldn't *be* that Lord of restraint: only the exiled Charles Stuart could be. The Protector was not only a usurper, but one who was too soft on Jews, Quakers and Papists. That indiscipline showed in the infrequency of communion in the Commonwealth. He cited records from Lincoln's Inn to show the vigilance of Benchers in previous reigns to ensure frequent attendance at the Sacrament of the Lord's Supper. He spoke wistfully of "the rod of the ancient Discipline of the Society". When he saw ministers refusing to administer the Sacrament, he prayed for a revival of the

"Godly Discipline" of the past.[43] And he hit (in the enforced absence abroad of *his* godly magistrate) on a bold way of achieving it. He urged parishioners to refuse to pay tithes to ministers who would not administer the Sacrament.[44]

"Landlords rent and tithes rent will stand or fall together":[45] this was an insight fully grasped by Prynne. On those grounds he would defend tithes in 1653 as "a charge, debt, duty, as well as their Landlords Rents". He would say the same again, against Quakers in 1659.[46] But in 1656 he would (as Baxter argued) borrow a *Quaker* weapon in the tithes debate; he would thus *in extremis* set aside even his deepest social fears, so high did he put the interests of discipline.

Baxter had no need for such desperate expedients, because (until May 1659) he could rely on the magistrate (in alliance with the clergy) presiding over a "holy commonwealth". Liberty in that ideal state certainly for "True Religion, true Faith and true Worship of God" but not for "False Religion, false Faith and false Worship" – a whole cavalry regiment of questions begged by Baxter in formulating that antithesis in the way that he did. But Sir Henry Vane's *A healing question* had made "liberty" the key principle in the "good old cause", and its vacuousness stung Baxter into a furious reply. "Liberty" to preach up "Popery, Mahometanism, Infidelity and Heathenism" – that was the "Libertinism" that had disfigured Laudianism previously. He spelt out the consequences: "a man that would deny the life to come, or revile Christ and the Scripture, or teach men to worship Mahomet, or the Sunne and the Moon, if he have liberty, and a plausible tongue, may look to have Disciples". Liberty plays havoc with family hierarchies and military discipline: it is "the Reign of Satan, and not of Christ"; "it is the loosing of the Dragon, and not the liberty of the Saints". To stop the magistrate from intervening in matters of faith and worship is to deliver "all the fruit of our Labours, Prayers and Victories into the Papists hands". Nor is it a defence of the Instrument of Government to say that "liberty" as an ideal is not extended in its provisions to "Popery and Prelacy". Baxter's point is that once accepted that liberty *is* the overarching principle, then Papist exemption from it will in the course of time seem unreasonable and discriminatory. For his part Baxter is sure that "the farre greatest part of the godly in the Land" – his *vox populi* – "abhorre the thoughts of Liberty for the Masse, and for preaching up Popery, Mahometism or Infidelity: Most of them desired the Acts for the Lords Day, which showeth that they are for no such Liberty".[47]

The "reasonable relief of tender consciences", the "stretching out the line of charity": these were worthy goals, but they were quite distinct from the abstract principle of "liberty". In stretching out charity beyond even the godly of the land it has been argued, though, that Baxter did come close to embracing Rome itself. Dr Boersma devotes a number of pages to this question, in his recent study of Baxter's doctrinal writings. If in the end he sensibly concludes that despite "eclectic agreement with some Roman Catholics, Baxter remains firmly entrenched within the Reformed tradition", he is impressed along the way by evidence from one of Baxter's last pamphlets in 1691 of the extent to which he was willing to pursue his "catholic" ideals.[48] Perhaps he was over-impressed. In that pamphlet Baxter did show how illusory were the supposed fixed dividing lines between Protestant and Catholic "in the doctrine of Predestination, Free Will, Grace, Merits, Justification, Redemption, Perseverance etc."[49] He there referred to his earlier work on this subject, *Catholick theology*. If we turn to that pamphlet, as Baxter asks us to do, we shall see, however, that Baxter is there making a double point. The *supposed* differences *are* slight, but the *real* differences are *unbridgeable*. And what are they? They are "about the Popish power and Church state, their Government, and worship as gathered hereunto".[50] And the title of the 1691 work is itself eloquent of his set of priorities: "*Against the revolt to a foreign jurisdiction*". This was the man after all who had said: "what is Popery but Errour in Politicks?"[51]

"Liberty" stuck in the puritan throat precisely because it opened the door to Popery. But we have also seen how it ran up against Calvinist ideals of "discipline". Can we say, therefore, that puritans needed to give up Calvinism before they could take aboard the principle of freedom? Liberty, lamented the puritan Thomas Jolly, is "the Diana of our times": long hair and bare breasts now get a favourable jury verdict, for fear of impugning "Christian liberty".[52] Calvin, he said, "would dy a 100 deaths before hee would suffer the profanation of the Lords supper".[53] Some later Muggletonians thought that their doctrine of the "two seeds" was liberating *because* it repudiated the Calvinist distinction between elect and reprobate.

The case for linking liberty with the retreat from Calvinism becomes more impressive if we think of some of its greatest seventeenth-century apologists. Milton's is the classic case: his *Areopagitica* is inseparable from his Arminian discovery of the importance of uncoerced choice. John Goodwin's defence of toleration is ultimately related to his Arminian perception of freedom, as even his adversary John Owen recognized.[54] As early as 1643 William Walwyn grounds his *The power of love* on the insight that "God ever intendeth unto man a pleasant and comfortable life ... he made him naturally a rationall creature."[55] Revolting against Calvinist determinism and pessimism, Baxter after 1649 extolled the "sapiential" rule of God as Rector. This made man not an independent agent, it is true, but "yet to be so far like God himself, as to be a kind of joint-determiner of many of his own Volitions and Nolitions, is part of God's Natural Image in Man". The corollary was that sin could be castigated as odious, "as it is the Act of a free agent".[56] In the 1630s, puritans like Baxter had attacked the Arminianism of Laud without (they admitted later) knowing what it was. The liberty it seemed to offer then was to them identical with *libertinism*, and with the encouragement of Popery. But Baxter's reappraisal of Arminianism began with his *Aphorismes of justification* in 1649: the enemy of discipline (he now recognized from first-hand experience with Roundhead army chaplains) was in fact the ultra-Calvinist repudiation of works. A puritan Arminianism was thus possible in the 1650s as distinct from the 1630s, and liberty could be given an altered dimension accordingly.

There is something very neat and attractive in an analysis that shows puritans discovering liberty as they retreat from Calvinism. But the reality is more complicated. Coleridge (a great admirer of Baxter) grasped it when he turned upside down the normal preconceptions. He called Calvinism "the lamb in the wolf's skin" and Arminianism "the wolf in the lamb's skin". His point was that Calvinism offered a bleak and pessimistic judgement to the human race, but comfort to individuals. The Arminian view of human nature, on the other hand, was generous and liberating, but it was cruel to individuals "for fear of damaging the race by false hopes and improper confidences".[57] This was Baxter's case against the "marrow" theology of Edward Fisher, who had expounded the classic statement of Calvinist *unconditional* grace in 1645. Of Fisher he would say "So the *Marrow of Modern Divinity* ... earnestly presseth believers not to look to their sins *as making them lyable to Gods everlasting wrath and Hell-fire, nor to crave pardon and forgiveness for them that thereupon they may escape that penalty.*"[58] Arminianism and Hell went together. Prayers and sermons reinforce the message that parishioners must be kept up to the mark, by reminding them of the need to fulfil the divine conditions. Hell-fire is the essential reminder of the consequences of that failure. The assurance of the elect comes not from the fact that there are no conditions (the "Marrow" error), but from the certainty that he will fulfil them. Baxter achieved notoriety by his vision of Heaven in one work as an old boys' reunion of the saints, such as Hampden and Pym; but it is his vision there of Hell, which is truly central to his theology. Hell he described significantly as "a *rational* Torment by Conscience, according to *the nature of the Rational Subject* [my italics]". Sinners, he said, "shall lay all the blame on their own Wills in Hell for ever". They cannot shelter behind determinism, and make it God's fault, not their own. The beauty of Hell is that "to remember their wilfulness will feed the fire, and cause the worm of conscience never to die". Always there is "an angry sin-revenging God above them". The lovers of earthly pleasures have their sublime come-uppance: "those Ears which were wont to be delighted with Musick, shall hear the shrieks and cries of their damned companions".[59]

The nineteenth-century interpreter of Muggletonianism, Thomas Robinson, certainly believed that his sect's break with predestination was crucial. With scorn he spoke of "the slavish worship of fear and trembling towards God", and even said in 1888 "I think you will see God did not decree before creation that any should be lost".[60] But we must not read back nineteenth-century developments to the seventeenth-century beliefs. It is true that in 1656, in the first edition of *A divine looking glass*, the Prophets exempt children from the doctrine of election and rejection, but this was "not for Persons of understanding", and they went on to denounce "Free-Will-Mongers" who put Man in a state where "he may be in a condition of Salvation Today, and Tomorrow be cast away".[61] The Prophets would complain in *A stream from the tree of life* of the doctrine of election as being "very coldly maintained", and regret not hearing it preached in contemporary sermons.[62] Although in March 1665 Muggleton told Thomas Tomkinson that "half the world will be saved", in May of the same year he was telling another correspondent of the importance of nurturing the distinction between elect and reprobate, and another again, a year later, that "many are called but few are chosen".[63] Tomkinson in his *Truths triumph* (first written in 1676 and amended in 1690) championed predestination against the Quaker Penn, who had called it "a cruell doctrine". There was nothing wrong with predestination; what was wrong was a dispensation in which the presence of "two seeds" (Faith and Reason) was not recognized as being present *in all mankind*. The arbitrariness lay in God, on this view, taking "one of Adams children" and rejecting "another, and yet they bee alike and all of one father". According to Calvin's doctrine, he claimed, until the time of Christ "the whole seede of Adam" had provided "nothing worthy of his Election".[64] Through the doctrine of the two seeds, certainly not through free will, Muggleton lifted from his correspondents the fear of witchcraft, showing how the maladies of the child, even in Muggleton's own case, could be attributed not to external agency (God's decree, or witch's sorcery) but to the fact that, at the time of conception, Muggleton's wife had the seed of Reason in her dominant over the seed of Faith.[65] Muggleton could put his correspondents' fears to rest – on witches, the Devil, eternal hell-fire – in a way that Baxter could not (for all his equal skill in casuistry). But this was not because Muggleton had been more receptive to Arminian influences than Baxter had: rather, the reverse. In 1704 Tomkinson called Baxter "an Eminent Preacher in Reasons Kingdom", and, from his *Saints everlasting rest*, attributed to him the belief that "Every man may be saved if he will". Tomkinson called such a doctrine "Right Develish", for "by this man is His own Saviour".[66] We shall see that Muggletonians did indeed give liberty a heightened importance, but clearly it could not be by this doctrinal route. The tension between origins and evolution in the movement is beautifully captured in the historian A. P. Gordon's obituary notice on the believer J. D. Aspland, who had introduced him to the movement: "Mr. Aspland was accustomed to express his own belief that tho' Universalism was to him a dream without warrant in Revelation, the number of those who would be finally outcast from God's love would be few indeed."[67] There survives in the Huntington Library, California, a pamphlet by John Owen, *The doctrine of the saint's perseverance*. It is an attack on John Goodwin's Arminianism in 1654. It was in the possession of a Welsh Calvinist, Richard Leggett, who wrote personal comments in the margin in 1792. He knew that Goodwin was a favourite of John Wesley, and kept drawing affinities between Goodwin and Wesley throughout the work. He revelled in Owen's attacks – the pamphlet is sprinkled with admiring phrases like "the Doctor is funny" – not least in Owen's recognition of Goodwin's dependence on Hell:

> I say that these persons should be most effectually stirred up to
> Obedience, by the dread and terror of that Iron rod, of vengeance
> and Hell, and that they should be so, by God's appointment, is
> such a new, such another Gospell, as if preached by an Angell
> from Heaven, we should not receive.[68]

Leggett correctly saw that Wesley, like Goodwin and Baxter, *needed*
Hell to complement his Arminianism.

Are we reaching the paradoxical conclusion that Owen's Calvinism
made him a *better* standard bearer for religious freedom than Baxter's
Arminianism made him? Owen argued for religious toleration against
the Scottish Presbyterians in 1649; he argued for religious toleration
against the Anglican authoritarian, Samuel Parker, after the Restoration; he argued for religious toleration against Baxter's "comprehen-
sion", both before and after the Restoration.[69] Moreover, he was not
weighed down (like Baxter was) with deference to imperial authority,
either arguing that the Church flourished best in the three hundred
years before it had a Christian Emperor (siding here with Milton and
Roger Williams) or – hedging his bets – that "great Constantine"
stood for liberty of conscience anyway.[70] In 1657, the Presbyterian
Daniel Cawdrey saw Owen's advocacy of toleration as "a prudentiall
way of these Erastian Polititians", and showed how inconsistent it was
with former statements by Owen.[71] Owen's defence in 1658 was that
fifteen years previously, when he had debated liberty, he had been on
the other side, because he was then a Presbyterian.[72] But this was to
miss Cawdrey's point, who had said that toleration "hath done much
more towards the rooting of Religion out of the hearts of many men in
7 yeares than the enforcing of conformity did in 70 years".[73] Compare that judgement with Owen's in 1658:

> How many professors have I known that would plead for their
> *liberty* as they called it! They could bear any thing, all things – all
> sorts of men; they would try all things whether they came to them
> in the way of God or no – they could do it, but their opinions they
> hated as much as any. What hath been the issue? I scarce ever
> know any come off without a wound; the most have had their
> faith overthrown.[74]

And in 1668 Owen could hymn magistracy, if not in imperial terms, then at least in Old Testament terms:

> We may also see hence the great use of *magistracy* in the world . . . the terror of him that bears the sword . . . When then there was no king in Israel, none to put to rebuke, and none of whose evil men were afraid, there was woful work and havoc amongst the children of men made in the world, as we may see in the last chapters of the book of Judges.[75]

And, far from seeing pluralism as a *virtue* (as Milton, Walwyn and Roger Williams in their different ways did), Owen saw it as a vice. Thus at the end of his life in 1681 he would lament the multiplicity of thoughts in men's minds – "what a hell of horror and confusion it must needs be!" And he would argue that the "design of conviction" was "to put a stop unto these thoughts, to take off from the number, and thereby to lessen the guilt".[76] Should the magistrate, he had asked even in 1649, let men get away with odious remarks about the Trinity? Certainly not.[77]

This is the context in which Cawdrey's critique of Owen as an "Erastian Politician" has the real force. It is not – as Owen tried to pass it off – that he had once been against liberty when he was a Presbyterian. What Cawdrey was saying was that he had *always* been against liberty, but was ready to use toleration as a pragmatic weapon of survival. Never was the game more blatantly given away than in Owen's reply to his own query in 1649, whether the magistrate had a duty to bring people to the truth. This was his answer:

> Were the precious distinguished from the vile, Churches rightly established, and church discipline so exercised that Christians were under some orderly view . . . an easy finger would untie the knot of this query. But being in that confusion wherein we are . . .[78]

In other words, best, a magistrate-ordered godliness; second-best, a toleration that allows it in miniature. Owen thought, when he was first chaplain to Oliver Cromwell, that the ideal *was* attainable; when he stopped thinking that, he worked in 1658 and 1659 for the separation of the precious from the vile by suspending ministers (the Savoy

Conference) and for the overthrow of the inadequate magistrate (by then Richard Cromwell). With a Stuart Restoration, the second-best (toleration) was the only way forward for the attainment of godly discipline: the identical diagnosis of his co-religionist Burton, a decade earlier, as we saw. No wonder Walwyn scorned the "liberty" credentials of these Independent ministers who, at the drop of a hat, would ditch sectarian colleagues, and find hitherto unsuspected virtues in cohabitation with the civil magistrate.

The aim – to separate the precious from the vile – whether it was performed by magistrate with the sword or clergyman at the Table was inimical to the concept of freedom; indeed, to some Calvinists themselves, it was worse than that: it was an act of blasphemy. This applied not only to Owen's "inner certainty" but even to Baxter's "outward holiness". Prynne's Calvinist defence of open admission was congruent with his anti-Arminian arguments of 1629:

> If God should cull out his Elect from among the reprobate, making an open division or separation from them here, by preaching the Gospel unto them alone; all Reprobates must needs presently despaire of his grace and runne into some desperate course.

It is precisely to avoid such breakdown of order that "Reprobates are intermixed and mingled with the Elect, as the weedes, the tares are with the corn and grasse".[79] Roger Williams took that logic one step further when he refused to let the magistrate, any more than the clergyman, take on that God-like power of discrimination. Williams agreed with Prynne that the tares and the wheat were *inextricably* bound together on Earth; in Heaven would come the reckoning, carried out with peculiar venom by avenging angels. This makes Williams neither a democrat (between the elect and reprobate there is an unbridgeable gap) nor a liberal (eternal punishment is for him a deferred gratification).[80] It does not make him an anarchist either. As a magistrate, he brusquely turns down the Baptist citizens' plea for exemption from the militia on religious grounds in 1655. He says then, "that ever I should speak or write a tittle that tends to such an infinite liberty of conscience is a mistake, and which I ever disclaimed and abhorred". The liberty he will give to "Papists, Protestants, Jews or Turks" is not to be "forced to come to the ship's prayers or worship" – in seventeenth-century terms an almost unimaginable generosity – but "notwithstanding this liberty, the commander of the ship ought to command the ship's course".[81] To which Oliver Cromwell would say "Amen". Like Williams, he would confine the magistrate's role to that of "keeping the peace", claim as his supreme achievement that of having prevented any one religion from imposing its views upon the others, and see his role as that of a "good constable", not that of an Old Testament prophet/king.

Clarendon once (wrongly) called Hobbes's *Leviathan* "a sly address to Oliver". Yet Cromwell *is* a very Hobbesian Christian Magistrate. On conventional readings of Hobbes, this, if true, would make Cromwell's puritan rule the obvious enemy of freedom. But conventional readings of Hobbes, and of Cromwell, and of the relation of both to freedom, have all been recently challenged. Professor Woolrych has shown how the puritan aims of the Long Parliament – discipline, not liberty – were being opposed as early as 1642 by Cromwell. At Naseby, and again at Bristol, parliament deleted whole passages from Cromwell's victory messages that put liberty of conscience at the centre of the struggle. When, as Lord Protector, in a much misunderstood passage, Cromwell said in 1655 that "religion was not the thing at first contested for, but God brought it to that issue at last, and gave it unto us by way of redundancy, and at last it proved to be that which was most dear to us", he was not saying that the English Civil War was initially *not* about religion. "Religion", as Professor Woolrych says, was shorthand for "liberty of religion".[82] So it was for Baxter, in his analysis of the Civil War, only with him this change is given a negative, not positive, gloss. Baxter says in retrospect that the English Civil War was not initially a "war for religion" and, like Cromwell's judgement, this has been wrongly taken as an argument that he thought it was initially a war about the constitution.[83] But, just like Cromwell, Baxter is using "religion" as a synonym for "religious liberty": what Cromwell praises as the outcome of the Civil War is precisely what Baxter condemns.

And, on this issue, surely Hobbes is on Baxter's side, not Cromwell's? Not if one reads carefully the key passage in the last chapter of *Leviathan* on the untying of the knots on men's liberty. The Papal, Episcopal and Presbyterian knots are dissolved, until we are reduced "to the Independency of the Primitive Christians to follow Paul, or Cephas, or Apollos, every man as he liketh best". This is "independency" as Walwyn visualized it, not as Burton or Owen practised it. He goes on to make the extraordinary claim that that way, "if it be without contention", is "perhaps the best". But the whole argument of *Leviathan* is surely that contention *is* the price paid for freedom, and it is one that is inordinately high. Yet when he goes on to say why it was the best, the passage does not read like a *reductio ad absurdum* at all:

> First, because there ought to be no Power over the consciences of men, but of the Word it selfe, working faith in every one, not always according to the purpose of them that Plant and Water, but of God himselfe, that giveth the Increase: and secondly, because it is unreasonable in those, who teach there is such danger in every little Error, to require of a man endowed with reason of his own, to follow the Reason of any other man, or of the most voices of many other men; Which is little better, than to venture his Salvation at crosse and pile.[84]

There is an uncanny similarity here with Walwyn's first defence of freedom, *A new petition for the Papists*, in 1641: "and therefore holds it unreasonable, to be forced to follow other men's Judgments and not his owne in a matter of so great importance as that of his salvation is".[85] Dr Richard Tuck has written persuasively about Hobbes's "civil religion". He shows that Hobbes broke decisively with the Apostolic Church, and with his Anglican friends, in Paris between 1647 and 1650. He then imagined a version of Christianity, which rejected an immaterial soul and eternal torment, with the intention of relieving men of their fears. No greater liberty could be offered than that; that is why Tuck calls *Leviathan* "the greatest of the English revolutionary utopias".[86]

But there remained a nagging qualification to the achievement of liberty from the knots. "If it be without contention", Hobbes had said, such independence was best. The evidence of the 1640s – not only that provided by the English Civil War but by the Thirty Years War – argued the opposite. Walwyn makes just such a claim for freedom's peace in 1641, but it is done defensively and apologetically: "it may be objected that the Tolleration would breede a greater confusion, but wee which know wee have the spirit, believe the contrary". Compare this with the confident tone of his utterances in 1649: "it were much better for the Common-wealth, that all mens mindes were set at liberty"; "the Nation will never flourish with that plenty of Trade and commerce" until persecution ends.[87]

Liberty and prosperity were coming to be seen as complementary, not antithetical, qualities: the pragmatic arguments for religious freedom were given new force in the later seventeenth century. John Owen is able to make mincemeat of Samuel Parker accordingly when the latter tries to say that religious freedom is not good for trade.[88] Owen gets more prominence than he deserves, as the champion of freedom, as a result; we have seen that his advocacy was in fact more muddled and opportunistic than has often been recognized. The Dutch commercial success was to become related in men's minds to religious toleration: they knew, after all, that it was bad for business to burn your clients. This pragmatic justification for freedom, however, could only be so effective when the ideological justification had already been conceded. Parker saw Hobbes therefore correctly as the villain. He calls the fifth chapter of his *A discourse of ecclesiastical politie* of 1670 "A Confutation of the Consequences that some men draw from Mr Hob's Principles in behalf of Liberty of Conscience". Only a future bishop could have the gall to say, against Hobbes, that "though Religion were a cheat, they are apparently the greatest Enemies to Government, that tell the World it is so". What Parker wanted from Hobbes, and didn't get, was recognition of "the Ties of Conscience . . . super-induced upon those of Secular Interest". What for Parker were ties, were for Hobbes, knots. Parker argued that, without them, kings were "nothing but terrible men with long Swords".[89]

That was how Hobbes did see them, and in that sense the stereotype of him, as the apologist for brute force, is not wholly false. He *wanted* kings to be terrible men with long swords (a desire shared by most puritans, as we saw in the last chapter). But that was all they were. They were not to pry into the souls of their subjects; they were not to take on the mantle of God (who remains unknowable). A commentator on the American novelist John Updike noted how the "vigorously pro-Caesar stance" of one of his fictional heroes is related to his Calvinism:

> Somewhere Barth says "What shall the Christian in society *do* but attend to what *God* does. What God does in the world is Caesar."
> Only by full acquiescence in established power, in other words,

can the salvation-minded Christian ready himself for "a way out of the crush of matter and time".[90]

Render unto Caesar the things that are Caesar's – and no holding back on that submission. Let Oliver Cromwell set up Triers and Ejectors (who disarm even an initial critic of them like Baxter, by their non-inquisitorial nature); let magistrate Roger Williams conscript Baptist ministers into national service; let President Johnson bomb Vietnam (as Updike argued elsewhere).[91] But render unto God the things that are God's. *Leviathan* is not *1984*. Hobbes would have rewritten the last sentence of Orwell's novel: Winston Smith would *not* "love Big Brother" (though Samuel Parker would have let the original sentence stand). Before Orwell wrote *1984* he had found in *Gulliver's travels* the meaning of totalitarianism. Swift showed how a subject's secret thoughts can be detected by examining his or her excrement:

> Because Men are never so serious, thoughtful, and intent, as when they are at Stool, which he found by frequent Experiment: for in such Conjunctures, when he used merely as a trial to consider what was the best Way of murdering the King, his Ordure would have a tincture of Green; but quite different, when he thought only of raising an Insurrection, or burning the Metropolis.

But in 1668 Hobbes refused even to enter a debate on whether the anorexic Martha Taylor passed excrement or urine: "I think it were somewhat inhuman to examine of these things too nearly, when it so little concerneth the commonwealth." Swiftian satire (and its extension in Orwell) could only work upon a world in which nothing was too little *not* to concern the commonwealth, and that world wasn't Hobbes's. It is in another Updike novel that a Calvinist hero is admired by his lover in these terms: "unlike most men he did not judge". The philandering Dutchman, Piet, responds somewhat complacently that he owes it all to his Calvinism: "Only God judged".[92] If at times – Marston Moor in 1644, Barebones Parliament in 1653 – Cromwell may feel a perfect identification with God's will, the more characteristic note is caution in trying to read "providences", and unwillingness to extend the magistrate's role beyond that of a "good constable, set to keep the peace of the parish".[93] It is the Calvinist John Cotton who argues against fellow Calvinist Richard Mather that it is better that hypocrites be admitted to the Sacraments than that one worthy person should be excluded. It is the Calvinist Increase Mather, Richard's son, who says that it was better that ten witches escape than that one innocent person be sent to the stake. It is the Calvinist Cromwell who says, "I had rather that Mahometanism were permitted amongst us than that one of god's children should be persecuted". And it was to his fellow Scottish Calvinists that he delivered his famous rebuke: "I beseech you, in the bowels of Christ, think it possible you may be mistaken."[94]

One can see why the nineteenth-century Muggletonian Thomas Robinson tried to explain his sect's commitment to freedom straightforwardly as a repudiation of Calvinist dogma. In doing so, however, he is mistaking the way Muggletonians were developing doctrine in his day from the way they had thought in the time of the Prophets. The secret lay elsewhere: in the Muggletonian conviction (shared with Calvin, Hobbes, Cromwell and Roger Williams) that God is unknowable. Free-will theologians were as blasphemous in Hobbes's eyes for pretending the opposite, as were medieval schoolmen. The key Muggletonian tenet (after 1661) was that God took no "immediate notice" of His subjects. Arden Bonell described its liberating importance in 1739:

> he who does his duty knowing God does not take immediate notice of him, is preferable to him who does it on account of Gods continual Notice, he therefore is called an Eye Servant since his Actions are the effect of his fear, when the others are the effect of their Love.[95]

In 1707, the Muggletonian, Thomas Tomkinson, would note with admiration "Learned Hobbes", who preached the "prerogative power of God in salvation and damnation" (no problems for *him* on that score), though he was opposed by almost "all sects and opinions".[96] Tomkinson's Calvinist defence of liberty of conscience in 1679, like Owen's, acknowledged the force of the economic advantages that would accrue:

> Then could men trade freely with one another and such as wher more conscionous than the Rest (being the onely Thriving people and the most wisest and Industreous of any) I say such would

trade freely to the greate benefit of the Common-wealth and the Commonwealth and State would in noe land flourish but only in that where the magistrate punisheth upon the breach of the civil law and for nothing besides.[97]

In 1725 a Muggletonian transcribed excerpts from Hobbes's *Leviathan*, and highlighted these specific points with approval: mortalism; angels as impressions on the brains of men; materialism; determinism; self-love as motivation; obligations to obey the ruler but the treasuring of inward dissent; Hell as internal.[98] If Tuck is right, and *Leviathan* is more than an analysis of how political societies are founded and conduct themselves, but is also "a vision of how a commonwealth can make us freer and more prosperous than ever before in human history",[99] then those Muggletonians who, later on, admired and transcribed Hobbes knew exactly what they were about.

Chapter Seven

Puritanism and capitalism

Max Weber, it sometimes seems, is chiefly famous for *not* having said that Calvinism created capitalism. The alleged causal connection he discovered is what many of his critics picked him up on, and they were wrong to do so. Weber never argued that ideal factors alone could be agents of change.[1] He wanted their importance recognized, however, *alongside* the material factors. Those material factors, which Weber recognized as much as his later critics did, are not our concern in this chapter. But the ideal factors very much are, because of the primacy that Weber gives to English puritanism in that story, and in particular to the writings of one of our three puritan protagonists, Richard Baxter.

The critics here too have sometimes been wide of the mark. That includes two of the earliest of them, Sombart and Brentano, who showed how critical Baxter actually was of the acquisitive society. But, as Weber pointed out in the second edition of his 1904/5 work, they had overlooked the fact that what he had been attempting to do was to show how "in spite of its antimammonistic doctrines, the spirit of this ascetic religion nevertheless, just as in the monastic communities, gave birth to economic rationalism because it placed a premium on what was most important for it: the fundamentally ascetic rational motives".[2] This is the claim that we will examine in the rest of the chapter.

Before we do so we must ask how far the controversy still has life in it. Two recent publications might suggest a negative answer. A team of experts produced a volume on international Calvinism in 1985 that hardly mentions capitalism.[3] To return the compliment, in the same year a Cambridge symposium, somewhat portentously focused on

"The European Miracle" – defined as the seventeenth-century trans-formation of Europe towards "capitalism, the Industrial Revolution and modernity" – had only 2 out of 14 contributors even mentioning the Weber thesis. Nor were their mentions very supportive: Alan Macfarlane touted the claims of England's "unusual politico-economic system" inherited from its medieval past, rather than puri-tanism, to stand at "the cradle of capitalism"; Peter Burke refers to the thesis as one that "has long been pounded by the batteries of histori-ans, who have scored at least a few palpable hits".[4] Where Weber *has* been more successful is in making historians address the problem of the "Protestant Ethic": that is to say, the crisis of proof which he diag-nosed for the seventeenth-century predestinarian Calvinist believer that, albeit *unintendedly* (the point missed by his critics), produces a spiritual sanction for labour.

The evidence here, too, is mixed. There is a kind of gut recognition of affinity that Weber appeals to, which is captured well in this obser-vation by John Updike (already used as a handy Calvinist benchmark in Chapter 6):

> His life smells of financial failure and of the guilt and shame that attaches to such failure in the United States. It is the inspiratory genius of Calvin to link prosperity and virtue, to take material blessing as a sign of salvation.[5]

Two striking local studies of life under a godly discipline in seven-teenth-century England – David Underdown's Dorchester, Keith Wrightson's and David Levine's Terling – are helpful to such an identi-fication.[6] An earlier Alan Macfarlane gave full weight to the Protes-tant Ethic in his explanation for the late sixteenth-century Essex witchcraft persecutions.[7] But recent witchcraft investigators have other explanations to offer, and other local studies of communities have thrown up a very different pattern from Dorchester and Terling,[8] leading Patrick Collinson to warn against a simple equation of "puri-tan evangelism" with "class war of a kind".[9]

It is no accident that England is seen as the country where Weber's thesis must be tested. Weber's essay, it is true, begins in Germany, with observations on the contemporary political scene there, but it stands or falls in the end by a German's view of English puritanism. A Ger-man historian, in a recent volume on the Weber thesis, can provide an essay with the title, "Weber the would-be Englishman"; [10] to complete the German/English connection the index to that same volume refers to the present writer as "Johann von Lamont". [11] But had the "would-be Englishman" found the legitimate key to capitalism in English puritanism, and in particular in the person of Richard Baxter?

Baxter was a prolific writer. There are 140 published works of his, and 1,262 letters in Baxter's calendared correspondence. Not all of these were exercises in casuistry (although the bulk of his letters were). Weber – and R. H. Tawney after him – drew overwhelmingly in discussing Baxter on one of his works, *A Christian directory*. There is nothing perverse about such a choice. Baxter claimed to have composed most of it in 1664 and 1665, although it was published in 1673. It was truly his *Summa Theologica*, bringing together in one volume much of his earlier writings. At one crucial point in the text – on what proportion of charity should go to the poor – he is content to reprint a letter written previously on the topic to Thomas Gouge. [12] Even if he does not raid earlier writings in such a direct way very often he is clearly building on earlier foundations.

Nor is it one of Baxter's shorter works. It may even count among his longest (876 large pages in one edition, for example). So much material for Weber, and Tawney after him, to plunder; and inevitably much of it to skip over. Tawney's wife published *Chapters from a Christian directory* in 1925, and her criteria for selection are interesting. Three out of the four sections of the book are represented in her collection: Section II, "Christian Oeconomicks" or "Family Duties"; Section III, "Christian Ecclesiasticks" or "Church Duties"; Section IV, "Christian Politicks" or "Duties to our Rulers and Neighbours". [13] The topics covered, in her edition, in Section II are the reciprocal duties of masters and servants, and directions to slave-owners. The one chapter reproduced from Section III is on directions for the poor. Section IV includes chapters on directions against theft, cases of conscience about theft, and directions against oppression and prodigality. What is missing is anything from Section I, "Christian Ethicks" or "private Duties", which contains the first 374 pages of a treatise running to 876 pages. This selectivity distorts Baxter's purpose in writing the book and obscures its most damaging weakness: that it *is a maimed work*. This is the point that will now be developed.

For Baxter, Section I is not only more than a third of the whole: it is the most important section. Section IV *would have been*, if political circumstances had been different, as we shall see. But it is the "private Duties" set out in the first section that are the basis of the family and "Church Duties" set out in the following sections. Yet a citizen, weighed down with the sense of his own inadequacy, is in no position to contemplate taking on these wider duties. As a pastor, catechizing his flock in Kidderminster or corresponding with the troubled in mind, Baxter had to combat that sense of melancholia – whether in parishioner or correspondent – that, in extreme form, would lead to suicide. He did so not by some tortuous *wresting of* Calvinist theology (as Weber would have it), but actually by *repudiating* it. That is the significance of the first work that he ever wrote, *Aphorismes of justification*, in 1649; the controversy that it provoked showed how the disputants grasped its importance. As one recent commentator on Baxter has pointed out: "he was obviously not a predestinarian theologian and to that extent, Weber's use of Baxter and of his prominent pastoral work, *A Christian directory*, was indeed not at all well chosen".[14] It was not well chosen because, among other things, the comfort he offered in that first section of *A Christian directory* was that offered by Richard Hooker and Hugo Grotius – what Professor Trevor-Roper has characterized as an expression of "the Pyrrhonist crisis" of the early modern period.[15]

Baxter told the "troubled Christians" that they didn't (false fear) doubt the truth of the Word of God, even when they thought that they did; *only the truth of their own sincerity*, and consequently of their Justification and Salvation. For, said Baxter, "it is no act of unbelief at all, for me to doubt whether my own heart be sincere". That is not unbelief (in whatever degree) but ignorance of self. For "God's Word doth no where say that *I am sincere*: and therefore I may doubt *of this*, without doubting of God's Word at all".[16] In 1675 he would offer the fullest statement of these doctrinal views, in his *Catholick theologie*. It includes a fascinating discussion of the nature of truth, emphasizing *probability* not *certainty* as the antidote to fear, and separating "objective certainty" from "subjective certainty". Men may be *uncertain* of that which is certain in itself, says Baxter.[17] But that same Pyrrhonist insight is precisely the comfort that he already offers to the anxious in Section I of *A Christian directory*: "And so the Truth of Gods promise of Justification to believers, is more certain, that is, hath fuller surer Evidence to be discerned by, than the Truth of my sincere believing." The rules of conduct that follow are based on the premise that the believer is capable of following them precisely because the burden of melancholia has now been taken from him; and it has been taken from him, not by a "crisis of proof", to quote Weber, but *by showing up that same crisis as self-induced and gratuitous.*

From this base, other comforts follow. Apparitions, witches and extraterrestrial spirits are not to be feared but to be seen as supplementary aids against unbelief. Very few now see the Devil: "This Fear is therefore irrrational, the Danger being utterly improbable." Gluttony is disgusting: the rich try to excuse themselves by doling out a few scraps to the poor. Meals should last a quarter of an hour; half an hour, if a guest were present. Gluttony frustrates the drive to create schools, alms-houses and hospitals by a diversion of resources. It rests on an inequitable foundation: "What an incongruity is it, that one member of Christ (as he would be thought) should be feeding himself deliciously every day, and abounding with abused superfluities, whilst another is starving and pining in a Cottage, or begging at the door?" He wants to provide the rich glutton with a basin and a feather, to vomit up his superfluities, and thus to save his body at least, if not his soul. The drunkard is "to the common-wealth as Mice in the Granary, or Weeds in the Corn". Baxter says to him that "it is a great part of the work of faithful Magistrates to weed out such as thou". The adulterer should ask the pastor to pray with his congregation for pardon and recovery: "begin thus to crave the fruit of Church Discipline thy self". Note the emphasis (as we saw in the two previous chapters) on puritan magisterial authority and on discipline, not on revolution or the liberty of the market. If all else fails, a cold bath is the best antidote to lust. "Millions of Glorious Angels" would execute God's Justice on the swearer in the hereafter. That champion of religious freedom, Roger Williams, shared Baxter's joy in angelic retribution in the hereafter; but with him it is *only* in the hereafter. With Williams it is a *substitution* for magisterial action now; with Baxter, it is both. Catholic Spain, not Rhode Island under Williams, turns out to be Baxter's model: "in Spain I have known a man sit in the marketplace the greatest part of the day gaping with a Gagg in his Mouth for swearing only *By the Life of God*". The public welfare is the ultimate yardstick: "every man is therefore bound to do all the good he can to others, especially for the Church and Commonwealth" and "this is not done by Idleness but by Labour". The slothful will keep up "in the secret receptacles of the body a dunghill of uncosted and excrementous filth". The callings that are most serviceable to the public welfare are those of "the Magistrates, the Pastors and Teachers of the Church, Schoolmasters, Physicians, Lawyers, and Husbandmen (Plowmen, Grasiers and Shepherds)".

Baxter elucidates the true meaning of Proverbs 23.4, *Labor not to be rich*:

> The meaning is, that you make not Riches your chief end . . . You are bound to improve all your Masters Talents: But then your *end* must be, that you may be the better provided to do good service, and may do the more good with what you have.

This could be little more than a pious aspiration (and would be in many of those who came after him). The point is that the pious aspiration, as we shall see, took embodiment in Baxter's case in very practical and detailed plans for "Holy Commonwealths" or "National Churches", which would be judged in turn by their ability to meet these criteria.

Idleness usually begets poverty. A poor man's sloth is in one respect more culpable than the rich man's: "he is under the pressure of Necessity". But that very reason makes him, in another respect, less culpable. The rich are burying the greatest talents and "they have not the crys of ther hungry Children to rouse them up". In Section II ("Christian Oeconomicks") Baxter claims that the first sign of a "mortall damnable state" is "when a man had rather have worldly prosperity than the favour and fruits of God in Heaven".[18] Christopher Hill gives another quotation from the same source, however, on the lawfulness of money-making as a function of God's stewardship. He caps this with a still lengthier quotation from Baxter. Baxter asked how the rich could justify property rights while the poor starved. Hill quotes Baxter's reply:

> Whensoever the preservation of life is not in open probability like to be more serviceable to the common good than the violation of property will be hurtful, the taking of another man's goods is sinful, though it be to save the taker's life . . . Therefore ordinarily it is a duty rather to die than to take another man's goods against his will.

Hill goes on: "'Property', said Baxter, anticipating Locke, 'is in order of nature antecedent to human government'." This second extract comes from the fourth section of *A Christian directory*: Hill actually quotes from Jeannette Tawney's 1925 selection.

What is being argued here is that this twin selectivity (Jeannette Tawney's in 1925; Christopher Hill's in 1972) distorts Baxter's message. On the basis of such quotations one can see why Hill makes Baxter the spokesman for a section of one chapter in his book *The world turned upside down*, entitled "The Protestant Ethic".[19] This is what the Winstanleys of his next section, "Beyond the Protestant Ethic", were fighting against. It is not that Baxter and other puritans do not have prejudices that match well with a "Protestant Ethic": the poor's responsibility for their plight, the importance of property, a horror of levelling doctrines, a recognition of the need to use one's time methodically, and so on. But the point that Weber made was a greater one: the prejudices match so well because they can be related to a particular tension within predestinarian belief. But what Baxter's first section showed (and he would expand this in his later *Catholick theologie*) is that there is a way of resolving these tensions, and that way is an *anti-Calvinist* way. We *have* faith, says Baxter, even if we *think* that we haven't: anxieties therefore can now be contained within this Pyrrhonist framework.

Weber, Tawney and Hill were wrong therefore to gloss over the huge first section of the work; they were equally wrong to pin so much faith on the fourth. They do so in the teeth of some pretty heavily signalled disclaimers from Baxter himself. The reader is not to be fooled, he says, by the title: "Christian Politicks" is not to retread the ground of his "Political Aphorismes" (the alternative title of his 1659 work, *A holy commonwealth*). Indeed it had better not: in 1670 after all he had retracted that work, and declared it to be *non scriptum*.[20] The tone of his opening remarks in the last section is astonishingly defensive and apologetic. Men of his profession should not meddle with matters outside their sphere. He is not giving "Directions", just a "few briefe Memorandums" to civil governors. He won't presume to speak further to his superiors; the "Memorandums" even will not be practised until we have a "Golden Age". He gives a coy non-answer to his own fifteenth question – "May not a Magistrate take the Subjects goods, when it is necessary for their own preservation?": "I answered the question once heretoofore in my Political Aphorismes. And because I repent of meddling with such Subjects, and of writing that Book, I will leave such cases hereafter for further Persons to resolve." When it comes to the fourth section, Baxter is making clear that what he is offering *is* a maimed work. Could his commentators miss that note? R. H. Tawney certainly didn't: it is precisely the self-consciously maimed nature of the offering that he exploits to make it the mainplank of his revision of Weber. Weber knew that there was human compassion in Baxter and other puritans, a genuine detestation of "mammonistic" practices. In practice, though, it was "unintendedly" diluted by the tensions within Calvinism. Tawney, recognizing that Weber was not talking of *intended* consequences, nevertheless still felt that he did not make enough of the disciplinary checks that puritan clergy would resort to, in order to prevent these unwanted consequences happening. That is why for Tawney the apologetic preamble to the fourth section is more significant even than the text that follows. It reveals Baxter's own consciousness that 1659 has gone for ever. No more "Holy Commonwealths", no more "directions" to rulers. *A Christian directory* is for Tawney the classic Restoration formula: sincere but toothless injunctions by a tamed clerical body to rulers to behave themselves. There is no call then, in Tawney's interpretation, any more than in Weber's, to impugn Baxter's sincerity, when in that fourth section he flails "unmerciful Landlords":

> how hard must it needs be to a poor oppressed Man, whose body is tired with wearisome labours, and his mind distracted with continual cares, how to pay his rent, and how to have food and rayment for his family? How unfit is such a troubled disinterested Person, to live in thankfulness to God, and in his joyful Praises? Abundance of the voluptuous great ones of the World, do use their Tenants and Servants, but as their Beasts, as if they had been made only to labour with toil for them, and it were their chief felicity to fulfil this will, and live upon their favour.

Baxter is appalled to think that one of his tenants "could live and maintain all his family competently" if he could have as much as his landlord "bestoweth upon one suit of Cloaths, or one proud Entertainment, or one House, or one pack of Hounds". But where does all this fine feeling flow towards? To this message of resignation: "But alas! Who shall first reform the Landlords? And when may it be hoped that many or most great Men will be saved?"[21] The treason of the clerks in seventeenth-century England is not hypocrisy (a vulgar misreading of Tawney). It is a failure of nerve, not compassion, which Tawney excoriates. At some point in the century puritans gave up on "Holy Commonwealths". Tawney thought that it may have been after the Barebones Assembly failure (a traumatic blow for Cromwell), or with the triumph of persecuting Anglicans at the Restoration. A whipped puritan body for whatever reasons made its peace with capitalism (although through gritted teeth).

This is a plausible way of decoding Baxter. But even in his deferential work of 1673 there are residual defiances. For instance Hill's seemingly damning quote from Baxter, elevating property above life, is not a simple obeisance before market forces. On the contrary Baxter's criterion is serviceability, in his own words, to "the common good". In "ordinary cases", he says, saving a man's life won't do as much good as his stealing does hurt. This is a shockingly insouciant statement: a reminder (do we need it at this stage in the book?) that seventeenth-century puritanism is not nineteenth-century liberalism. Hill, however, doesn't quote the next lines from Baxter, and they are worth quoting: "But in case that the common good doth apparently more require the preservation of the Persons Life, than the preservation of property and Keeping of the Law in that instance, it is then no sin (as I conceive)." Later on Baxter can foresee another circumstance in which the individual life may be jettisoned:

> But yet it must be confessed that some few Persons may be of so much worth and use to the Commonwealth (as Kings and Magistrates) and some of so little; that the maintaining of the honour and success of the former, may be more necessary than the saving of the lives of the latter.[22]

We confront here – as we did in Chapter 5 – the lengths to which the seventeenth-century puritans would go in praise of magistracy: no knee-jerk jacobinism here. But praise for the magistrate is given only if he does what he was set up to do: that is to say, to be of use to the Commonwealth, to fulfil his imperial mission. If these ends are frustrated, then the lives of even a Charles I or a James II are not sacrosanct, as we saw.

The objection could be raised here that the "common good" is so woolly a phrase that, to elevate it as a principle to which the lives of "ordinary people" (and also, note, Papist-leaning magistrates) are forfeit, is not to say anything very much at all. But Baxter had a very clear idea of what the "common good" meant. He knew it at first-hand experience from ministering to his parishioners at Kidderminster in the 1650s. It is Baxter's record of his activities there that is drawn upon most perceptively by Eamon Duffy, in an article that challenges the conventional picture of the godly at war with the poor. As he points out, the crucial question is: who *were* the poor? Ralph Josselin was a minister who had three categories of poor in his parish of Earles Colne: the committed godly (all 34 of them); the "sleeping hearers" majority; finally, "the ruder sort". But Baxter offered 12 categories in his parish of "three or four thousand souls", of whom 1,800 "or more" were at the age to be communicants. His 500 "precise" were the equivalent of Josselin's 34; supplemented by 100 or so outwardly sincere. Other categories include "tractable and willing", Anglican loyalists, "secret Heathens", knowledgeable sinners, pelagian ignoramuses, idle tipplers, antinomians, Anabaptists and papists. What Duffy is arguing against is a simplistic two-culture polarity, and he is drawing heavily upon Baxter to make this case.[23] It is Baxter's sophisticated understanding of the complexity of responses in his parish that fuels his hopes for catechizing, which he came to see as the way forward for England in the 1650s. But just as in A *Christian directory* Baxter starts with the (critically neglected) first section – private duties – and in the subsequent three sections (family, Church and rulers) builds on that foundation, so Baxter's perception of the "common good" began with Kidderminster, and upon that model created the Worcestershire Association, and upon *that* model fashioned the network of County Associations of Ministers that spread across England in the 1650s. This was Baxter's "Holy Commonwealth" ideal that he wrote up in 1659. It was not a democratic ideal: the majority remained ungodly.[24] But one did not give up on them, any more than one had done in Kidderminster. The weapons used on them were the same: intensive catechizing ensured a "ripening" process by which "catechumens" would be gradually brought into membership of a National Church. Baxter boasted in his memoirs that enforcement of the new moral order in Kidderminster had been made possible by "the zeal and diligence of the godly people of the place who thirsted after the salvation of their neighbours and were in private my assistants".

Michael Walzer cites this passage, against Weber, Tawney and Hill, to demonstrate the conceptual distance between the seventeenth-century puritan spy system and the world of bourgeois trust and contract.[25] Tawney – perhaps more than Weber or Hill – was aware of that gap, but his point was that puritan theocracy went out of fashion with the Barebones Parliament.

Baxter's "Holy Commonwealth" *is*, however, a "theocracy". It is the word he himself uses to describe his ideal government. But "theocracy" he defines, it has to be said, in a way that would not be recognized by Tawney and by most other historians.[26] The word is normally taken to denote clerical control over the laity, but that is not what Baxter is on about. On the contrary he is talking about a *partnership* between minister and civil magistrate. The role of the Protector (first Oliver, then Richard, Cromwell) is crucial. So too is Parliament: Baxter lobbied sympathetic MPs like Harley and Swinfen about his detailed proposals. Baxter believed that what was wrong with Scottish Presbyterians was that they subordinated the laity to the clerisy: the tenth chapter of his *A holy commonwealth* is devoted to proving how wrong this was.[27] Baxter, like other English puritans, was heir to the magistrate-led reformation tradition; only at the end of his life would he concede that he may have been misled by this tradition, into doing an injustice to the alternative Scottish model.

The "Holy Commonwealth" did not in the end happen. Richard Cromwell was overthrown by a military coup. After the Restoration Baxter had to come to terms with a wholly different political situation. His adjustment came a little later than that of his fellow English puritans, and in a more dramatic form. He had publicly (in 1670) to swallow his brave words of 1659.[28] Yet in essence, Tawney would argue, his experience was not radically different from that of his fellow puritans: "the Religion of Trade" now displaced "a Godly Discipline".[29] This was not the swap of one fervently held dogma for another; rather, a resigned recognition that the rules had changed for good. *A Christian directory* did not have to be a hymn to this new religion of trade; from Tawney's point of view, the defensive, apologetic tone of the fourth section strikes the wholly appropriate note for this shift in puritan aspiration.

But this in turn presupposes that the shift was sincere and permanent. There is compelling evidence to the contrary: that, at least in the key case of Baxter, the shift was both insincere and temporary. Those pusillanimous public statements, about clergymen giving up their right to monitor the behaviour of magistrates, are given the lie by the contrary evidence from Baxter's private papers. In the year of the publication of *A Christian directory*, Baxter expresses incredulity to a would-be historian of the Civil War who neglects to consult his by-then publicly disclaimed *A holy commonwealth* in order to find out the *real* explanation of why the war had happened. He similarly takes pleasure in the opaque language in which his recantation of 1670 is wrapped up.[30] There is a huge hole in *A Christian directory*, of which Baxter is fully aware. The edifice carefully constructed – from individual, to family, to Church – and which should have its summit in "the state", collapses in a hideous anti-climax. "But alas! Who shall first reform the Landlords?" is the most depressing sentence in the whole treatise.[31] Baxter shrugs his shoulders.

But this is not in fact the end of the story for Baxter, or for his fellow puritans. The Glorious Revolution could not have been anticipated by him in 1686 when he found himself in prison, but the millenarian studies undertaken in prison then (of which, more in the next chapter) would provide the basis for his revived hopes in a reforming magistracy under William III. The last year of his life, 1691, sees the publication of three works on that theme (*Against the revolt to a foreign jurisdiction*, *Of national churches*, and *The glorious kingdom of Christ*). And one that was not published: *The poor husbandman's advocate*.

This 1691 timebomb did not explode until (perhaps appropriately) the year of the General Strike. His biographer, F. J. Powicke, found the manuscript in Baxter's archive that had been suppressed by Baxter's literary executors, Matthew Sylvester and Daniel Williams, and he, probably correctly, believed that it had been too radical for them to publish. Certainly they had published in 1697 another posthumous Baxter treatise on doctrine, to answer slurs on his orthodoxy. When Powicke published this social treatise in 1926, not only – and this is significant – was it too late for Weber, but it was also too late for Tawney, who had given the Holland Memorial Lectures, on which *Religion and the rise of capitalism* is based, in 1922. If they had seen it, would they have altered the way they had read Baxter, and, by extension, their view of the godly response to the poor?

Baxter's treatise is a "request": that the misery of the English poor be addressed. The German failure to do so had produced the Peasant

Revolt. Long leases had given way to rack-renting. The yields for the majority of husbandmen could not support the maintenance of wife and children in food and clothing. Their diet is often healthier than that of the rich, but their labour is repetitive and boring, and they have to endure the extremes of heat and cold. They are too worn-out with labour to be fit for anything but sleep at the end of the day. When they fall ill, they cannot pay their bills and are ripe for exploitation by mountebanks. Ministers argue for tithes to recompense *their* labour, but few work harder than those husbandmen who pay them. Poverty debases the national spirit – look at France and Muscovy! Poverty causes ignorance: the prerequisite of Popery. Charity to the poor is enlightened self-interest; it is how God will judge the steward; it is the essence of Christianity. Follies of the oppressed are no excuse to those who oppress them, who are equated in sin with Tiberius, Nero and Domitian. There are no absolute property rights, except God's. The excusatory plea, that one saves to provide for one's children, is the "last self-deceit".

"The Great Dog will not be moved by argument or Oratory to give up his bone or carrion, nor to let the little dogs partake with him", concedes Baxter. But "the publike welfare of the nation" should ensure that landlords reduce rack-rents by a third; concern for health should facilitate the renunciation of a lavish table; self-interest, as his friend Thomas Gouge showed, advanced philanthropy. Lawyers and doctors should reduce costs to the poor in their charging of fees. Baxter, though, "is not for levelling or equality". This does not stop him, nor should it, from telling lords and knights how they should live. Any more than it had Christ, who had told the rich man, *Goe and sell all that thou hast, and follow me, and thou shalt have a treasure in heaven.* If this doctrine seems to "savour of the Levellers or Quakers", Baxter asks: "What would you have done if you had lived when the Spirit of Love made all the Christians sell all that they had and live in common?" And if the rich plead the tax burden, Baxter comments: "Who should pay money but those that have it? and who should pay dearer for the publike safety than they that have most to loose?" There is a monstrous disequilibrium of service: "*You* do but give your *money*; but poore men give their *lives* for the publike Service by sea and land. While you sit warme at home out of fear and danger, they are night and day in suffering and peril." To claim that "the Levelling Spirit of Popularity" has inspired the tract, "to teach the people to cry down Monarchy and cry up a Common Wealth", draws his angriest response. It is "ignorant Sots" who equate "Commonwealth" with "Democracy" (and this is wholly consistent with his earlier argument in *A holy commonwealth*). For although in 1691 neither a populist nor an anti-monarchist, Baxter is emphatically for a "Common Wealth", even if he is more inclined to use now the less provocative term, "National Church". Respected contemporaries like John Selden and Sir Matthew Hale knew what the word "commonwealth" meant, whereas "the Ignoramuses seem not to know that the common welfare is so essentially the *Terminus* of the Policie, that to exclude it is to dissolve all the Policie, Kingdom and State".[32]

The last chapter turns to consolatory advice to "poore unrelieved Husbandmen" in default of voluntary action by the rich. There follow trite and predictable pleas for temperance and frugality. In that sense the treatise is as anti-climactic as *A Christian directory* was in *its* last section. The continuities between the two run deeper than that. Baxter was not markedly less sympathetic to the poor in 1673 than he was in 1691. There are quotations given earlier in this chapter that are every bit as telling against "mammonism" as the passages quoted from the later work[33]. He is calling in both works ultimately, without too much conviction, on the rich to reform themselves. In what sense then is *The poor husbandman's advocate* a watershed? It is a watershed because of the context in which it is written. In a number of works published in 1690 and 1691 (and in a number of unpublished archive papers) Baxter outlined his idea of a "National Church". Fifth Monarchists propagated their fantasies of Christ's rule on Earth, and missed the actual achievements of Christian magistracy in the past. "Would they have the Churches have the full power of Church discipline, to separate the precious from the vile", then that is precisely what happens when the right Protestant ruler sits on the throne.[34] It had happened in 1659 in the brief rule of Richard Cromwell; it was to happen again in 1691 with William III. It was the prospect of a recrudescence of "the full power of Church discipline" in 1691 (he now thought kindly, if belatedly, about the Scots[35]) that made these later admonitions anything but the toothless pieties of 1673.[36] The point became clear in an exchange of correspondence between Baxter and his friend John Humfrey in 1691. Both were then arguing the merits of a "National Church", but meant very different things by the term. Humfrey was thinking of an Erastian framework, with the minimum of ministerial discipline. But for Baxter the discipline was the *point* of a "National Church": Kidderminster writ large in 1691, as it had been (briefly) in his reform programme of 1659.[37] There was the same rigorous attention to details in his *Holy Commonwealth* as in his *National Church*.[38] Christening by baptism, in 1691, would not be "an Infant Ceremony" but one where parents were taught to know what was meant by entering their child into a covenant. Adults should have their own baptismal covenant. The pastor should know his parish. Unrighteous Canons would be discarded. Ministers would not impose unnecessary terms for communion. Bishops should ordain in synods. The scandalous should be kept out of the Sacrament (at the heart of his dispute with Humfrey). The universities should be purged until there are only "godly careful Tutors". Toleration was not an absolute right, but dependent on the will of the law-giver, "who can difference between Man and Man when the Law cannot". There must be "a wise and godly King that must be the principal means to accomplish all this": Richard Cromwell in 1659, William III in 1691. The "common wealth" and monarchy were, as he argued, terms that were complementary, not contradictory. And what would destroy a "National Church"?:

Sins of Injustice and Unmercifulness, especially Rich Mens oppression of the Poor, Landlords grinding their Poor tenants, and Judges, Justices and Lawyers unrighteousness in Suits and Judgments, are sins threatened by the Prophets as the forerunners of Destruction.

It is significant that Baxter's last testament should be devoted entirely to spelling out the implications of what is meant by the rich oppressing the poor. But even though it would not be until 1926 that the general public would read it, it needs to be restored to its 1691 context before its importance is properly registered: these are homilies that derive their force as part of a whole, of an ambitious plan in 1691 to restore "the full power of Church discipline".[39]

The life and death of a Boston merchant reflects the tension between ethic and discipline, and shows up both the strengths and the weaknesses of the Weber thesis. James Henretta draws a picture of a man, in Robert Keayne, who not only seems to have been the embodiment of the Protestant Ethic, but indeed to have stepped straight out of the pages of Weber. Here we have a puritan migrant in 1635 who turns his religious convictions to economic success in the import business. He boasted of his diligence in his will, left an estate of £4,000 on his death in 1656, but found time all the same to produce three weighty tomes of biblical exposition. But Keayne was not destined to be the model citizen of Massachusetts Bay; rather, the reverse. In 1639 he was accused of "taking above six-pence in the shilling profit; in some above eight-pence; and in some small things, above two for one". He was fined £200 by the General Court; the elders of the Church came close to excommunicating him. The General Court bore the imprint of Governor Winthrop's convictions, which saw it (as in 1640) intervening vigorously to protect the interest of debtors from their merchant creditors. When earlier in the Antinomian Controversy, Anne Hutchinson (wife of a merchant) challenged a gospel of works, most merchants supported her because, as Henretta argues, they feared a close communal regulation of their spiritual, as well as their economic, lives. But they lost, and Henretta argues that Massachusetts Bay became "an authoritarian state, a holy commonwealth on the model of Calvin's Geneva".[40]

These American tensions were well known to Baxter. A witness against Anne Hutchinson in 1637 had been John Eliot, who became Baxter's most faithful transatlantic correspondent. Eliot's *Christian commonwealth* and Baxter's *A holy commonwealth* not only *sound* similar, and were published (if not written) in the same year (1659), they are the fruits of a common commitment to a godly discipline. When in 1691 the "Holy Commonwealth" ideal is revived by Baxter under the title of "National Church", it is another American minister, Increase Mather, who has replaced Eliot as the confidant of shared millenarian dreams.[41] Baxter would express, in debate with Humfrey, his wish that the world had "more such Nationall Churches as New England is (if a Province may be called a Nation)".[42] And in his *The poor husbandman's advocate* Baxter apologizes for his copious recitation of "Scripture texts for good works" because of the need to combat the influence of Anne Hutchinson's antinomian contemporary, Tobias Crisp, whose works had been republished in 1690. His sixth chapter ends with a plea to the reader to "peruse the Texts that I have so largely cited, and then nothing but obstinate prejudice or contempt of Scripture, can keep you from abhorring this *Crispian, Anti-Christian Libertinisme*".[43]

A later generation of Robert Keaynes (in England as well as America), in a more relaxed intellectual and social context, would find much that was congenial in the writings of a puritan minister like Baxter. When a Birmingham button manufacturer in 1790 invited his workmen to his home to read together edifying works, the readings were mostly from Richard Baxter's writings, beginning with "'Saints Everlasting Rest', where he recommends our reproving the ungodly and inviting them to return to Christ".[44] On such anecdotal evidence the links between puritanism and capitalism are often forged, but note (as we see so often in these controversies) it is an extrapolation of nineteenth-century or eighteenth-century experience back into the seventeenth century. But restore the crisis to its seventeenth-century setting and we know now where Baxter stood: not with Keayne and Hutchinson, but with Eliot and Winthrop; not with "the religion of trade" but with "a godly discipline".

If we remove Baxter from the first section ("The Protestant Ethic") of the sixteenth chapter of Christopher Hill's *The world turned upside down* – and I think we should – that does not mean that we should necessarily rush to reinsert him into the second section of that same chapter ("Beyond the Protestant Ethic") alongside radicals like Winstanley, Coppe and Nayler. It is true that Baxter reminds his readers in his last tract that so-called Leveller and Quaker practices were really those of the Primitive Christian Church. He made this point earlier in his *A treatise of self-denial*, written in 1660 but republished in 1675. The "Charitable Community" that he describes movingly in that pamphlet was not the same as a "Levelling community", and he was careful not to seek to abolish private property altogether. But the ethic he invokes is a world apart from possessive individualism:

There was so great vigour of true Charity, as that all men voluntarily supplied the wants of the Church and poor, and voluntarily made all things as common that is, *Common by voluntary communication* for use, though not *common in primary title*: And so no man took any thing as his Own, when God, and his Churches, and his Brethrens wants did not call for it. O that we had more of that Christian Love that should cause a *Charitable Community* which is the true Mean between the *Monkish Community* and the *selfish tenacious Propriety*!

119

And, weighing the profit motive against Levelling, Baxter does not resort to a plague-on-both-your-houses resolution: "Levelling hath not destroyed one soul for ten thousand that an inordinate love of Propriety hath destroyed."[45]

Baxter, however, was no Winstanley. Lady Katherine Gell was one of his most persistent correspondents. Ridden with melancholia, she wrote to Baxter for counsel and was rarely disappointed. A casuist of genius, he resolved her fear of the dark, her temptations to sin, her immoderate love of her children. But what happens (on 15 December 1657) when she raises with him the problem of usury? Baxter's tone changes to one of distinct unease:

> As to the case of usury I am a very unfitt person to give you advise in it, because I am not satisfyed myselfe how far usury is unlawfull, whether it be any where unlawfull where it is not oppressing or injurious I cannot affirme.

He even suggests a less than heroic compromise whereby, if she feels scruples about profiting from usury, she could allow her money to be handled by another "able faithfull" person with a more robust conscience.[46]

Twenty-four years later Baxter is no clearer on the problem. One fellow minister who was, Samuel Shaw, corresponded with Baxter. He sent him his manuscript on usury that had been held up in the press. We don't have Baxter's reply, but we have Shaw's reactions to what were clearly critical comments on his manuscript. Shaw, respected by Baxter as a "Learned and Worthy Man", gracefully acknowledged Baxter's superior erudition, but wished that Baxter would speak out on this controversy with the tongue of "Moses and the prophets". Instances of usury having done good, which Baxter clearly must have cited, could be replicated, according to Shaw, by simple examples of "lending without usury".[47] When Shaw's pamphlet appeared the following year, in 1682, it was an unequivocal attack on usury. "*Controversie about Usury*, did I call it?", he asked briskly, and then wondered what made it a controversy. Only in the past hundred years had a defence of the practice been so much as ventured: "although Usury be a very old Sin, yet the Defence of it seems to be a very new one". The name stank, so men dressed it up with the politer-sounding "interest". Reiterating the point made in his letter to

Baxter, Shaw argued that it was not the case that some sorts of usury were lawful, but that there were some lawful things that *looked like* usury, but were not. There always will be the poor to be provided for, but they should not have to beg. Begging is not their sin, therefore, but that of the rich, and of the magistrates, who do not prevent it happening. Shaw explained that he first saw the light in an earlier encounter with a Bible-quoting beggar woman. He quoted to her, at his own door, the biblical injunction against the righteous, begging for bread, but she was equal to it, who "premising a little Sigh, answered me very readily, True, Sir, the Psalmist does say so but yet he knew there was a time, when he himself was forc'd to beg his Bread". David's example was what Shaw then took to his heart, "and it made me kind to her at that time, and to think more Charitably of that whole Tribe of Mankind ever since".[48] We miss that incisiveness in Baxter. He was no Moses, he was not even a Samuel Shaw, but on the other hand neither was he the domesticated pet of Birmingham button manufacturers.

Baxter has dominated this chapter as he dominated the works of Weber and Tawney. Do we gain any extra insights from reflections on Prynne and Muggleton? Prynne wrote no casuist works as such, but there is enough evidence from his political and religious writing of his social prejudices. This was not the man to be swayed by the pleas of a beggar woman, however rich in scriptural knowledge. He had hated Laud as, among other things, a social upstart "raised from the dung-hill".[49] His history provided Prynne with a pious homily:

> That persons sodainly raised from the lowest degree of man, to the highest pitch of honour, proove commonly the most insolent, domineering, ingenious, tyrannical and mischievous of all others such preferments being unable to weld or manage the greatnesse of their fortune.[50]

When Prynne taxed him with humble birth at his trial, Laud replied that "all this if true no fault of mine", and added, "my father had born all offices in the Towne save the Mayoralty".[51] Prynne thought that the case for tithes was proved by his conviction that "Nine Parts of Ten of the present Petitioners against our Ministers Tithes (if strictly examined by the poll) will appear to be poor mechanical persons".[52] That disposed of the case against tithes then. Prynne illuminatingly contrasted the social class of Sir George Booth's royalist rebels with that of the regicides: "The one were Gentlemen of conceit and considerable Families, and could not better themselves with a Warre; the other upstarted Mushrooms, and could not have risen but by a Warre."[53] Sir Richard Baker detected a social discrimination, even in Prynne's war on stage plays: "But perhaps because Tragedies are the Gentry, I may say, of plays, he is so generous as to spare them for ther Gentry's sake; but ther Comedies, which are but the Commonalty of Plays are like to pay for it."[54] One writer even suggested that Prynne's opposition to the entry of Jews into England was based on social grounds: "surely the party who writ so furiously against the Jews coming in, was afraid his chambers in Lincolnes-Inn should have been for ther habitation, or else his Mannour of Swainscomb or Swainswick; of which he writes himself Esquire".[55] That snobbery in Prynne was picked up by another critic, who hoped that "William may have liberty to write against Prynne, Prynne against the Esquier, the Esquier against the Utter Barrister, the Utter Barrister against the Bencher of Lincolnes Inne, and to retrograde, till he himself (when he shall become himself) thinks fit to have leasure to desist and to be quiet."[56] Predestination was right, thought Prynne, above all *because* it was arbitrarily elitist: "hence worldly honours, favoures and preferments among men, are stiled grace, because they are conferred upon few, and that without any merit or demerit of theirs, not cast promiscuously upon all". Conversely, he thought that Arminianism was wrong, because it was subversively egalitarian: "to throw down all the hedges, all the inclosures, of his more speciall love? to lay them common unto all without distinction?"[57] Baxter, the poor husbandman's advocate, pressing for good works, and craving a discipline that separated the precious from the vile, seems at the opposite end of the spectrum from Prynne, the encloser, the determinist elitist, and the opponent of clerical discipline. In one sense, that view is correct. In another sense it is not correct. Prynne the ineffable snob, champion of the House of Lords, enemy of the Levellers and Quakers, naturally found in the maintenance of tithes the key to stability. It was not just the fact that nine-tenths of opponents of tithes were "poor mechanical persons", and many of them Quakers to boot. Worse was the fact that, without the payment of tithes, ministers would be dependent upon "the meer arbitrary uncoercive Benevolence of the people (who being generally profane, covetous, vicious, and enemies to all godly Ministers, will not voluntarily contribute one farthing towards them)".[58] To resist opponents' suggestions that ministers could always support themselves by manual work, Prynne proved with his usual copious documentation that Christ and St Paul had never in fact laboured with their hands.[59]

And yet Prynne aligned himself with these same despicable tithes-refusers in the late 1650s. Why? Because ministers were not offering the Sacrament of the Lord's Supper to their parishioners, who should therefore refuse to pay them their tithes. The Lord Protector's Proclamation of 25 November 1658 condemned the spread of this subversive tactic.[60] For Prynne, it was subversion that was justified by religion, and it is a reminder to us again of the priorities of the seventeenth-century puritan. Prynne's opposition to clerical suspending powers can correctly be called "Erastian", not in the caricature sense of a lay indifference to religious niceties, but in the technical sense of being in line with Erastus's own arguments against George Withers on this issue.[61] Neither Prynne nor Erastus was hostile to discipline; they just thought that the clergy didn't have the exclusive rights to exercise it. When Prynne argued for free admission to the Sacrament it was therefore not (as his opponents alleged) because he was against discipline; it was the frequent and open administration of the Sacrament that *was*, in Prynne's book, the "godly discipline". Because Prynne was no fan of "Holy Commonwealths", and because his idea of "discipline" was what Prynne's opponents saw as its opposite, we should not therefore assume that in a clash between "discipline" (as he defined it) and social and economic motivations, Prynne would in the end choose any differently from Baxter. His stand on tithes demonstrates this. To put it another way, to preserve his Manor at Swainswick he would keep Jews out of England, but to ensure regular communion he would be prepared to see it destroyed. These are the *seventeenth-century* priorities that the historian of puritanism must recognize, and so often fails to do.[62]

Professor Reay has shown that, in their earliest years the small number of Muggletonians were drawn largely from the class of wholesale and retail traders and artisans.[63] That pattern seems to have been maintained in the later history of the movement. The Frosts were Derbyshire brassfounders who moved to London around the year 1800 and their line is a dominant one in the nineteenth-century history of the sect. They were able to administer discreet patronage to the poor of the faith, very much along the lines commended by

Muggleton himself in 1683.[64] But that dominance and patronage must be put in perspective. For all their financial clout, the Frosts were unable to prevail in will over the caretaker's husband, Thomas Robinson, beneficiary (as he acknowledged) of the *largesse* of "those dear loving kind genuine and practical believers Mr and Mrs Huntley", when it came down to the crucial question of whether the 1656 or 1661 edition of *A divine looking glass* were the authentic one. The will of one of the last Muggletonians, Charles Crundwell of Bournemouth, in 1960 contains a bequest of £100 "to the trustees of the Muggletonian Church and Meeting House for general charitable purposes". Thomas Tomkinson's definition of Muggletonian principles in 1695 is the most robust defence of the poor, who are "filled with the Substance of spiritual Truth, when as the Rich in Reason, Notion, and Argument, are sent empty away".[65] From Muggleton himself there were more equivocal signals. He boasted to cousin Roger (his one convert) in 1678 of the family's *low* social origins, but at the same time pointed out that the tailor-as-Prophet phenomenon was not after all so strange, since "a Taylor is more honorable with kings and princes and noblemen of this world than Heards-men and fishermen".[66] Muggleton was, in truth, not much of a class warrior. He *boasted* to a follower in 1663 that, in contrast to turbulent Quakers, *his* people could live quiet lives by forbearing meetings, and by paying their tithes and taxes.[67] He allowed rich followers to attend public church services, even if he hoped that they wouldn't (and regretted in the last years of his life his laxity on this point). He diverted a query about trade in Antigua with this disclaimer in 1678: "I leave it to Mr Saddington to give you an Account of it for I have not Commerce with any men of the World". His parting shot was: when in Rome, do as the Romans do.[68]

How far does Muggleton then fit into the Weber model? It is the puritans' piety and liberty that link them in Weber's mind to commerce, as a recent commentator notes:

> Puritan peoples everywhere have been immune to Caesarism, Weber reports, concurring with Montesquieu who notes that the English "have progressed the farthest of all peoples of the world in three important things: in piety, in commerce, and in freedom". For Weber, Puritan piety gave rise to commercial superiority and free institutions.[69]

The formulation is too tidy, as we have seen. In Chapter 5, puritans are shown not to be immune to Caesarism, and certainly Muggleton is one who is not (whether in his uncensored rhapsodies to Cromwell in the 1650s, or in his subsequent care to obey the law after 1660). More important, as we saw in Chapter 6, piety and freedom were often contradictory, not complementary, puritan traits, and that is why Commons and Army could not agree on what should be left in the text of Cromwell's victory communications to the Speaker.[70] Professor Norman Jones has provided the most comprehensive recent study of how the Commons dealt with usury. He believes that the piety of the 1571 Commons' debates on the issue had given way to the freedom of the Usury Act of 1624. He argued that puritans in England did create "a rationale that sanctioned economic self-aggrandisement", and for them the Act was welcome primarily because it *internalized* the sin of usury. For by then, he argued, puritans were learning "the moral from the theology that you could do what you felt was right".[71]

Professor Jones's study is a valuable record of a sea-change that was occurring among members of Parliament, and he supplements this material with references to contemporary puritan casuistry. But how puritan *were* early Stuart MPs? One remembers Professor Conrad Russell's half-joke, that Ignatius Jordan was the single *real* puritan MP in the Jacobean Commons![72] To most puritans, a theology that "you could do what you felt was right" smacked of antinomianism; it would be perverse to argue that, as early as 1624, it had now become orthodoxy.

However, it is no bad summary of the position that Muggleton himself had reached in 1661, when he banished from his followers the expectation that God took "immediate notice" of their actions. He told rebels Medgate and Buchanan that, without external sanctions, "I do well to please that Law written in my heart, so that I might not be accused by that Law written in my owne Conscience."[73] At the age of 22, in his posthumous memoirs, he recalled working alongside William Reeve as a journeyman, the brother of his later co-Prophet:

> He was a very zealous *Puritan* at that time, and many others of that Religion came to him, and disputed with me about the unlawfulnesse of lending Money upon Pawns, because they pleaded it was Usury and Extortion, and did alledge many places of Scripture against it.[74]

To do what you felt was right, to be answerable only to a law in your own conscience: this was the liberation by Muggleton from the old "puritan" scruples, offered now to those who followed a "third commission" of the Spirit that transcended Law *and* Gospel (the first two commissions), and which banished an intervening God. But it *did* sound very antinomian. That was particularly embarrassing, because Muggletonians had recruited many in their ranks from former Ranters. Worse, the dead John Reeve was being traduced in 1663 as a parasite or drunkard, because of the confusion, said Muggleton, in the accuser's mind with his brother William, who did go on to become a Ranter.[75] These were circumstantial points; more serious was the way in which Muggleton's stand against "immediate notice" carried with it the antinomian virus. The fifth of Muggleton's nine points against Medgate stresses that the Prophet's love can uphold corrupt nature: "this was not Christ's practice when on earth to cast off corrupt natural men *that believeth in him* [my italics], neither doth the prophet". Hence, as we saw earlier, Muggleton's reluctance to condemn the scandalous, *but believing*, William Cleve. The seventh of Muggleton's points contains the same message. Medgate claimed that the Prophet's blessing, on his line of argument, actually supported the wicked. Muggleton replied that, when transgression occurs, where else but from the Prophet could the sinner expect to receive support?[76]

An unfettered conscience and unfettered trade went together: that was the Muggletonian Tomkinson's argument in 1679.[77] Earlier in America it had been the argument of the merchants who had supported Anne Hutchinson. Weber's trinity of piety-and-freedom-and-commerce came together in fact in antinomian theology, but it was an equation roundly repudiated by Winthrop and the Founding Fathers, and by Baxter in 1691. When Baxter becomes the poor husbandman's advocate, he looks to a "Holy Commonwealth", an alliance between magistrate and clergyman that he calls a "theocracy", to bridle the acquisitive appetite. And he knows the enemy: "Crispian, Anti-Christian Libertinisme". The reprinting of the dead Crisp's antinomian sermons in 1690 is, for Baxter, the major calamity of his last years. And, against Crisp and his contemporary Saltmarsh, Baxter recites "the Scripture texts for good works".

We seem to be concluding with a paradox. It is Baxter's Calvinism, according to Weber, Tawney and Hill, which makes him end up, however unwillingly, as capitalism's friend. The argument advanced here is the opposite: that it is Baxter's commitment to good works, as evidenced in his posthumous last treatise, which makes him capitalism's enemy. Is there no connection then between reformed theology and the rise of capitalism? There is, but it is not the one that Weber, Tawney and Hill make. The theology that "you could do what you felt was right" was never at the centre of Calvinist beliefs, but it is correctly associated with its antinomian wing. The passing of the 1624 Usury Act says something about a changed temper in the Commons, but not about a changed temper in puritanism as a whole. Calvinist believers like Governor Winthrop could continue to hold the line against antinomianism, and the freedom of the market, in the 1630s and 1640s, but their successors would find it progressively more difficult to do so. Even so, Tawney is probably wrong to believe that the pass had been sold by the time of the Restoration in England, and certainly wrong if he based that belief on the (enforced) caution of Baxter's *A Christian directory* of 1673.

If, by the end of the seventeenth century, the merchant successors of Anne Hutchinson's followers had less to fear from interference by clerical busybodies than they had in the 1630s, there were material factors at work here that lie outside the remit of this chapter, and which are in fact recognized by Weber, Tawney and Hill. In so far as ideal factors can be brought into the equation, however, there *were* developments within puritanism that helped this loosening-up process. They were to be found (though not exclusively there) among those who were seen as antinomian. It is the paradox we encountered in the previous chapter, in our search for the links between puritanism and liberty: the knots on the individual's liberty were most loose when the magistrate stuck to the task of keeping outward order (Hobbes, Oliver Cromwell, Roger Williams); when the clergy preached but did not discipline (Hobbes, Oliver Cromwell, Roger Williams); and when God ceased to terrify men and women with the spectre of Hell (Hobbes). Emancipation from all three knots made the individual conscience sovereign, and the arguments for religious toleration on the grounds of commercial advantage irresistible: that was the gist of Samuel Parker's critique of Hobbes and of toleration in 1670.[78] The Muggletonians, who would transcribe Hobbes later, satisfied all of his requirements: they outwardly obeyed the magistrate, they made the wearing of a clerical collar a cursing offence, and they banished an external Hell and an intervening God, in endorsing Muggleton's repudiation of "immediate notice". Freedom of religion, and for trade, were obvious correlations in Tomkinson's arguments of 1679.

Antinomianism at the end of the seventeenth century was nothing new. If Crisp was Baxter's enemy in 1691, it is to be remembered that he had been dead for nearly 50 years. That was precisely what was sinister to Baxter: the republication of Crisp's works in 1690, and their (seeming) acclaim by the mainstream divines of his day. If the climate was now right for the propagation of such views, so much the worse for the climate. And Baxter accordingly buckled down to the task of writing his corrective, *The poor husbandman's advocate*. This is the time when he is also in the grip of millennial dreams (on which, more in the next chapter). It draws him into controversy with Thomas Beverley, a millenarian of a more literal cast of mind than Baxter's. That wouldn't be so bad, if Beverley didn't also profess an admiration for Crisp's antinomianism. For Baxter, the combination of millenarianism with antinomianism was lethal: he had opposed it in Crisp and Saltmarsh in the 1640s, and did not want to see its recrudescence in the 1690s. Against liberty, Baxter now preached discipline; against the market, Baxter now preached sovereignty; against complacency, Baxter now preached compassion. We might even perhaps call him a seventeenth-century Tawney.[79]

Chapter Eight

Puritanism and millenarianism

Puritanism and millenarianism come together in the creation of America. This is a truism that no longer seems to us true. We need in fact to get America out of the way before we can assess what millenarianism really meant to English puritans in the seventeenth century. Events like Waco in April 1993 cast a lurid, and deceptive, shadow. Eighty-six members of a religious sect perished in that Texan siege, including its charismatic leader, David Koresh. But that sect did not come from nowhere. The "Branch Davidian" movement was an off-shoot of the Seventh Day Adventists. They, in their turn, were an off-shoot of the Millerites, following upon the failure of William Miller's prophecy that Christ would return on 22 October 1843. In the world of apocalyptic prophecy, as a famous sociological study has shown,[1] nothing succeeds like failure. The great evangelical successes of Seventh Day Adventism would come with the leaders of the Millerite secession, like Hiram Edson and Ellen White. It would be Ellen White's protégé, John Kellogg, who would invent an appropriate diet for the return of Christ, and so revolutionize the world's breakfasts, if not its religions. We can press back further still on origins. Behind the Millerites were English prophets like Richard Brothers, "Nephew of the Almighty", and Joanna Southcott, "The Woman Clothed with the Sun", and contemporary with them American movements like Shakers and Mormons.[2] If Joseph Smith had not been a different type of leader from Koresh, we might easily have witnessed a Mormon Waco in 1844.

It is good historical sense then to see Koresh, not simply in pathological terms (as, fatally, the Texan authorities did), but in eschatological terms, as belonging to a long tradition of American puritan millennialism. But how far back should we push it? Some would begin with its own millennial beginnings. This was certainly the belief of Lyndall Gordon's teacher, as she found, when she came from South Africa to America, to begin her postgraduate literary studies:

> Sacvan Bercovitch declared to the American seminar that "to be an American is to have a vision in your head. There are two Americas," he went on, "the geographical United States, a place of scramblers as the West opened up, and the America of the dream, Winthrop's dream in 1630 of a *city on the hill* – that's how he saw it in his prophetic dream on the *Arbella*, the flagship of the great Migration: a vision of an exemplary society that would become a model to all the nations."[3]

Bercovitch developed this theme in a number of important works.[4] His "splitting" is interesting: the materialist scramblers (bad); their idealistic predecessors (good). We saw, in Chapter 7, how John Updike described a very different history of America, which he depicted as a seamless process by which an initial theology of justification by success would make possible, and indeed sanctify, all those later scramblings. But we also saw that there was at least one high-minded scrambler, Robert Keayne, who would find the Winthrops of his world anything but accommodating to scrambling, however high-minded. Winthrop was not soft on scramblers, that we can now accept, but it doesn't follow either that this was because he was into the business of model-making for future idealists.

His 1630 sermon has, in truth, had its importance grossly inflated. It wasn't published in Winthrop's own lifetime, and, when it was, it was usually quoted out of context. Here is the controversial passage:

> We shall find that the God of Israel is among us, when ten of us shall be able to resist a thousand of our enemies; when he shall make us a praise and glory that men shall say of succeeding plantations "the Lord made it like that of New England". For we must consider that we shall be as a city upon a hill [Matthew 5:14–15]. The eyes of all people are upon us, so that if you shall deal falsely with our God in the work we have undertaken, and so cause him to withdraw his present help from us, we shall be made a story and a by-word through the world.[5]

Theodore Bozeman is the best deconstructionist of this text.[6] The message of the sermon, as he points out, is sombre, not euphoric. The "eyes of all people" may be upon the migrants, but *it is in anticipation of their failure*. The hope, such as it is, rests with "succeeding plantations", not with the founders. Susan Hardman Moore's careful researches have reinforced this picture.[7] She depicts a flight from "popery" rather than pursuit of a dream. Flight denoted cowardice: were the migrants quitting the scene prematurely? This was a good question to ask in the 1640s, when that scene embraced an Archbishop in the Tower, and a New Jerusalem in the pulpits. The answer (for many) then would be *reverse migration*: an under-reported phenomenon in American historiography. Stephen Fender has documented well the tensions between those who stayed and those who went. Nehemiah Wallington, for instance, had once seen his friend John Cole, at least until his departure in 1635, as a "Job in bearing of many seasons". Cole would defend himself to Wallington with scriptural justification, invoking David's flight from Gath. But it was David's friendship with Jonathan which Wallington preferred to quote in his counter-reply in 1642: their own friendship, seemingly indissoluble once to Wallington, had now been wrecked on Cole's false decision seven years earlier.[8]

Some "eyes of the people" may not even, as Wallington's, have been censorious; they could just have been blank. There *was* a "city on the hill" for some English puritans, Karen Kupperman has argued, but that city was Providence Island, not New England. For leading puritan grandees like Saye and Brooke, Massachusetts was a side-show, and an irritating one at that, when its rulers seemed to be bent on making approved godliness a prerequisite of citizenship. For many puritans in England, it was the victims of a theocracy (as they saw it) – men like Roger Williams, Gorton and Vane – who cast the most impressive figures. When Providence Island was collapsing in 1640, English puritan leaders wanted to shore it up by a *remigration* of the New England settlers.[9] The failure of Hispaniola in July 1655 was the end, therefore, of one puritan millennial dream. Blair Worden has shown brilliantly how it related in the mind of Cromwell to "the sin of Achan", and ultimately to his decision to reject the Crown.[10] For men steeped in "providences", the failure of Providence Island was as unignorable as Hispaniola would be later.

When Cotton Mather, in his 1702 *Magnalia Christi Americana*, said that "whether New England may live any where else or no, it must live in our History", he was delivering a powerful truth. It was New England's later historians who would rewrite the experience of the early settlers in their own image, and, in their "jeremiads" against a "declension" from former purity, would sow the seeds of a belief in America's "exceptionalism". Mather was quite open about it: "In short, the *First Age* was the *Golden Age*: to return unto That, will make a Man a Protestant, and I may add, a Puritan."

It has taken us eight chapters, but now, it seems, we know who "puritans" are: they are the ones who recognize that the "First Age" was the "Golden Age". That was the time when an example was set "to them first", and then by them, to give "a *specimen* of many Good Things, which he would have His Churches elsewhere aspire and arise unto". John Cotton called such model-building arrogant, but he said this in 1650 when he was *living in* a "Golden Age" rather than *writing about* one.[11]

Who was right: Cotton or Cotton Mather? Were John Cotton's contemporaries, Prynne, Baxter, and Muggleton, aware that a "city on the hill" was being erected in America? Certainly not Muggleton: a very English home-spun Prophet, who found even the thought of a follower contemplating emigration to Virginia deeply shocking.[12] Prynne has not much to say about America either, except as a handy arsenal for cautionary tales about antinomian excesses. The puritan who does seem best to fit the mould is Baxter. He certainly had contemplated migration in the 1630s, according to an unpublished prison note in 1686. The details are scanty, but he and his friend had even picked out a likely spot on the basis of a rather obscure map. From then on, even if he stayed behind, he was an informed observer of the American scene. His sympathies were engaged with orthodoxy's attempts to bridle the antinomian Anne Hutchinson; like Prynne, he would regale the reader with stomach-churning details of the providential "monster births" of the heretics, Anne herself, and of Mrs Dyer.[13] John Eliot had been a witness against her at her trial, and he became a regular correspondent with Baxter. But Baxter, like other English puritans, worried about the dangers of the authorities overreacting to her excesses. The demands being laid upon New England communicants were too close for comfort to the exactions of John Owen and his Independent colleagues in their 1658 Savoy Declaration. There was palpable relief, therefore, for Baxter in the "half-way

covenant" compromise agreed by the New England ministers in
1662. There had been a convergence of reformist hopes in the 1650s
in the Baxter–Eliot correspondence of those years, which would yield
the near-identical titles in 1659 of Baxter's *A holy Commonwealth*
and Eliot's *Christian Commonwealth*. There were times, though,
when Baxter had to apply the brakes, when Eliot's enthusiasm was in
danger of getting out of hand.[14] Similarly, at the end of Baxter's life,
Increase Mather, who had replaced Eliot as the repository of his
shared confidences, held a belief in a future millennium at variance
with Baxter's own convictions.[15] Mather had to acknowledge that he
himself was unusual, among New England divines, in even having
such interests. Eliot was an earlier example, and if his correspondence
with Baxter is less explicitly on millenarian themes, that says more
about Baxter's shifts at the end of his life, than it does about the relative significance of the millennium to these two American divines.
For, by the later date, Baxter had become an enthusiast for "National
Churches", and as such would express a heartfelt wish that "the world
had more such Nationall Churches as New England is". This is perhaps the most direct statement we have from him of the significance
of the American experiment for English puritans. But we must not
overstate the point. Baxter adds the rider: "if a Province may be called
a Nation".[16] Here we have the essence of the relationship. New England is honoured, just as Scotland is by him at this time (and he was
never so enthusiastic about the Kirk before, as he apologetically conceded), as representing two "provinces" that had cracked the problem
of Church discipline. And discipline was what mattered most of all to
Baxter in 1691; without it, his *Poor husbandman's advocate* would
have been merely words. But this didn't make either New England or
Scotland "Specimens", to which the halting English Church might
aspire. Theirs were real, but at the same time *provincial*, achievements
that deserved more recognition than they often got. "Golden Ages"
are what Baxter dismissed in his *A Christian directory* of 1673 as the
never-never land of unfulfillable dreams. He always put "Second
Ages" above "First Ages", as he had been taught to do by Foxe: better
the imperial achievement than the pristine promise. This would make
him – on the Cotton Mather test – not a "puritan". There is another
moral that can be applied: we shouldn't go to later American puritans
(or their historians) to find out about the earlier English ones.
    And if not to America, where should we go for insights into the

original beast? One scholar, Peter Burke, has an interesting line of investigation to offer, and he starts with the *Oxford English Dictionary*. In England between 1630 and 1650 he notes the coining of new words: *literalism, literalist, literality* and *literalness*. He associates this development with the Reformation, and particularly with the puritan wing of the reformers. Richard Hooker had quarrelled with puritans famously over their belief "that the Scripture had set down a complete form of church polity". They had failed to realize that known laws "may be varied by times, places, persons and other the like circumstances".[17] Hooker's "puritan" is something of a strawman, as the sensitive study by J. S. Coolidge has shown.[18] It was Catholics who were the more literal-minded on the Mass, and on Hell. The Catholic Bellarmine and the Lutheran Osiander would be equally literal-minded in their rejection of Copernicus' heliocentrism. Galileo's sophisticated "allegorising" of the Book of Joshua cut no ice with Protestant fundamentalists, but neither did it with literal-minded Dominicans.[19] But when we have resisted a simple-minded division between "literal-minded" puritans and "allegorist" opponents, we can't ignore what the title of the recent Ford Lectures reminds us, namely that the Bible is "the religion of Protestants".[20] For "hotter sorts" of Protestants to leave the mysterious sayings of St John, in the last book of the New Testament, as a mystery, would prove an impossibility.

But "hotter sorts" of Christians in the medieval past had been equally attracted to Revelation, and as Norman Cohn showed, the results had been unsettling for emperors and popes.[21] St Augustine taught Christians to look for the "heavenly city" in the hereafter; the Council of Ephesus in AD 434 pronounced on millenarianism as a heresy. Heresy and subversion came together in medieval peasant insurrections, but millenarianism could also have counter-revolutionary implications. The Emperor of the Last Days and the Angelic Pope were conservative models drawn from Revelation; Joachim of Fiore and Francis of Assisi showed how millenarianism could stay (just) this side of orthodoxy. The three stages of Muggletonian history – Law, Gospel, Spirit – are pure Joachim. John Foxe tied the Apocalypse to imperial political theory in his famous work *Acts and monuments*, which was ordered by the Elizabethan Privy Council to be chained in every parish church.[22] That work was twice the length of the Bible, and almost as influential upon English Protestants. Professor

Collinson has discovered a man of the 1620s who had read the Bible right through ten times, Foxe seven. John Taylor, "the Water Poet", produced a "thumb-bible" in 1614, a verse summary of scripture bound in a volume that measured only one inch by two. His second successful "thumb-book", a year later, was predictably Foxe's *Acts and monuments*.[23] The omission of Foxe from both works by Norman Cohn[24] and Michael Walzer,[25] which attempt to show a correlation between millenarianism, puritanism and revolution, is a major solecism. The one millenarian group of the English Revolution which is unarguably revolutionary is Captain Venner's Fifth Monarchy Men, as Pepys' diary entries show;[26] but Professor Capp has shown how unrepresentative this activist wing was of the movement as a whole. It has led historians, if anything, to underrate the less showy aspects of millenarian interest. Capp points to no fewer than 77 mentions, in a sample of sermons between 1640 and 1673, which show a millenarian interest as against 34 who don't.[27] He puts Baxter in the 34 who don't; we shall see that he belongs with the 77 who do. That doesn't mean that Baxter (or the other 77) are card-carrying Fifth Monarchists, but it does mean that they would share many of the assumptions (if not the conclusions) of those who were.

Muggleton would seem a stronger candidate than Baxter to be placed in the millenarian world; that was where he came from after all. Muggletonianism hinges on the identification of the two tailors as the Two Last Witnesses in Revelation, and yet we immediately confront a paradox. Nobody could be less respectful than Muggleton of the author of Revelation: St John of Patmos. Nobody, that is, except D. H. Lawrence when, as a dying man in 1929/30, he wrote *Apocalypse*. Was Lawrence a "puritan"? This was a key question at the later trial of *Lady Chatterley's Lover* for obscenity. Richard Hoggart said that he was, drawing on that moral earnestness in the English novel that he shares with George Eliot. The prosecuting counsel claimed that he was not, drawing upon four-letter words in the text. The different connotations of the word could not be more tellingly exposed. Professor Kermode has shown how Lawrence's novel is actually bathed in apocalyptic imagery.[28] This was argued in an essay, not in the court – would his insights, if offered there, have strengthened the defence, or weakened it? Lawrence, like Muggleton, knew that one way to tame Revelation was to allegorize it, as St Augustine had successfully done for Catholic orthodox thought, and for both that way

135

was inadmissible. Lawrence explains "actually, then, the Apocalypse has appealed to men through the ages as an 'allegorical' work. Everything just 'meant something' – and something moral at that. You can put down the meaning flat." But it's the flatness which repels: "fix the meaning of a symbol, and you have fallen into the commonplace of allegory". One can't fix the meaning of a symbol, but what one can do is *fix St John's meaning when he uses it*. But this is not by allegory but by something approximating to what R. G. Collingwood counselled in his *Idea of history* as the historian's "imaginative re-creation". To re-create the experiences of St John in writing down his version is not to sympathize with him: on the contrary Lawrence informs us breezily that the Apocalypse is "the work of a second-rate mind". And that is why, he says, it has had "a greater effect on second-rate people throughout the Christian ages, than any other book in the Bible". Lawrence never quite says that what St John needs is a first-class mind to interpret him, but that is the point of the book that he goes on to write. Muggleton was never quite as rude as that, but we smell the whiff of parricide in the air, in 1661, as he sets to put St John to rights. For both of them, St John is a rather pitiable figure – probably old, certainly an exile, never quite up to the job. There is one point where Lawrence can claim that a certain passage had a "very deep meaning, too deep for John of Patmos". Maddeningly, though, he was the one who had been chosen by God as the vessel for divine truths. For Muggleton the important truth was the naming of the Two Last Witnesses; for Lawrence it was the identification of the final struggle as one between the God of Love and the God of Power. Both men were intrigued by one particular passage in Revelation: "And before the throne there was a sea of glass like unto crystal: and in the midst of the throne and round about the throne were four beasts full of eyes before and behind." Lawrence called this "splendiferous imagery". But it was also "distasteful because of its complete unnaturalness".[29] "Naturalness" is what Muggleton also sought, and he too found this passage in Revelation a hindrance to understanding. When God spoke to Reeve in 1652 it was a "natural" encounter. So it was when God spoke to St John. If it *seems* "unnatural" to us now, it is only because St John has presented it to us in that way. The task of reinterpretation is, therefore, to recover that "naturalness". How should we then respond to "the sea of glass like unto crystal" reported by St John? Lawrence had called it "distastefully unnatural". First, we must recognize that *it happened*. St John did not lie: "who should gain say it?", asks Muggleton. But neither should it be explained away "as an allegory, as many do vainly imagine, but a real spiritual substance".[30] For the trouble with allegory, as Lawrence understood, was that it "can always be explained and explained away", and then for him "the real interest is gone".[31] William Blake's recent interpreter noted his hatred of allegory: "The 'allegorical' is a negative term in Blake's rhetoric, associated with delusions masquerading as absolute truth."[32] "Absolute truth", argues Muggleton, compels recognition of the "sea of glass" as "a real spiritual substance":

> For this must be understood by the reader, that God created or made all creatures of something; he had matter and substance to make every creature of. He did not make living substance of an allegory, that is, as if he should say God made all things of nothing; For an allegory is nothing, and of nothing comes nothing.[33]

The Muggletonians' materialism cannot be emphasized enough. It lay behind their contempt for allegory as used by Behmenists and Quakers in the Prophets' days; and as used by Swedenborgians and Spiritualists in their successors'. Matter pre-existed God. The soul was mortal. God *became* the Man Jesus, all five feet of him. Heaven is a few miles up in the sky. The Devil is a construct of men's imaginings. The Fall has conventionally been seen as an allegory of the human condition, but an eighteenth-century Muggletonian blacksmith knew better: "what a great deale adoe has beene abought the eateing of an Apple".[34] (A personal note here. The Last Muggletonian had been asked by his then young daughter what Heaven was. I was startled when she told me his reply: "a place without apple trees". My mind raced to profound allegories about the Fall. I should have known better. He was making a joke: for a Matfield fruit farmer, what better Heaven could there be?) Eve's eating of the apple didn't produce the Fall: it was her impregnation by the serpent that did. William Blake presented the Fall in pictorial form in just those Muggletonian ways (one more link in the chain connecting Blake and the Muggletonians, in E. P. Thompson's challenging hypothesis).[35] Dreams signify nothing, except fear in those who dream. So much for James Birch's reliance upon dreams and visions to authenticate *his* meeting with God in the eighteenth century. What is missing from his account is the down-to-earth solidity (one might even say, stolidity) of Reeve's report of his conversation with God in 1652.

In the light of Peter Burke's observations on the importance of the concept of "literalism", one should note the ferocity of the Birchite counter-claim that "literalism" was the distinguishing mark of their "orthodox" Muggletonian opponents. In the eighteenth century, believers were very much taken with "spiritual songs". But they sing, says Birch in a letter of 1778, to please the Spirit of Reason. They turn other men's writings into verse, and call the finished product hymns. "Do you think", Birch asks scornfully, "there is any Difference Between Their Singing and the Litteral Muggletonians singing in the sight of the Lord?"[36] (Muggleton's point, of course, was that none of them *were* in "the sight of the Lord": hymn-singing and praying were both, in that sense, gratuitous exercises.) But note the "Litteral" tag. In another letter at the same time he claims that *his* prophecy is one not to be found "by Litteral Signs and Observations according to the Spirit of Reason". Thus literalism equals the False Seed, whereas his truth is discovered by "the Spirit of Faith assisted by Divine Revelation from Heaven". His parting shot is to leave "the Litteral wandering Muggletonians that will wander in the dead Letter to the World's End".[37] Their literalism becomes an excuse for political inaction. They won't even, jeers Birch, name the day of the winding up of history. In the seventeenth century Reeve and Tomkinson had seemed confident of its imminence.[38] Dates get bandied about in the later history of Muggletonianism as likely candidates (such as 1787, 1851, 1914, 1938 and 1957) but with no real air of conviction about them. From America one reformed Birchite, Roger Gibson, took a different view of the "literalist" accusation from his earlier one. He had been then deceived by correspondents from England into thinking that "Traditional Litteralists" were those people who disbelieved in James Birch, and who were therefore wrong. But it is their literalism, he now realizes, that enables them to see through Birch's own writings as "a cunning artful piece of Plagery". Their style of writing was "Mystical", that of "Jacob Behemens Theosophick Philosophy", and not that of the great "plainess of speech of the Commissioned Prophets and Apostles".[39] "Literalism" was not therefore a reproach to be levelled at Muggletonians; it was their glory.

Reproach or glory, was it true? When Reeve and Muggleton wrote *A divine looking glass* in 1656, their attack was not on allegorists, as we might have expected, but on "Trinity Literal-Mongers".[40] *The witch of Endor* is Muggleton's denunciation of a belief in witchcraft that rested (among other texts) on a literal-minded reading of Exodus 22.18, "Thou shalt not suffer a witch to live". This was the very text on the title-page of Matthew Hopkins's *The discovery of witches* when he justifies his brief reign as Witchfinder-General.[41] When Muggleton warned an implacably unforgiving mother that she was bringing Hell on herself he was not speaking in metaphors, but out of a profound literalist conviction that Hell was a state of mind (though not the *conventional* literalist one of fire and brimstone).[42] Muggleton can override literalism – in his handling of the Trinity, witches and Hell – not by allegorizing, but by imposing his own insights on to the reading of disputed texts. As the Prophet of the Third Commission of the Spirit, he transcends those of the first two, of the Law and of the Gospel. With his unerring spirit, the Prophet liberates his followers from conventional obeisance before the texts of both Old and New Testament. Blake similarly would describe "'the Bible or Peculiar Word of God' as an 'Abomination'".[43] The Bible, "by having its meaning arbitrarily fixed", Lawrence tells us, "imposes on us a whole state of feeling which is now repugnant to us".[44] The letter kills, but so do fancy allegories. The rescue for "second-rate minds" comes from reposing their trust in a first-rate one (Muggleton, Blake and Lawrence). There are "positive" texts, explains Muggleton, which *can* only yield to a literalist reading (like the Two Last Witnesses in Revelation), but they are few and far between. Therefore commentators who attempt to dazzle the readers by the sheer quantity of scriptural references are wasting their time (a real Hobbesian touch this).[45] The great majority of texts are "privative", not "positive". That is not open-house for any allegorical conceit that springs to the interpreter's mind, but it does mean a yielding on matters in dispute to *better-informed* minds. The biblical text, "In the beginning God created the heaven and the earth", is then *not* to be interpreted literally (the Quaker William Penn therefore misses the point when invoking that text against Muggleton's materialism). This is a "privative", not a "positive" statement, and as such stands correction by the Prophet: "Moses set the cart before the horse . . . he spake that first that should have been spoken last."[46]

St John's inadequacies must be redressed, no less than Moses's. He was, says Lawrence, "second-rate", "a strange Jew: violent, full of the

Hebrew books of the Old Testament, but also full of all kinds of pagan knowledge";[47] he was, says Muggleton (more politely), "a banished man, before those things were acted upon the earth, which maketh his writings the more hard to understand, and much more hard to interpret". He concludes: "So that it must needs be true wisdom to know the mind of the spirit in these mystical sayings of his."[48] Like those other blunderers, Moses, Augustine, Aristotle and Penn, St John clung to the illusion that God *could* make something out of nothing.[49]

Lawrence and Muggleton agreed that the worst illusion fostered by St John was that of a 1,000-year rule of the saints. Lawrence saw it as the second-rater's form of class revenge, in which the mighty are toppled from their thrones. Muggleton is kinder. It is an illusion, "imagined by Men of rare parts, in the devout of many People, that before the general Judgment-Day Christ would come again personally to reign a thousand years on the Earth with his Saints",[50] according to him, but, however understandable, it is still an illusion. Why is it an illusion? Because it is grounded in the twentieth chapter of Revelation, *which is already fulfilled*. If Christ came back personally to reign with His saints, what more felicity could they enjoy than that which they had already had? It is the mark of the False Prophets (Tany, Robins, Fox) that they tell "of great Signs and Wonders, which they expect shall come to pass by inward Voices, or Visions, from the imaginary bodiless God".[51] The same signs would expose as false the later claims of Prophets like James Birch or Martha Collier. The Book of the Apocalypse is "too mysterious to be understood by the Achitophels of this Perishing World", according to Muggleton.[52] No "Signs and Wonders" then for the two tailors? Not quite: in *A divine looking glass* they would ask "what is the Ground think you of so many dreadfull Fires this Year in the City, and other Parts, above the Meaning of Man?" The answer is not in natural causes but in "a Divine Power, as a Forerunner of the eternal burning of this World".[53] Ten years later the Great Fire would be such an omen, and so too in later times would be for Muggletonians the American War of Independence, the Great Exhibition ("the triumph of Reason"), the First World War and biological warfare. But these were omens portending the winding-up of things, not the inauguration of a millennium.

The true meaning of Satan being bound for 1,000 years, and his being loosened for a little season, said Muggleton, was that 300 years had expired (not 1,000) and *then* the people were deceived for a further 1,350 years. In other words, the millennium was AD 0–300, and 300–1651 was the loosening of Satan, that is to say up until God's message to Reeve. But why *should* we read the (literal) 1,000 years as being no more than 300? Here believers simply have to defer to a prophetic reading, against a literalist one, of a "privative" text: "For the revelation of faith doth not count or number as reason doth, only to keep the seed of reason wholly in darkness, concerning heavenly and spiritual things, and that might reveal them to his own seed."[54]

Foxe believed in a past millennium (300–1300); Brightman in a second, part-future one (300–1300, 1300–2300); Milton in an imminent future one, but a best-past period (0–300). Milton's best-past period in history actually was the same as Muggleton's past millennium. Since the loosening of Satan had ended with the appearance of the Two Last Witnesses, all that the Muggletonians now needed to expect was the winding-up of history at an indeterminate date. So, although the Muggletonians have come down to us as a classic millenarian sect, and in their literal-mindedness (what, after all, could be more so than for two cousins to say that they *were* the Two Last Witnesses?), as a supreme example of Burke's Law, paradoxically they were also perhaps the most formidable opponents of what we take to be millenarianism, thrown up by English puritanism in the seventeenth century.

This would be equally true in later times. The characteristic of a Muggletonian meeting, at almost any period, in what has come down to us from their records, is a refusal to take *anything* on trust from Scripture. Blake, even if he wasn't one, would have fitted in well in such company: "at the root of Blake's attitude to the Bible lies a hostility to the very notion of the pure text, the text which gains authority for its claim to be sacred, invariable, and original".[55] The literal claims of a 1,000-year kingdom ran up against this craggy textual independence. Believers expected from their co-religionists the same exacting standards. Richard Huntley tells Flo and Fred Noakes in 1931 that the weekly meeting had examined a strange letter from America from a correspondent there, one Mrs Simmons: "one feels sure she is of the elect seed by the beautiful way of starting her letters, then she goes right off the deep and rambles so vaguely that starts me thinking (that on the natural rule) there surely must be a link missing". The millenarian claims of the contemporary American revivalist Billy Sunday elicit from the Muggletonian Alfred Hall in 1914 a confession of hate. In 1871 Thomas Robinson explained to a believer that there were three strengths of faith – "some thirty, some sixty, some a hundred" – and the "hundred" were not just the prerogatives of "Apostles and Prophets": "I believe there has been in all the Three Commissions many Believers possessing the hundred and have arrived at eminence in knowledge." He hastens to add that this power was itself derivative from the primary belief in the Third Commission, but it meant that even the Prophets could have their judgements questioned later, by believers who possessed "the hundred" (on the premise that the dispute was a "privative" matter) – and so Arden Bonell could query, early in the eighteenth century, the efficacy of even the Prophets' curses on named opponents. If Muggleton and Reeve can nod, why not God himself? Thus Thomas Robinson, "Upon New Thoughts", in May 1885, raises the ultimate question, whether even God could have "seen and visited the Extent and Infinite Boundless Space, or can He ever fully do so". Audacity could surely go no further than this, but Robinson applies *seventeenth-century precepts* to the question that he has raised. If it would seem a presumptuous one, "I remembered what the Prophet Muggleton wrote, Answer to Penn, 2nd Chapter, Faith is not tied so as to know no more than what is written in Public, Then I resolved to apply to the Prophets Writings." And his conclusion was startling:

> there is no end to Infinite Space, therefore it is safe to conclude that it is everlastingly impossible for the Eternal Infinite God and Creator ever to see that which there is not, but that He will be eternally advancing in Space ever New, beholding new Scenery, new objects, new company of Birds, Beasts, and Fishes, on the Earth, and in the Waters.

The *limitability* of God is, he insists, no eccentric doctrine but one that is grounded in Muggleton's technique, and is indeed anticipated in "that remarkable saying of the Prophet to W. Penn, and in the Occasional Discourse, D. Looking Glass, that God did not know all Things Past, Present and to come". When three years later than the latter text quoted, Muggleton writes with scorn to fellow believers of "the slavish worship of fear and trembling and awe towards God", he is recognizing the intellectual liberation that he himself gave his fellow believers, when he told them that God took no "immediate notice" of them.

The autodidactic self-confidence of the artisan was a feature, also, of the later popular millenarianism studied by John Harrison in his book *The Second Coming*. In the Muggletonians' case, though, it was directed, not simply against rival millenarian Prophets (as Muggleton and Reeve had begun their movement by taking on John Robins), but against the whole *idea* of millenarianism, as a tenable proposition in itself. This autodidactic self-confidence can topple over into absurdities (Alfred Hall: Isaac Frost, 19 September 1880: "I never did believe in the imagination of the Newtonian principle"; eighteenth-century debates about Adam's erection in Paradise; eighteenth- and twentieth-century debates about which animals would go to Heaven, and so on), but there is a weight given to the individual's judgement, as against a literalist obeisance before the Bible, which makes the Muggletonians a sect that refuses to recognize the existence of any "no-go areas", be they witches, devils and patriarchs in the seventeenth century, or spiritualism and dreams in the nineteenth. In 1901 Mrs Huntley looked back on a debate 35 years earlier in Putney, when she was 17, with a university graduate about cosmology and the reading of Scripture:

At last he got into such a rage, he said – who are you to contend with a man brought up at the University? I said this is the difference – you were brought up in the University on earth and I in the University of heaven. How I dared to say it at the age of 17 I cannot tell, when I knew so little.

When Alfred Hall winced at the millenarian errors rampant in 1926 he reached back to seventeenth-century parallels, and to their common grounding: "It must have been a conspicuous element in O. Cromwell's dictatorship, for I notice the Prophet Reeve in chapters 41 and 43 'Divine Looking Glass' of the great error in their supposition and reason in the interpretation of scripture." Mrs Lee writes to Mrs Noakes in 1927 of her belief (this long-standing Muggletonian obsession) that there are "no repulsive animals in Heaven". As Robinson and Hall did before her, she finds her inspiration in Muggleton's way with biblical texts: "I remember the Prophet Muggleton says that faith is not tied to know only the things which he has written down so I venture to think that this is so." Birch and his followers had tried to discredit his Muggletonian enemies with the epithet "literal-minded", but it is because they were not that they were able to see off, not only false pretenders such as Birch himself, but all those deluded people who were simple-minded enough to expect Christ to return, and to set up a 1,000-year kingdom on Earth.[56]

If, in Muggleton, we can now see an anti-millenarian millenarian (a prophet in a sense created by St John's text, who then deconstructs it), in Baxter we can see the opposite: a millenarian anti-millenarian (a man who spends a lifetime exposing its inadequacies, only secretly to embrace a form of it at the end). From his first publication in 1649 to his pamphlet in 1684 that led to his imprisonment in 1686, what emerges is certainly a profound disbelief in traditional millenarian speculation (this is what had put Professor Capp on to his false scent). He notes how few commentators on the prophetic texts agree with each other, that those who take them up are usually neurotic and unstable creatures, and that even the central Protestant *credo* – Rome is Antichrist – rests upon pretty dubious scriptural grounds. When Baxter lodged in Coventry in the Civil War, he shared rooms with a Major Wilkie. The experience was enough to put Baxter off the whole tribe of apocalyptic prophets. Here was a man steeped in Scripture, subject to visions and dreams, who read in thunder intimations of parliamentary victories, and who named 1648 as the start of the millennium. His ending was exemplary: a drunkard, spending his days in darkness, lying in bed on the Sabbath, and deported "starke mad" back to his native Scotland.[57]

Baxter could have been composing a rationalist tract. That, however, is the type of snap judgement to avoid (a point developed in Ch. 9). "Rationalist" Baxter could see evidence of Wilkie's "starke mad" condition in his readiness to read military victories in claps of thunder. But this was a little bit rich coming from a man who himself believed in God's capacity to destroy selective church steeples by lightning.[58] And his moral from the Wilkie anecdote is not a "rationalist" one, but an anti-Papal one. He says: "'tis more than probably that there is some blacke Jesuiticall Art that hath drawne up the whole design". Wilkie becomes, on this reasoning, a Jesuit double-agent, bent on persuading people that "a perfecter Revelation is to be expected". The Papist interest in this is self-evident: "Their maine drift is to Disgrace the Scriptures as Insufficient . . . which is the master point of our differences with them. If they gett this, they thinke they gett the day." What better way to do this than to shake the Protestant bedrock certainty that the

Pope is Antichrist?[59] It was the charge that he was to make against another Jesuit/Quaker double-agent, James Nayler, and which Nayler had to deny.[60] Baxter, however, for all his bravado, harboured his own doubts about the scriptural grounds for the position that he was defending. His anti-Catholic (and anti-Quaker) prejudices are displayed to maximum effect in his *A key for Catholicks* of 1659, but when it comes to the question raised in it as to whether the Pope is Antichrist, there is not the expected defence of Protestant orthodoxy on this point, but rather a distinct shiftiness in tone:

> But I must profess here to the Reader that though my modesty and consciousness of my weakness, hath made me so suspicious, lest I understand not the Apocalips, as to suspend my judgment, whether the Pope be the Antichrist, the Beast etc., yet the readings of their serious immodest arguings, to prove the Pope to be the Vice-Christ on Earth, doth exceedingly more increase my suspicion that he is *the Antichrist*.[61]

Baxter was in a cruel double-bind. As a puritan, he could not ignore the last Book of the New Testament. He knew the utility with the vulgar of the belief that the Pope was Antichrist. But this was a belief to which he could not, hand-on-heart, subscribe. The exasperated claim by the Scot Robert Baillie that all English puritans were "expresse Chiliasts" is exaggerated, but not by very much.[62] After the failure of English Presbyterianism in the 1580s, the Scots continued to go for a system (a presbyterian classical one) while the English went for an eschatology. In 1684, Baxter's friend John Humfrey, encouraged him to write a paraphrase of the New Testament, which perforce could not stop short at the Book of Revelation. The luxury of suspending his judgement (as in 1659) was no longer possible to him. He did not equivocate this time. The Pope was not Antichrist. This work landed him in jail, after his notorious encounter with Judge Jeffreys. His enemies wrested meanings in the text that were not there, to show that he was seditious, but his friends were no less dismayed by what (in their view) he had conceded to those same enemies. One might say that he lost his liberty on trumped-up grounds, and his reputation with fellow Protestants on real grounds.

The use that he made of this loss of liberty, as an old, sick man, is impressive. He immersed himself in apocalyptic studies. There were two fruits of these researches. The first was the scholarly underpinning of his agnosticism about Antichrist. Scripture did not cast the Pope as the embodiment of that concept. The second, however, was a realization of the firm basis for Foxe's claims that Christian empire was based upon the Apocalypse. The "immodest arguings" of the apologists for the Papacy had made him *suspicious* that it was Antichrist in 1659; it made him *certain* that it was in 1686. The certainty sprung from his later millenarian researches in prison. He now *knew* that Christian magistracy had its warrant in Revelation, and that the act of usurping that role showed that the Papacy was Antichrist, even if there was no clear scriptural proof of the accusation. The title, as much as the content, of one of his last works expresses his optimism: *The glorious kingdom of Christ* will be established on Earth, even if for a very short time, before the winding-up of history. The millennium was the past one: the time of Christian empire. Now in the last, fifth stage of history – the conflict between Christ and Antichrist – England did not lack Christian emperors to take on the Constantine mantle: Henry VIII, Edward VI (but too short), Elizabeth I, Oliver Cromwell, Richard Cromwell (but too short), William III. These were rulers untainted with the fatal Stuart propensity to succumb to the attractions of "French" Catholicism. Foxe's history, like Baxter's, breaks off before the culminating vision of the New Jerusalem. Neither Foxe nor Baxter is, therefore, technically a millenarian at all. A recent study is right to ask the question, in the very title of its article: "was John Foxe a millenarian?" In an interesting comparison of the different editions of Foxe's *Acts and monuments*, the author shows how the 1570 edition differs from all its predecessors in its apocalyptic superstructure, and he is the first historian to make intelligent use of Foxe's posthumous commentary on Revelation in 1587. The author recognizes from this evidence that Foxe, by the end of his life, does look *forward* to the period of time between the fall of Babylon and before the end of the world: "a this-worldly future and penultimate time of peace and victory for the Protestant cause, however short". When Marjorie Reeves examined the influence of Foxe on seventeenth-century puritans, her conclusion was very similar to his: "though no millenarian, Foxe used the prophetic tradition to read the signs of a new age dawning".[63]

Foxe, therefore, does not only teach Baxter good history about the *past*; he gives him cheer for the *future*. Foxe uses the prophetic tradition to anticipate the new age dawning; Baxter in turn uses Foxe *as prophet* to anticipate his own new age dawning. He cites the case of melancholic Mrs Honiwood. She was assured by Foxe that she would shake off her malady and live to a ripe old age. She threw a glass to the ground in disbelief. It bounced back intact and, noted Baxter, "fulfilled his Prophesie".[64] Foxe attained his insights by no ordinary route. God directed him, insisted Baxter, "by Revelation, by sudden irresistible impulse (equally to a voice, tho' not a voice)."[65] It was just this equal to – but not quite – formula that orthodox Muggletonians found upsetting about the pretender James Birch, and indeed about the primary source for all millenarians, John of Patmos himself. Why not – as with Reeve – just *have a voice?* Foxe once did come near to such an experience. Baxter thrilled to its narration by "that holy credible man". Foxe was lying in bed of a Sabbath and became confused with numbers when doing his apocalyptic count: "it was answered to my Mind as with a Majesty, thus inwardly saying with me, *Thou foole, count these months by sabbaths as the weeks of Daniel are counted by Sabbaths*: The Lord I take to witness thus it was."[66]

Baxter, like Foxe, believed that the apostolic Church had been preserved for 300 years until it "ripened" into a Christian empire. Those first 300 years were the best of times, argued his opponents, Thomas Beverley and Henry More; they *were* the millennium, argued Muggleton and Reeve. The rot set in with Constantine, said all his critics; Baxter told More that his "hopes in Christ" would have been shaken if indeed he believed that.[67] Men like Beverley looked to a future millennium, he argued, because they were not good enough historians to have understood the blessings of the past one. But there was a mutual respect between Baxter and opponents like Beverley and Increase Mather, despite their differences, which was founded on what they had in common.[68] That was why Mather wanted Baxter to publish *The glorious kingdom of Christ*, even if he did not share either Baxter's scepticism about a scriptural identification of Pope with Antichrist, or equally his conviction of a past millennium. What then did they have in common? They shared the following beliefs: that Revelation contained the key to salvation; that the Pope was Antichrist (as a usurper, if not in Scripture); that there *was* a new age dawning, a "Glorious Kingdom of Christ", before the winding-up of things, headed by the Christian Prince:

> The description of New Jerusalem and of the finall judgment
> fully proveth that Christs Kingdome as instituted and consumate
> containeth his sword government, of which Apostles and Men
> are official substitutes. All the millenaryes maintaine the Royall
> Kingdome, except they be sworne self-contradictors.[69]

The Major Wilkies and the Captain Venners were just such self-contradictors, pursuing the shadow of godly rule and missing the substance: "It is a far more glorious Christian Monarchy which Christ by Constantine set up, than most of the Millenarians give any probability of . . . The knowledge of what hath been long ago would have prevented any men's expectation of the same."[70] In his 1691 work, *Against the revolt to a foreign jurisdiction*, Baxter acknowledged that he had ruffled a few feathers with his apocalyptic revisionism, but he was impenitent. John Foxe, with his "Divine Revelation", was "much to be regarded".[71] In what way was Baxter expecting, at the end, Christ's Second Coming? He distinguished four ways, three of which he had no trouble with: His Coming to destroy Jerusalem by the Roman armies; His Coming to put down the Pagan empire, and to reign by Christian emperors (Foxe); His Coming to "finally judge all the world" (indeterminate, but soon). The fourth way was what bothered him: His Coming to "head a sabbatisme of Holyness" for 1,000 years before that final judgement. Even this interpretation he would grant "as very probable at least"; but it wasn't *certain*, as his other three convictions were, and he would not pretend otherwise.[72]

Baxter was the man for distinctions. He would, said one critic, "distinguish himself into a Fart".[73] If Christ's Second Coming had four meanings, Revelation could be read in five ways. The first way he calls, significantly for our argument, "meerly Literall", which is presented by him as "contrary to Reason" – the world of the Venners and the Wilkies. The second way he calls "cabalistical", which he describes as "fictitious and presumptuous", and its oracle is Thomas Brightman. The third is "Conjecturall", that is "by reasons which seem plausible to each man as prejudice and fancy dispose him". With his disarming candour, he owns up to a dash of this vice in himself, when he pronounces on the Number of the Beast, for instance. The fourth way is "Rationall", that is to say "fetcht from the context of former prophecies", and that was how Baxter liked to characterize his own approach on most of the disputed apocalyptic points. What could be higher than that? The answer is that there was one way even higher, "By Propheticall Inspiration or Vision", and it was a way denied to him. Perforce his experience is a second-hand one, "the context of former prophecies". Of those which he studied, no prophecy enthralled him as Foxe's did. Foxe's access to his imperial truths was a "Revelationall" one. Baxter noted that Foxe "sweareth by an Appeal to God that he had" just such an experience as he described. Baxter adds humbly that "I can boast of no such thing", any more than he could earlier date with precision the time of his conversion, to his real chagrin. Baxter was not a visionary prophet of the millennium, even at the end of his life, but he knew one when he saw one. And he saw one in Foxe, in his prison cell in 1686.[74]

Prynne was no more of a visionary prophet than Baxter was. Indeed he was less. He did not write about the millennium in print; we have no access to personal papers; his pamphlets are not confessional in nature. It would be easy then to leave him out altogether of a discussion of puritan millenarianism. Why it would be wrong to do so only becomes clear when we look at the "root and branch" debates about bishops in 1641. Before that date, we can isolate three main themes in his writings: fear of Rome, loyalty to the Crown, and belief in a purified Church of England. After 1648, and indeed for the rest of his life until his death in 1669, these same three themes persist. In the interim period, although the fear of Rome does not abate, loyalty to the Crown is strained to breaking point, and bishops are seen as needing a "root and branch" overhaul. We might put it another way: before 1641 the chained books, Foxe and Jewel, chain him and other puritans psychologically; 1641 witnesses the snapping of these chains. Prynne's *The antipathie* and Milton's *Of reformation* are both openly "root and branch" works of propaganda. They attack, obliquely, Foxe, and directly all that he held dear – Constantine, Cranmer, the martyrs, Grindal, the Elizabethan Church.

Milton said of Camden that he loved bishops as he loved old coins, for antiquity's sake. The same could be said of Prynne, but it did not prevent him from ending up, not on Camden's side, but Milton's, in 1641. For although Prynne was an antiquarian, who marshalled his case against the rogue bishops in the 1630s with battalions of lawyers' precedents, we should not therefore – the recurrent danger – secularize the man. This puritan shared the *intimations*, as well as the *conclusions*, of his much-quoted Foxe. One of the best historians of millenarianism captured well its appeal when he asked: "was not the Book of Revelation almost wholly written in terms of 'past wonders' and 'great, marvellous' signs in heaven and full of references to fire and blood and war and death?"[75]

Prynne's *A quench-coale* of 1637 is, for much of its length, a dry constitutional argument against Laudian excesses, prompted by Camden-like respect for the antiquity of bishops. But it is also much more than that: it is a search for "visible prognostickes from heaven". On 23 February of the previous year he found one in Sussex (and in other places). Between eight and nine of the morning (plenty of supporting evidence for this) three suns were observed together in the sky. This was not unique, but three of them *with a rainbow* was (there had been one previous precedent only, to be exact). It was no ordinary rainbow. It boasted seven distinct features. It was not seen in clouds. It stood south-east to the sun. It was higher in the sky than other rainbows. It was seen about 30 miles distant. It lasted an hour. It was static. It was peculiarly shaped. The last point was the strangest of all. Usually rainbows stand with "horns downward" like this:

$\cap$, this appeared all the while with the horns upward thus: $\cup$

The significance of this shape is related to the bow. When the archer turns the bow (as in the second shape) to himself, it augurs vengeance. The application is obvious, says Prynne: "*God hath a bow* (a warlike Instrument) *as well as man, which scriptures often mention*"; when God inverts the bow "in an unusuall miraculous manner", he means business. And how do England's citizens respond to "his pestiferous quiver"? Instead of arming themselves with "publike fasting, prayer, humiliation and repentance" – which would be the classic weapons of another army in another decade – they respond with "feasting, dancing, masking, playing, chambring, dallying and what not". Prynne trembles at the outcome of this terrible misjudgement about priorities.

But it *had* happened before (once). It was also in England, and "portending the heaviest woefull dayes and tidings to it, that ever it heard or saw before". The "month, time of the day, forme and continuance" were identical; the only difference was the day of the month, and the presence of two, instead of three, suns in the sky. Foxe had written it all up in his *Acts and monuments*. The rare prodigies occurred on 15

February 1555, seen at Westminster, Cheapside and many other places, and testified "by a great number of honest men". Prynne quoted Foxe's marginal annotation: "strange sights seene before the coming in of King Philip and subversion of Religion".[76]

History did not have to repeat itself, but the omens were disturbing. Although he had not abandoned hopes in King Charles and a moderate episcopacy in the mid-1630s (and would not formally do so until 1641), there were signs that Prynne was being attracted, even by then, to more radical solutions. Thus, in another work of 1637, he uses apocalyptic prophecies from Scripture to point to the imminent downfall of the whole episcopal order. But in the same pamphlet, he cites Foxe's work for its exposé of only *some* prelates' wrongdoing, and even these were directed against "our Martyrs".[77] Four years later "our Martyrs" themselves would not be spared from his total attack on bishops. In 1636, fears that episcopacy might be doomed were tempered by hopes of reform through a change of heart.[78] In another pamphlet of that year, bishops were compared to devils, but he adds "if you amend then and become new men the Parallels will soon grow out of date". Foxe backed his reading of Church history as an eternal struggle between "Prelates" and "Puritans", he claimed, but conceded that "I know some Bishops have been godly men, and Gods deere Saints, and I doubt not but there are some few such men, though their cowardice and silence in Gods cause, in which they dare not publickly appeare, be inexcusible". Twice, in this pamphlet, when alluding to bishops' cruelties he cites respectively "*the Booke of Martirs* and present experience" and "*the Booke of Martirs* and dayly experience". "Present" or "daily" experience in the late 1630s was used by him as a *supplement* to Foxe; in 1641 it would be used as a *corrective* to Foxe.[79] But it is interesting that even in November 1641 he was presenting Foxe's volumes as a gift to his own local church in Swainswick.[80]

There would be, however, no recognition of any of "Gods deere Saints" among the bishops whom he denounces in his *The antipathie* of 1641. On the contrary "Divine Providence", he claimed, had set him on the task of showing that all bishops were foul by virtue of the fact that they were holding that office. He acknowledges its propagandist purpose. Like Milton, in his *Of reformation*, at the same period, he was agitating for a "root and branch" solution to England's religious problems. England and Ireland were shaking off the yoke; Scotland already had. Foxe's heroes bite the dust in 1641. Cranmer, "our religious Martyr", as he had called him in 1630, was now a man with no fewer than nine heavy question marks against him.[81] Foxe had praised him, among other things, for opposing the Six Articles; Prynne simply noted that they had been "made and devised in the Archbishops time".[82] Whitgift – once (implausibly) claimed by Prynne as a puritan godfather – is now written off as "a stately Pontificall Bishop".[83] Abbot was a (correctly) suspended homicide, said Prynne, in 1641 (but became the victim of a trap set by Laud, in Prynne's version of events three years later).[84] Williams was a trusted confidant of Prynne when they were fellow prisoners in the 1630s[85] (overtrusted by him, on the basis of the evidence in Williams's personal papers at the time[86]). On his return from exile in December 1640, Prynne was consulting with Williams, who by then had become the focal point of anti-Laudian episcopalianism.[87] But in July 1641 *The antipathie* is published, with its "root and branch" message, its admiration for the Reformed Churches of Scotland, France and Geneva, and a bitter personal attack on Williams for "his late extraordinary stickling (much spoken against) to maintain the Lordly jurisdiction, and secular authority of our Prelates".[88] In between December 1640 and July 1641 Prynne had come to embrace ecclesiastical radicalism. We could put it another way: he had swapped Foxe for Brightman.

Thomas Brightman's *The revelation of the Revelation* of 1615 is the (politely expressed) answer to Foxe's interpretation. Like Foxe, he draws upon medieval prophetic tradition – the medieval number symbolism of seven, the Joachimite angels of the Apocalypse as God's human agents, the New Jerusalem on Earth – to offer an optimistic message. Like Foxe, he places the period of Satan bound in the past (300–1300), but unlike him he interprets the text "And they lived and reigned with Christ a thousand years" as the blessed age of the "first resurrection" (1300–2300). Therefore he grafts a future millennium on to a past one, acknowledging all the time his debt to "our John Foxe", much as the PhD student bows to his Professor before destroying him.[89] His point is that events have moved on since Foxe's days. By 1615 (and, *a fortiori*, 1641), it was possible to see the weaknesses in Foxe's dependence on the Elizabethan Church, now written off by Brightman with its "hotch potch lukewarmeness" as the type of Laodicea in Revelation (with Geneva and Scotland, the zealous, identified with Philadelphia).[90]

"Mr. Brightman's stupendous Revelations", was how one admirer described them;[91] "the Prophet of the Centurie, the bright burning light of our age, Master Thomas Brightman", claimed another.[92] Here was provided the apocalyptic justification for sweeping away all bishops, though not necessarily with a corresponding specific attachment to any one alternative form of government. But "root and branch" would prove stronger on negatives than positives. Robert Baillie, we noted, was deploring the fact that most English puritans were chiliasts. But that was in 1645. Four years earlier the popular association of Scotland with Philadelphia actually worked to the Presbyterians' advantage. Vines pointed out in 1656 that Brightman's prophecy had led to the rejection of episcopacy as "loathsom", but not necessarily to a separatist solution. Ball, believing that Brightman was "consonant to the nonconformists principles", agreed; Canne argued the opposite.[93] The point was that, in the period around 1641, it was possible for a separatist like John Goodwin, and a non-separatist like Thomas Edwards, to join in approval of Brightman's rejection of a totally, corrupt lukewarm episcopacy.[94] Hanserd Knollys claimed Brightman for support of a full millenarian position (actually with his double millennium, half past, half future, Brightman had hedged his bets here too).[95] Thomas Fuller noted his value to ecclesiastical radicals; it was on arguments learned from Brightman that Thomas Case urged the taking of the Covenant in 1643; the Laudian Pocklington had seen Brightman and Cartwright as the two key figures in the growing threat of English radicalism in 1637; Heylyn had linked Prynne and his colleagues with Brightman in the same year, when in Prynne's case it should have been four years later.[96] Edward Symmons in 1645 explained how he had questioned parliamentary prisoners at Shrewsbury as to why they had taken up arms against their sovereign:

> they answered me, That they took up Arms against Antichrist, and Popery, for (said they) 'tis prophesied in the Revelation, that the Whore of Babylon shall be destroyed with fire and sword, and what doe you know, but this is the time of her ruine, and that we are the men that must help to pull her downe.[97]

On the other side, the Cavaliers' attitude was summed up as: "the fulfilling of the Revelation but a puritanicall presumption and arrogant phantasie"; this was from an anonymous prophet of 1642, whose pamphlet has been wrongly attributed to Prynne.[98]

When the puritan ministers produced their extremely important apology *Scripture and reason pleaded for defensive armes,* they claimed that Parliament began the war with aggressive aims against bishops, but by 1643 were warning them: "let them remember Mr. Brightmans Propheticall Interpretation of the spewing out of the Laodicean Angell".[99] Through these ministers, Brightman's influence was distilled. In their sermons before the Commons of 1640–42, both Holmes and Symonds quote directly from Brightman, and Holmes's description, of the "New Jerusalem" about to be built, follows the account of Brightman remarkably closely.[100] But, indirectly, almost all the sermons show a similar indebtedness to Brightman: in the importance attached to zeal; the devaluing of Constantine and the Elizabethan episcopate; the pressure for what Fairclough called a "reall" reformation; the total rejection of bishops; the attacks upon lukewarmness; the ethical craving for reform expressed by Case in the words, "Oh if it might be reported in heaven that England is reformed – that such a drunkard, such a swearer, such a covetous man . . . is become a new man."[101]

It was this ethical craving that is seen to be characteristic of Prynne's attitude in 1641, and which comes out strongly in his dedicatory epistle to the Earl of Essex in a pamphlet of 1643: "I shall in my daily Prayers recommend your Honours, Persons, Forces, and Military proceedings, till through his blessings on them, the house of the Lord shall be established in the top of the mountain, and exalted above the hills."[102] He does not *quite* say "a city on the hill". In a dedicatory epistle to another general, Fairfax, in a pamphlet of 1645, he referred to the settlement of Church discipline "according to Gods Word, and the Purest Times" as "one principle end of Your and Our taking Defensive Armes".[103] It seems fair to assume that Prynne's ethical concern was, in part, a reflection of the influence exercised on him by the London "root and branch" ministers of the time, both because of our knowledge of the type of pressure that they exercised, and of Prynne's links with them, and approval of their aims.[104] Moreover, curious supporting evidence is provided by Prynne's withdrawal from such radical courses in that same year. In 1645, he now attacked too much devolution of power into the hands of ministers, because he had become sceptical of their ability to deliver the desired ethical reforms. The London ministers remained for him admired figures. They were the men, he noted with approval, who were constant advocates of a "thorough and compleat Reformation" in their sermons, and who had warned their audiences persistently that "lesse will not be accepted of God or good men".[105] But by 1645 – this was the crucial point – he now recognized that their zeal was *atypical*:

That though there be sufficient choice of prudent, discreet, learned, conscientious, upright Ministers and Christians in and about London, fit to be united into Presbyteries, classes and trusted with Ecclesiasticall Censures; yet in most places else throughout our three Kingdomes (except here and there a City or County Town) there are very few, if any such Ministers or Lay-Elders to be found for the present.[106]

Prynne became by then a leader of the Erastian attack on the Scottish Presbyterians, because they couldn't deliver the goods (even though their *London* counterparts could). Well might Robert Baillie deplore the chiliasm in the bones of English puritans – how naïve to expect New Jerusalem to be built overnight (though they *had* promised as much in 1641)! When Prynne (of all people) could urge in 1645 that "moderate Christians ought in all things to avoid extremes",[107] this was too much for one former ally, Herbert Palmer. The terms in which the rebuke is delivered are of prime importance. For Palmer accused him of deserting party by deserting Brightman:

Mr. Brightman (whose interpretation of Revel. 3 concerning Sardis and Laodicea, have been to Admiration and neare to Propheticall) makes England, as you know, the Anti-type of the latter: surely whoever thinks he is at all in the right therein, and withall have seen that lukewarme Angell so strangely spewed out, almost to the destruction of the whole State ... ought to take speciall heed, that they themselves degenerate not into like lukewarmnesse.[108]

We don't know if Brightman tugged at Baxter's heartstrings, as he did at those of Prynne and other "root and branchers" in 1641. Baxter's thoughts on the origins of the Civil War are all retrospective; though, as we saw, some were more retrospective than others. The earliest of them make much of the negative feelings that were incurred by the Irish Rebellion in October 1641 (which had a similar effect on Prynne). On the positive side, however, there is only the tantalizingly oblique reference in 1657 in a Baxter letter to the fact that he had been much caught up in apocalyptic speculations some "20 years agoe, or nigh, my juvenile fancye being more daring".[109] Daring enough to have at that date swallowed Brightman, the man whom he was to write off, at the end of his life, as a "cabalistical" interpreter of Revelation, that is to say one who was "fictitious and presumptuous"? Perhaps, but there is no documentation to prove it. What we do know is that apocalyptic speculations in his last years, even if they don't inspire tender feelings towards Brightman, do arouse expectations of a "Glorious Kingdom of Christ" (the title of his 1691 pamphlet). Paradoxically it is Muggleton – at first sight the most obvious candidate for connecting links between puritan and millenarian – who is depressing such expectations in his followers, and only asking patience from them as they await the winding-up of things.

The most obvious way that puritanism connects with millenarianism is in fomenting revolution. When the Cavaliers called "the fulfilling of the Revelation but a puritanicall presumption and arrogant phantasie" in 1642, they were delivering a self-fulfilling prophecy. The more that millenarianism was associated with militancy, the less likely it was that sober puritans like Baxter and Prynne would own up to personal delight in it. One thinks how Baxter recoiled in disgust from Major Wilkie (as he, and others, would later from Captain Venner), and it took a prison sentence, and a lot of intensive study, to win Baxter back to an appreciation of John Foxe's interpretation of the millennium. And even then, when he was awaiting his "Glorious Kingdom of Christ" (and it should not be forgotten that the great Victorian revivalist C. H. Spurgeon would reprint chunks of Baxter under the adventist title *The Second Coming of Christ*), he wanted to keep his researches secret. When millenarian views were combined with antinomianism, as they were in the case of Major Wilkie, the results were catastrophic. That was what he had against his friend Thomas Beverley. He was daft to name the year when the millennium would start (1697); he was dafter still to compare the imminent advent of the Lord (which Baxter himself expected) with a specific 1,000-year earthly kingdom; he was daftest of all in failing to recognize that the hoped-for millennium had already happened. But Beverley's worst fault, even above all these, was to combine millenarianism with support for the antinomian doctrines of Tobias

Crisp. As Baxter pointed out, in his *Glorious kingdom of Christ*, there was a dreadful mismatching at work, when it was the antinomians, who least understood the millennium, who "lay much of their Religion on it". The consequences were appalling: "For if Christ Reign not till then, he maketh no Laws till then; He setteth up no Magistrate till then, to be Governing Officers in his Kingdom; He executeth no Discipline in his Church as King."[110]

Millenarianism plus antinomianism meant, for mainstream puritans like Baxter, an assault on what they most held dear: magistracy (see Chapter 5); discipline (see Chapter 6); a communalist ethic (see Chapter 7). However, *if one read the Book of Revelation properly*, there was no better guarantor for all three precious principles than what was to be found in the Apocalypse.

That is why the Wilkies and the Venners misrepresent the mainstream puritan interest in the millennium; their notoriety, if anything, drives that interest underground. No man was more woundingly funny than Hobbes about sectarian fancies; but *Leviathan* itself is steeped in an apocalyptic eschatology.[111] *Apocalyptic Marvell* is the title of a recent major revaluation of our great seventeenth-century poet (reinforced since its publication by the author's discovery of a new Marvell manuscript).[112] Another lost manuscript has transformed the secular Ludlow into *Apocalyptic Ludlow*.[113] Ralph Josselin's manuscript diary – not the later printed editions except the last – gives us *Apocalyptic Josselin*.[114] It is actually when he is talking about matters other than Revelation that we now can recognize more clearly *Apocalyptic Bacon*.[115] What we are seeing in all these cases is a tension between a world-we-have-lost millennialism of the seventeenth century, and its pallid re-creation in Victorian nonconformity. It is not that the nineteenth century did not have its millenarian cranks (like Edmund Gosse's father, in his son's famous memoir[116]), but it was then generally seen as crankiness: it was no longer perceived as a mainstream concern. Foxe's work would not be neglected in the nineteenth century; on the contrary, it went through numerous editions. But by then it had been abridged into Foxe's *Book of martyrs*, and in the process had become marginalized as an anti-Catholic tract of the times. What was missing was the eschatological grandeur of the original design of the *Acts and monuments*.

We conclude with a paradox. It was the enemy within who was best placed to attack that millennial hegemony in the seventeenth century.

Lodowicke Muggleton stepped out of the pages of Revelation to tell his followers that there *would be* no 1,000-year rule of the saints, no New Jerusalem, not even a "Glorious Kingdom of Christ". D. H. Lawrence spoke dismissively of "a curious being, this old John of Patmos" and saw in his revelation, not pieces of several books, but one book in several layers. There was at the core of the book Muggleton's "positive" truths, but there were innumerable false "privative" layers that had first to be removed. It was not by fixing the meanings of allegories that later generations would recover those earlier truths, but by relying on the insights of prophets (Muggleton, Blake, Lawrence), in order to re-create the experience of "the intelligent pagans of St. John's day". There was no shortage of "unintelligent Christians" in their own times (Fifth Monarchists in Muggleton's, the Salvation Army in Lawrence's) to claim for themselves that prophetic role. It was the unintelligence of Christians like Anne Hutchinson and Major Wilkie that repelled mainstream puritans like Prynne and Baxter. But what of "intelligent Christians" who claimed that they could read Revelation – men like Foxe and Brightman, with luminously sane and stabilizing interpretations to offer? That was another story, and it indeed turns out to be the story of the majority of seventeenth-century English puritans.

There was, however, a third way, which by-passed *both* "intelligent" and "unintelligent" Christians, and which sought to recover the experience of "intelligent pagans" of St John's time. Foxe and Brightman had tamed St John and made him accessible to puritans like Baxter and Prynne; Muggleton and Lawrence, however, destroyed him. Their prophetic gifts gave them access to the "very deep meanings" in Revelation that, alas, "were too deep for John of Patmos".[117] The trick was to get behind the words of St John, which he was imperfectly communicating, *to the experience of his listeners.* The Apocalypse, in a word, was too important to be left to St John of Patmos.

Chapter Nine

Puritanism and reason (witches and science)

From puritanism to the age of reason was the title of a book published some 40 years ago.[1] It is a good book with a bad title. Its badness resides in the encouragement it gives to a view of puritanism as the agent of modernization; this was the view that C. H. George challenged in the article quoted in Chapter 1. And when seventeenth-century puritans were indeed (in previous chapters) examined for their links with modern abstractions like "revolution", "liberty" and "capitalism", C. H. George's scepticism was on the whole to be found vindicated. Puritans were also linked with "millenarianism", but that at first sight didn't seem like a step to modernity. And yet we found that that was exactly how it was treated, by American historians in particular: the "errand into the wilderness" *was* the birth of a nation. Puritans have also been linked with the rise of science and with the persecution of witches: again two seemingly contradictory claims but both of which will be found, as with all these other controversies, to be related to a similar quest for modernity.

"Science" is an obvious candidate. It is the missing piece in the jig-saw. If puritanism is the natural ally of "revolution", "liberty" and "capitalism", then we only need to add "science" and we have conjured up the figure of Benjamin Franklin (always provided that we *can* claim him for "puritanism"). But "witchcraft" is another matter. Here we are not moving into an Age of Reason, but are plunging precipitately backwards into a pre-Enlightenment mental world. Yet again we see in the historiography of puritanism, above all in its American branch, a determination that "witchcraft" should occupy a central role. This would seem to have little to do with modernity, and yet the conviction that it does would inspire Arthur Miller's best play. Such a

159

conviction is only intelligible if one recognizes that "witchcraft" is only the other side of "millenarianism": both concepts that are seemingly throwbacks to a pre-rational age, but which are in reality perceived as being equally formative in building the modern American nation, as were the more obvious abstractions of "revolution", "liberty", "capitalism" and "science". This point is well grasped by the best recent historian of the Salem witch trials:

> The study of witchcraft within it, of the injustice, offers the test of faith and poses the question of whether the original journey held a true promise in a land that executed the innocent . . . The failure of America to live up to the dream Europe imagined it, becomes contained in dark Tituba's voodoo-inspired hysteria of young girls in the time of Salem, in the abiding faith that a threshold of superstition had been crossed in 1692.[2]

We might summarize it thus: no American dream, no American nightmare; no *Arbella*, no Tituba. Richard Baxter saw how the two were connected:

> If any are Scandalized that New-England a place of as serious Piety as any I can hear of under Heaven, should be troubled so much with Witches, and with Melancholies, and self-murders, as Mr. Mather tells us, I think it is no wonder: where will the Devil shew most malice, but where he is hated and hateth most?[3]

There is something disproportionate about the attention that historians have given to the events at Salem that prompted this despairing comment from one of them: "if Puritanism is responsible for the hanging of 19 people in Salem, what was responsible for the burning of 900 people in Bamberg?"[4] Perry Miller described Salem as a "blip of sorts" in the total history of New England puritanism;[5] the failure of other historians to see it in these terms, ironically, owes as much as anything to the success of his own "errand into the wilderness" explanation of American origins.

We can now see that the Salem episode was not typical of New England puritanism; the small number of 19 persons executed was more than the entire total of previous witchcraft executions in New England's history. We can go further and query how "puritan" it was.

Most puritan ministers opposed the trials, and some of them did so at great personal risk. The two of them who were seen as most influential, Increase and Cotton Mather, admittedly have ambivalent roles to play. The new governor, Phips, was the protégé of Increase Mather. Phips set up the special court to try the witches, and he included in the body members who had already been encouraging the prosecution of witches. Increase Mather may have only attended one trial, that of the minister Burroughs, but he supported there the guilty verdict. In the end he enlisted Phips' aid to stop the trials, but by then credibility had drained away when the accused were now extending to such impossible categories as men and Mrs Margaret Thatcher (widow of a Boston clergyman). Still his *Cases of conscience* (endorsed by puritan ministers) is an impressively liberal document: it accepts that witchcraft is real, but lays down scrupulous guidelines for its proof. The work appeared almost at the same time as his son's defence of Salem, *Wonders of the invisible world*, which has not done wonders for Cotton Mather's reputation. Nevertheless it needs to be borne in mind that only five days after the hanging of the first witch, he published *The return of several ministers* with its damning condemnation of the spectral evidence that had secured her conviction. His model was the English puritan minister Samuel Fairclough, who, in Suffolk in 1645, first established with his congregation the reality of witchcraft, and *then* established the importance of authentic proof.[6]

That Cotton Mather referred back to England in 1645 is not an accident. More witches died in that one year in England than any other in the century: it was the reign of terror of Matthew Hopkins, Witch-Finder General. But Hopkins's crusade has been as overblown in English history as Salem has been in American. His defence of his actions is notable for three things. It was published in 1647 (after the First Civil War had ended). It was a justification addressed to the Norfolk Assizes when efforts to restore older proprieties were being made. It was (thinly disguised) a rationalization of the use of torture, confessions, and physical marks on the accused as evidence in the trials. The pamphlet may have come with a scriptural epigraph – "thou shalt not suffer a witch to live" – but it doesn't read like a work driven by scriptural literalism. Salem itself, of course, actually flatly contradicted that scriptural injunction. It was the accused who confessed to being witches *who were spared*; it was those who said that they were not, who perished. Only when (late in the day) confessing witches were also put on trial did both confessions and trials dry up. What England in 1645 and Salem in 1692 had in common was that, in exceptional circumstances, normal judicial processes were not safeguarded; there were therefore rich pickings for the men on the make. Nothing rings with more feeling in Hopkins's defence than his claim not even to have covered his expenses;[7] no such problems for the sheriff of Essex County in 1692 who milked the estates of the accused. There was obviously more to the persecutions in these two dramatic episodes than just crookedness; there was also, however, *less* than a simple application of literalist-minded puritan doctrine. There were wonders of the visible world, as well as those of the invisible. The low incidence of witch persecutions in New England before 1692 (quite apart from the revulsion afterwards) should concern us, and with it the matching lack of interest by English puritans after 1645 in making the extermination of witches one prerequisite of a "Holy Commonwealth". Jim Sharpe notes that "even [why "even"?] the Puritan ascendancy in the 1640s and 1650s did not see a marked rise in tension over witchcraft in official circles".[8] In fact, as another critic has noted, the English puritan *unofficial* circles in the Commonwealth period – as reflected in newspaper comment – bracketed witchcraft with "buggery, bestiality, adultery and murder" as "the natural crimes of the Country" that the Scots, with a different national culture, turned into "venial sins", and supernatural portents.[9]

Old myths die hard, however: never more so than when they are part of an energetic demythologizing. Michael Walzer sets Weber and Tawney to rights. "In the Marxist world of economic reason", he thunders, "beggars are duly whipped" but witches are "left untouched by the flame". If he is only saying that seventeenth-century puritan man agonized more over demonism than over the just price, this is unexceptional and probably right. But it is the underlying assumptions behind the aphorism that need to be contested. He assumes that puritans *do* whip beggars and *do* burn witches (hang them actually: but that is a myth that is as hard to dislodge for Salem as for England[10]). His complaint is not therefore that both of these assumptions are false,[11] but that it is the relative weight that they are given by Marxist historians that is false. They reverse the seventeenth century's own priorities. Their "world of economic reason" is what he objects to: it leads (and with Weber too in his book) to a will-of-the-wisp search for an ascetic rationalism in puritan forebears *which is not there*.

Walzer's "world of unreason", on the other hand, embraces puritanism (mainstream that is, not merely its wings) as precisely the creed for millenarians and witch-hunters. Can we therefore say that Walzer at least is one historian of puritanism who has given us a history not driven by teleology? That is precisely what it is: his *Revolution of the saints* is explicitly designed to show Calvinism as a "modernising" ideology.[12] But he doesn't confuse modernity with rationalism (as he alleges that Marx and Weber do). Therefore ministers preaching zeal, discipline and organization are harbingers of the "modernity" that interests *him*. The puritan, chasing witches and building a New Jerusalem, is looking forward, not back, in this reading of history. But we have exchanged in the end only one teleology for another. Millenarianism, it is true, is given due weight, but not those interpreters of it (Foxe, Brightman and Mede) who *domesticated* its potential wildness. Foxe is not mentioned at all in Walzer's study of puritanism; Jewel only for his "kind of spiritual alienation from England".[13] To the latter one can only say – some spiritual alienation this to end one's days as the writer of the classic defence by a bishop of the Establishment! Walzer is not therefore against a teleological reading of puritanism; only ultimately of Marx's and Weber's *kind of* teleology.

Teleology of a sort can be found in humbler sources. Richard Ward is no mega-historian like Weber, Marx or Walzer, but his little-noticed biography of his friend Henry More, in 1710, reveals something of the strain felt even at that date in taking his man out of the age of puritanism and into the (now seen as respectable) Age of Reason. There is no strain evident at first on anyone else except the reader, because Ward does go on and on about More's "rationalism". But the compliments dry up, Ward nervously clears his throat, and prepares the reader for the worst. "I am now on a ticklish Subject", he confides. The "ticklish Subject" is revealed to be More's fascination with prodigies and signs from Heaven. Ward records, in the spirit of better-get-it-over-with-and-out-of-the-way, that "the Doctor hath seriously related that from his Infancy he had this thing firmly imprinted on his Mind; that lying one Moon-shining Night in the cradle awake, he was taken up thence by a Matron-like Person, with a large Roman Nose, Saluted and departed there again". But Ward hastens to put this episode in perspective: "the Doctor was far from over-valuing, or laying any great Weight on things of this Nature". If such experiences came his way, well and good: they were "Prodigies, and of use". Even so they were to be received "with the greatest Caution and Humility imaginable". Another More "real Conjecture", as Ward described it, was that, in 7,000 years time, the inhabitants of terrestrial regions will be communicating with those of ethereal ones. But Ward noted that "in his Exposition on the Revelation, and in other Representations of the Glorious times, he wisely takes no notice of it". In a word, scholarship and fantasy were kept apart.

The scholarship went into his millenarian studies. Ward noted that here his great mentor was Joseph Mede (for Newton too). More showed why the Pope was Antichrist on other than scriptural grounds. Baxter agreed, but went further than More in saying that no other grounds than his (including scriptural) *were* tenable. Both agreed that Christ would not come down in Person to head a 1,000-year reign of His Saints. More thought it better to look for "an inward regeneration of spirit into the living Image of Christ" than to rely on the "external Person and Voice of Christ". Or, as he put it epigrammatically, "better for a Horse to be turned into a perfect Man, than to be rid by the bravest Heroe there is". More thought that the first few hundred years of Church history were the best – "the Symmetrical times" – but since he wasn't a Prophet, he couldn't, like Muggleton, at a stroke change a figure (300, 400) into 1,000, and make *that* the past millennium. Like Baxter, More combined disbelief in a future millennium with belief from Revelation in a better future; the counterpart to Baxter's hopes for an earthly "Glorious Kingdom of Christ" was More's sense that "things in Christendom would be in due time very much changed; and that for the better".[14]

More is therefore easy to place within the millenarian milieu that was described in Chapter 8, but that's not where Ward wants to place him. He holds him at arm's length with a pair of tongs: a good man fallen into the seventeenth century. That was also how Coleridge saw Baxter: a wonderful divine, but, oh, those "Irish stories" he lapped up so credulously![15] Rational deist John Toland found the Cromwellian soldier Ludlow useful – but only when his millenarianism had been removed for eighteenth-century consumption.[16] Ralph Josselin's millenarian dreams and suppurating navel escaped all the published editions of his diary, except the last, and that was in 1976.[17] F. J. Powicke saw Baxter moving to the Age of Enlightenment with his refusal in 1684 to call the Pope Antichrist.[18] But Baxter only objects, as we saw, to its scriptural basis; he *supports* its non-scriptural attribution. And the last year of his life sees him as a sort of communist millenarian, defending witches and ghosts: not quite the portrait of him that Powicke wants us to accept. But the fact that Powicke wants us to accept it is itself significant. As with these other examples, it illustrates just how hard it was to make the puritan fit into the mould of a later "rationality".

Some of the best recent historians of science have made a good case why they shouldn't even have tried. No monocausal explanation of the rise of science will satisfy, nor will confinement of interest to one country, or to one century. One work for instance compares Islam and China with the West; another honours the medieval antecedents of seventeenth-century developments in England.[19] The first work still remarks on the impact of the Reformation on the West, and the second work on the break with the esoteric in the activities of the Royal Society. A third study specifically focuses on the contribution of Robert Boyle, and his fellow virtuosi gentlemen, in establishing a code for truth-telling that transformed the study of science in England. Steven Shapin remarks on the fact that "the rejection of authority and testimony in favour of individual sense-experience is just what stands behind our recognition of 17th-century practitioners as 'moderns', as 'like us'." Shapin emphasizes the importance of the consensus that gathered around John Locke's prudential maxims of testimony: assent being given only to testimony that was plausible, multiple, consistent, immediate, derived from knowledgeable or skilled sources, convincingly presented, and based on sources of acknowledged integrity and disinterestedness. Equally important was ontological openness. "Wonders of the world" were to be combed out for scrutiny to redress previous reliance on common and familiar examples. In 1638 Wilkins argued the probable case for the existence of an inhabited world in the moon – inhabited perhaps by the matron-like women with large Roman noses who swooped down on terrestrial Henry More? Boyle saw it as the function of the "Christian virtuoso" to show "the vulgar catalogue of impossible or incredible things to be far greater than it ought to be". Bishop Sprat, the first historian of the Royal Society, rebutted the charge that the Royal Society dabbled in "incredible stories" by claiming that "many things which now seem miraculous" will not be so "when we come to be more fully and philosophically acquainted with the compositers and operaters".[20]

The world of Boyle is also Baxter's. In a sense the appearance of Baxter's *The certainty of the worlds of spirits* in 1691 would seem to be as badly timed as Cotton Mather's defence of Salem a year later. Just when he should be gliding into the "Age of Reason", he reveals himself as a sucker for "Irish" stories of ghosts and apparitions. The text shows something else: a defence of witches certainly, but one infused throughout with respect for the Lockean maxims of testimony. One of his chief witnesses is Boyle, "a Man famous for Learning, Honesty and Charity, and far also from weak credulity". Every case study is studded with supporting material. The candour with which he exposes his weaknesses on occasions is itself impressive. Thus a story about one spirit is one that was picked up by Baxter from a Mr Illingworth, "who can't remember it now". However, Mr Cooper heard Mr Franklin tell it to Sir Philip Woodhouse. But who was Franklin? All that Baxter knew about him was that he was a minister in the Church of England in a town "whose name I know not" in the Isle of Ely. No one could accuse Baxter here of overplaying his hand.[21]

The links between Baxter and Boyle were close. Besides Baxter's correspondence with him, there are also many letters from Baxter to Boyle's brother and to his older sister (whose salon has a claim to be at least one of the obvious precursors of the Royal Society). The voluminous diary of Boyle's younger sister, the Countess of Warwick, has not been plundered enough by historians: Baxter's prominence in her diary, as friend, counsel and recipient of charity, is well documented there.[22] Robert Boyle is the person whom John Eliot writes to about the printing of Baxter's works in New England. François Perrault's *The divell of Macon* – that would be drawn heavily upon by Baxter in his 1691 defence of witches – was a work first translated by Peter du Moulin in 1658; Boyle covered the expenses of publishing it.[23] In 1690, in the dedicatory epistle that he wrote to Cotton Mather's discoveries of prodigies, Baxter says of the French account that it was "witnessed by the Honourable and Credible Mr. Boyle".[24] In 1660 Baxter wrote to Boyle to ask him "when I may find you at home"; this would be the prelude to his recommending Boyle, as "a worthy Person of Learning and a Publike Spirit", to the office of Governor of the newly founded Corporation for the Spread of the Gospel in New England. Three years later Baxter was asking John Eliot for the number of native Indians to whom he had access, since doubts on that score had impeded the progress of the proposal of Boyle, "a man of great Learning and Wealth, and of a very publick and universal Mind", to hold a public collection "in all our Churches" for ministers who were prepared to join Eliot's missionary work. In 1665 Baxter would acknowledge the gift from Boyle of his "many excellent books" on theology, and his generosity in paying for the publication of Edward Pococke's translation of Grotius's *De veritate religionis christianae*.

This letter would also express Baxter's tribute to Boyle for the way in which his philosophy and his theology were interwoven: "I read your Theologie as the Life of your Philosophie, and your Philosophie as animated and dignified by your Theologie; yea indeede as its first part for God himselfe begineth the holy scriptures with the doctrine of Physicks." In their mutual exploration of the natural and the supernatural both men were invoking a rationality that undercut a simpleminded appeal to "Reason" (with its atheistic overtones). As Baxter put it to Boyle: "He that hath well learnt in the Alphabet of his Physicks, wherein a MAN doth differ from a Beast, hath laid such a foundation for a Holy Life, as all the Reason in the world is never able to overthrow." Boyle responded to this tribute in kind: "there are divers things that speake you to be none of those narrow-sould Divines, that by too much suspecting Naturall Philosophy tempt many of its Votaries to suspect Theology."[25] It was "suspect Theology" that inspired Baxter, in retaliation to it, to write the very first of his many books as early as 1649. He wrote *The aphorismes of justification*, having been traumatized by the shock of his experiences as an army chaplain in the Civil War. There he encountered the doctrine of Free Grace in its rawest form: chaplains like Saltmarsh and Dell who were telling the soldiers that the elect were justified and could not fall; or Coppe, who was preaching to the garrison at Coventry as a neighbour of Baxter in the Civil War, "with his hat cockt, his teeth gnashing, his eyes fixed, charging the great ones to obey his Majesty within him".[26] Against such doctrines, Baxter developed his crucial definition of God as not only *dominus*, but *rector* "of free-agents, and making their Laws to Rule their own volitions and actions, he doth by these Laws oblige their reason and will, to restrain and resist some natural or sensitive appetites and inclinations, and so to resist some natural motions of God in nature, in which he is pleased to operate by several courses but *in tantum* and resistibly".[27]

That was the point: God obliged men to exercise their "reason and will"; no prostrating of themselves before God's irresistible (and incomprehensible) Grace. And, as Baxter told the ever-melancholic Lady Katherine Gell, "Grace itself doth usually worke according to the way of nature".[28] For all their superficial differences, Cromwell's former chaplain Peter Sterry and Thomas Hobbes shared the same determinist fallacy: "overlooking and undervaluing God's Design in Making and Governing free Intellectual agents, by his Sapiential Moral Directive Way". Man, said Baxter, is not an entirely free agent, but Baxter makes him fall not far short of it. He is "so far like God himself, as to be a kind of joint-determiner of many of his own Volitions and Nolitions". Baxter claimed this to be part of "God's Natural Image in Man".[29]

The emphasis that Baxter placed on reason in his theology offended old-guard Calvinists. John Owen accused him of "Socinianism". Thomas Edwards's *Baxterianism barefaced* of 1699 is one of the most savage assaults on him. He recited Herbert Palmer's character of a Christian in Paradoxes, "who was an ancient worthy Presbyterian Puritan, and yet an abhorrer of Baxterianism, which is another Paradox amongst some, though not all of them". First of Palmer's 85 Paradoxes, quoted approvingly by Edwards, was: "A Christian is one who believes things which his Reason cannot comprehend".[30] Baxter saw this as a ludicrous but worrying doctrine: he persuaded his friends Sylvester, Manton and Bates to co-sign the seminal 1676 work, *The judgment of non-conformists, of the interest of reason, in matters of religion*. By then, Baxter and his friend Joseph Glanvill saw Roman Catholic fideism and sectarians' antinomianism as related enemies.[31] As Jackson Cope has shown, Glanvill was drawn to Baxter precisely by his commitment to *rational* investigations of "providences".[32] Their correspondence together (and with Henry More too) – on witches, ghosts and apparitions, – shows the lengths to which they went to satisfy themselves that such occurrences met the strictest canons of rational inquiry.

That work began, as many of the good things in the seventeenth century did, in the 1650s. As early as 1655, Thomas White had written to Baxter, asking him to use the contacts he was already making in his Worcestershire Association of Ministers, to elicit from ministers records of "Providences" and "Spirituall Experiences". Virtue was not sufficient as a guarantor of a witness's truth: "many pious persons are somewhat too credulous". White thought that ministers of the calibre of Calamy and Vines, as well as Baxter, could judge "the prudence as well as the piety of ministers".[33] This germ of an idea would be taken up by Matthew Poole, and developed into a full-blown co-operative venture for "registering of Illustrious Providences", with a secretary in every county reporting material to Poole. We are in the milieu of the creation of the Royal Society, or of *one* of its creations, at least, and note how interconnected these projects are with the Ministerial Associations already begun by Baxter[34]. Baxter thought that Poole's "designe about gatheringe Extraordinary Providences" was "very noble and excellent"; he rued only the fact that it had not been attempted up until now. But just as the Ministerial Associations looked outwards – through John Durie to the Swiss Churches abroad, in pursuit of ecumenism – so Baxter urged Poole to enlarge *his* project beyond national frontiers: "Pray get some Merchants to procure you the certaine narrative of the many hundreds said to be possessed of late in Germany".[35] Poole's project collapsed with the Commonwealth itself, but Increase Mather organized meetings of his Massachusetts ministers in 1681 on the basis of Poole's manuscript. Baxter was an intermediary, telling Mather "I am so much taken with your history of prodigies that I propose to put my scraps in your hands."[36]

Even a European figure of the stature of Comenius did not come up to the rigorous standards of investigation that Baxter demanded: "when he abjured the prophet to speak truth, and put him to swear as before the Lord that it was truth; this seemed enough to confirm his belief of him".[37] Comenius was a loner, whereas Baxter breathed a Baconian faith in the values of *collective* activity, based upon the pooling of knowledge. Nothing less than the most exacting of standards would do in an area notorious for its minefields. There were too many of the cheats and the credulous, both of them combined in Henry Jessey's three-volume record of strange occurrences in England between 1660 and 1662.[38] So deficient was this study in rational checks that it discredited the whole enterprise, complained Baxter, "and made the very mention of Prodigies to become a scorn".[39] Baxter's medical know-how could have made him rich pickings, he claimed, if only he had "the design and conscience of a Papist". It would be an easy job for the practitioner to convince the common people "that I had cast out a Devil". So caution was essential: "at this very time while I am writing this, I am put to dissuade a man from accusing one of his neighbours of witchcraft, because his daughter hath the disease, and cryeth out of her".[40] A local case fascinated him.

A 15-year-old girl, who was alleged to have been bewitched, "daily voided" a considerable amount of flint stones "as plaine flint as any was in the fielde, till they had large measures full of them." Baxter kept one specimen for three months, and "Mr. Boyle told me that the Earl of Southampton, Lord Treasurer, for his Satisfaction had got a great number of them".[41] A witch was hanged as a result, but not before the most searching enquiry:

> lest there should be any deceit (partly at my device but principally for his owne satisfaction) the learned godly prudent Minister of the towne, Mr. George Hopkins, my speciall beloved friend now with God took care that they might search her to be sure there was no deceit. And the witch was judged and she delivered.[42]

The quality of witnesses and the time span were telling factors in the verdict: "the thing was so long in doing, and so Famous, and so many Pious Understanding Persons marked it, that suspition of Fraud was by their Diligence avoided".[43] The investigating minister Hopkins had a brother who was an MP, "oft pained as he thought with the Spleen, but not at all Melancholy", who confided to Baxter his conviction that he was possessed ("meaning, I think, Bewitcht"). Baxter chided him with being "Fanciful and Melancholy", but then lost contact with him. He heard subsequently that he had died in pain, but just before his death, "a piece of Wood came down into the *rectum intestitum*, which they were fain to pull out with their Fingers". His wife told Baxter it was the length of one's finger, and that he, and they, were sure that he had never swallowed such a thing. Baxter's reflection was that "the best Men it seems may be thus Afflicted, as Job by Satan". On another occasion a woman, with her sister as a witness, had come to Baxter in 1662 with a revelation, not specified by Baxter, which she had had from God about Charles II. She had asked God to give a confirmatory sign and had promptly come out in black spots. Baxter chided her for thus sinfully testing God, but as to whether "it would prove a truth or a Falshood, it was not I, but the Event that must tell her, and therefore that she must wait in Patience and Innocency, and lay no stress on such a sign". It would prove in the end to be a delusion. Baxter was even more brusque with a man who came to him, peddling his vision of a "thousand years reign of Christ on Earth". He ploughed Baxter's viva disastrously. His vision had come "not by any hard Study, nor Zeal in Religion, nor by Reading any Book for it, nor by Concourse with any of that Opinion". Instead, "it was by seeming Revelation, finding him Ignorant and Enthusiastical, I displeased him by asking him to suppress his Papers; and I after heard that he had turned distracted". He had turned out in fact to be just another Major Wilkie, Captain Venner, or John of Leyden.

The Apocalypse and witchcraft were fields crying out for *rational* investigation. The men to be warned off from such pursuits were those who were most attracted to it: the antinomians. Hence Baxter's grief when Thomas Beverley put himself outside the circle of trusted friends exploring the supernatural, when he began dabbling in Tobias Crisp's antinomianism.

In the end Baxter would not accept Hopkins's self-diagnosis of bewitchment. He was not an antinomian and he was not a melancholic: both tell-tale signs normally of deceits. He was, though, a bit of a hypochondriac (not, incidentally, in Baxter's own class). He had made a genuine mistake, Baxter thought, and "swallowed in his Meat a piece of a Flesh-prick, and think it was a Bone, and forget it; though I could not persuade his Wife and Neighbours to believe it". His life had been shortened, in Baxter's view, not by his having been bewitched but by his *delusion* that he had been.[44]

Boyle, like Baxter, did not think that the age of miracles was in the past. He had been impressed by Greatrakes's claims to have cured his patients by "stroking", but saw himself, in this and other matters, as properly poised between scepticism and credulity. He never felt that it was wise to be over-sceptical, because all rational explanations carried with them a reservation clause, which acknowledged "where the irresistible power of God, or some other supernatural agent" might alter the course of nature.[45] Joseph Glanvill, Baxter's friend, authenticated Greatrakes's "stroking" by the testimony of "several inquiries and deep researches of the ROYAL SOCIETY". Boyle, Baxter and Glanvill knew what supernatural occurrences *should* be given credit. As Glanvill put it:

> these things were not done long ago, or at far distance, in an ignorant age, or among a barbarous people, they were not seen by two or three only of the Melancholick and Superstitious, and reported by those that make them serve the advantage and interest of a party. They were not the passage of a Day or Night, or the

vanishing glances of an Apparition; but those transitions were *now* and *late, publick, frequent*, and *of divers years continuance*, witnessed by multitudes of competent and unbyassed Attestors, and acted in a searching incredulous Age.[46]

Baxter's defence of witchcraft in his last year of life could at first sight therefore have been represented as a blow against rationality, and as a confirmation of the links between puritan irrationality and witchcraft. What we have seen is that it is nothing of the sort. Puritans have no monopoly of interest in witchcraft in the seventeenth century – as we have seen, a familiar canard – but, when they do display an interest in it, they do so for the most part according to the prudential maxims of testimony laid down by Locke. A better case can be made for aligning Baxter therefore with "science" in his 1691 defence of spirits, as arising out of an interest in "rational" theology that informed the circle around Boyle. Baxter's work seems weak and credulous only against the standard set by David Hume in the eighteenth century: "no testimony is sufficient to establish a miracle, unless the testimony be of such a kind, that its falsehood will be more miraculous, than the fact which it endeavours to establish".[47] Baxter fails the Hume test, but it is anachronistic to make him take it; almost all of the seventeenth century would fail it too. There was a mean between credulity and scepticism, which Baxter and Boyle both sought, and which is one important element in the development of a scientific outlook. The author of a comparative study of university textbooks in the first half of the seventeenth century, which includes England as well as continental countries, makes an important point:

What we find completely absent from any of the [earlier] textbooks is the Baconian vision and Galilean practice of using knowledge to get control over the forces of nature. There is absolutely no notion of putting knowledge to work, or manipulating natural things to discover the capacities, in short, of a truly practical science. Practical purposes seem to be considered utterly irrelevant to natural philosophy.[48]

This is what we do get in the middle of the seventeenth century in England, persuasively summarized in Charles Webster's *The Great Instauration*.[49] He shows the impressive quickening of interest, particularly in the 1650s, in practical solutions to philosophical problems by collective action, whether it was reform of coinage, agriculture, trade, language, education, the legal system or religion. This was the climate that saw the creation of the Royal Society. Webster's title presses us to see this development as the logical climax of Baconianism, although Julian Martin makes a better case for Louis XIV's Académie des sciences, rather than Charles II's Royal Society, as the true embodiment of Bacon's vision.[50] Nor can one see the 1650s reformers as any more specifically "puritan" in character than they are "Baconian": as Michael Hunter notes, "many of the most active scientists of the Interregnum were neither Puritans nor collaborators with them".[51] But some of them were, and of these none would make a more important contribution than Robert Boyle. Baxter's links with Boyle and his circle are manifest in his own interests: in the "rational" theology he defends, the "providences" he collects, the new university he wants to found (in correspondence with Lewis), the ecumenical schemes he favours (in correspondence with Durie); the missionary work with native Indians he fosters (in correspondence with Eliot); and finally in the vision of a "Holy Commonwealth" that would answer *all* these expectations. Why the 1650s were so energizing for "commonwealth" advocates is made clear in an astonishing letter written to Baxter in 1653:

> doe not we see in Common Weales how after ages perceiving the failing of the people in the observation of some precedent laws doe ad remedies to such transgressions and new conditions to old laws, or make new laws where the other are imperfect, or the present condition of affaires require? and for invention have we not some whose braines have brought forth some new forms of government very rationall?[52]

When Baxter defends the existence of witches and ghosts in 1691 he is drawing on the intellectual capital of (and sometimes his historical examples from) the 1650s, when he and Matthew Poole first set about injecting some rationality into the collection of what had hitherto been mere anecdotage. His *The certainty of the worlds of spirits*, far from being the last gasp of puritan irrationalism, is proof of the opposite: it is a work that Robert Boyle would have been proud to have written.

Not all commonwealth reformers, however, were puritans, as we have been reminded, and not all puritans were commonwealth reformers. Prynne spent the 1650s trying to destroy commonwealths, and to restore kings. The puritanism-to-the-Age-of-Reason scenario makes little sense with a character like him. He has little to say on witchcraft persecution, except that he's for it (how else to explain metamorphosing Jesuits?), or on scientific developments, except that he's against them (Copernicus is as much a rascal as Arminius). His research student at the Restoration, Anthony Wood, got him right surely when he saw him then as a "Jacobean" figure?[53] By that time he would seem to have been stuck in some time warp: an anachronistic figure, still thinking that arguments could be resolved by precedents, not reason. This was how the parliamentary diarist Milward captured him, in one of Prynne's last appearances in the Commons in 1668:

> Mr. Prynne affirmed that the Lords had the only power to hear and determine this case of Skinner and the merchants, and not Westminster Hall, but he argued it so poorly and impertinently against reason that it was not worth taking notice of his discourse, and so it was judged almost by the whole House, although he said it had been anciently done, as appears by Parliament rolls.[54]

Milward was an unfriendly witness, but there is enough evidence that survives to confirm that impression. Here we have a dinosaur from the age of Coke, preaching precedents and the Ancient Constitution in an age that saw them as irrelevancies, as indeed being "against reason", in Milward's words[55]. It would be foolish to argue the opposite and to claim Prynne as some harbinger of "modernity". But a *caveat* even here may still be entered. Prynne was, in Milward's account, defending the Lords, on an important question of privilege. He always did have a soft spot for the peerage. In execrable verse in 1641, he had expounded his core beliefs. He had there argued that pride was a characteristic of "Worthlesse upstarts, beggars, peasants vile", whereas it was men of higher worth who were distinguished by their humility. He showed how Christ – "the patterne of Humility" – went to a mountain top to preach that virtue:

> Showing hereby, that pride more oft doth dwell
> In lowest valleys, and the meanest Cell;

Than in the greatest Mounts, Men, Minds.[56]

By 1647 there was good reason to fear for the continuation of the existence of the Lords, in the worsening political situation. In January 1648 Filmer's *The freeholders grand inquest* was published. It provoked two replies from Prynne, in February and March, respectively: *The Levellers levelled to the very ground*, and *A plea for the Lords*. This was not the normal cut-and-thrust of debates in which Prynne was involved. Filmer had attacked Prynne. A contemporary wrote across his copy of Filmer's work the shrewd comment: "in a considerable degree an answer to the exceptionable doctrines in Prynnes *Sovereignty of Parliament*". But what is interesting for us is *how much of Filmer* went into Prynne's replies – not merely from the fact that he cites him four times positively in his *A plea for the Lords*, but from the way that he allows Filmer to take over his entire thesis.

Filmer's work, as Professor Pocock has shown, was a memorable assault on the "Ancient Constitution" – that ragbag of myth that had furnished Prynne hitherto, and his great mentor Sir Edmund Coke, with their arguments for the sovereignty of the Commons. Filmer showed how shaky was the history that underlay those claims. Drawing upon election writs, he showed that the Commons were not historically part of the Common Council. It was the Lords who were summoned to treat with the King. The Commons' antiquity was denied. They did not belong to Parliament until the reign of Henry I, and they were not regularly summoned by writ until 1265 (the first extant summons of knights by the sheriff's writs). Filmer pointed out that Prynne's 1643 work on the sovereignty of Parliament had only established a clear case for the antiquity of the baronial element in the Common Council:

And if Mr. Pryn could have found so much antiquity, and proof for the Knights, Citizens and Burgesses, being of the Common Council: I make no doubt but we should have heard from him in Capitall characters: but alas! he meets not with so much as these Names in these elder ages![57]

Filmer claimed that Prynne had distorted discussion by treating the King as one of the three Estates (although it is the King's own unhistorical Answer to the Nineteen Propositions which should be blamed for *that*).[58] The Lords' judicial power was derived from the authority outside the Estates: the Crown. He pointed out that the nobility were created by the grace of the King, which was "contradictory and destructive of that naturall equality and freedom of mankind which many conceive to be the foundation of the Privileges and Liberties of the House of Commons". The antithesis between Grace and Nature (assumed as a matter of course by Filmer, and by Prynne too, but, as we saw, not by Baxter) would have ensured eternal discord between the two Houses had they really been founded on these two distinct bases. But they had not. They had been founded on one: "nothing else but the meer and sole grace of Kings".[59]

What is unusual (perhaps even, one would say, unique) in Prynne controversies was the extent to which he here conceded the merits of his opponent's case. He fashioned them to a different end, of course: in 1648 he was still anti-royal, while Filmer was the champion of royalism. These distinctions, though, were breaking down. Prynne's enemy was increasingly seen as the barbarians within the gate; his first response to Filmer is in a pamphlet with a title aimed at Lilburne and his Levellers. He accepted, in both of his replies, that King and Lords *were* antique in a way that the Commons is not. He recognized that the writ, issued by the King to the Commons, conferred upon them a status inferior to that of the Lords. The Commons were formally limited to the discussion of matters originated by the King and Lords. But he subordinated the Commons, to the ancient law of England, which required *the co-operation of the King and Lords*, not to the King's will, as Filmer did.

There are a number of ways in which Prynne's change of mind can be played down. There can be no doubt, though, that he *had* changed his mind. In 1643, for instance, he had said that "every Baron in Parliament doth represent but his owne person and speaketh in the behalfe of himselfe alone. But in the Knights, Citizens and Burgesses are represented the Commons of the whole Realme, and every of them giveth not consent only for himselfe, but for all those also for whom he is sent".[60] But by 1648 Filmer's revisionism was not uncongenial to a man who was naturally hierarchical, fond of the Lords, and increasingly restive with claims made by radicals to sovereignty in the Commons alone.

Professor Pocock's argument holds good, both that the clash between the concepts of "ancient constitution" and "feudal law" is fundamental to our understanding of seventeenth-century English political thought, and that Prynne has an honourable part to play in this clash as a convert/critic of the "ancient constitution". For he preferred Filmer's reading of history to Coke's, in the final analysis not just because it suited his political prejudices (although it did), but because *it was rooted in better history*. Filmer drew on the work of previous antiquarians to establish his thesis about the novelty of the Commons; the importance of his work lies not in its originality, but in its transference *to political use* of what was original. His work was authentic because it drew upon the original records, not on commentaries on them, or on myths that had been allowed to perpetuate unchallenged. In *A plea for the Lords*, Prynne wanted to see ancient parliamentary Rolls and journals transcribed and published to preserve them from the threat of fire or war.[61] In July 1648 he wrote another pamphlet that attacked the irresponsible use by the Commons of Ordinances. Coke had been wrong to think that the consent of King, Lords and Commons was necessary for an Act of Parliament, but not for an Ordinance, which needed only one or two of them. Prynne made it clear that ordinary circumstances *required* the royal assent to an Ordinance, as well as to an Act. Only unwillingness to go behind Coke's authority *to the primary sources* had caused men to believe the contrary: "which errour hath been principally propagated by Sir Edw. Cooks venerable authority and assertion ... whose misallegations and mistakes are too frequently embraced for Oracles of truth for want of close examination."[62] By 1659 Prynne's complaint was that colleagues were not taking enough notice of the historical records he was collecting, and that they were still in the bogus historical world of Sir Edward Coke. In the same pamphlet he ridicules Coke's belief that the *Modus Tenendi Parliamenti* was written in the time of Edward the Confessor. Coke's gullibility about the dating of the document, he argued, showed "how little insight this great Lawyer had in Histories, Antiquities or Records, as to be cheated, besotted with such Impostures and bottom his Discourses of our Parliaments upon such spurious rotten Foundations as these".[63] These deficiencies Prynne could at last make good once Charles II had appointed Prynne to the post of Keeper of the Records in the Tower of London in 1660, and our greatest historian Maitland called him then "heroic", as he set about this task of preserving our historical records.[64] It was "heroic" in a double sense: in the physical sense of his working to rescue documents from the dust and the chaos in which they had been kept, and in the intellectual sense of his recognizing the primacy of the original manuscript as the weapon in the historian's armoury. Nearly a decade on from his appointment, Prynne could draw on these records to show why "our learned Antiquary Sir Henry Spelman" was right, and Coke was wrong to think otherwise, to go for the much later dating for the *Modus*.[65] He deplored the uncritical reliance still invested in Coke "yea by many Members of Parliament in the Debates, Conferences, without the least examination of the Originals". A year earlier he had attacked those "who through ignorance, laziness, or over-much credulity, vouch and cry up his [i.e. Coke's] misquoted, mistaken or misapplied Records and Antiquities (which he had little leisure to peruse himself) as undoubted Verities, and infallible Oracles".[66]

Prynne used internal, as well as external, testing to date a key document like the *Modus*. He noted in 1664 that the attention given in that work to the concept of the Committee of Twenty-four strengthened his belief that it was "contrived, compiled by some Leveller or creature of Richard Duke of York . . . from 7 till 33, H. 6": it was a pleasing doctrine for Levellers of that time, and for that matter of his own. Every Parliament was a new court, he argued, petitioned for by the Speaker, and granted by the King with cautions and reservations. Those reservations limited the extent of the privileges that members of the Commons could claim, and privileges began and ended with their convening and dissolution. The idea that privileges extended for 20 days, both before and after sessions, was dismissed by Prynne both in the pamphlet and in a debate in the Commons. Prynne argued *à la Filmer* that it was from the grace and indulgence of the King that "all the other Members Parliamentary priviledges only flow".[67] It followed, therefore, that the King, not the Commons, was the proper interpreter of privilege. So sceptical was Prynne of the Commons' claims to privilege that he even opposed a proposal on 17 December 1660 that letters of MPs should have free postage.[68]

The Commons had based their false claim to sovereignty upon a false right to judge privilege. This had been true of the Rump, but it had been no less true of Charles I's political opponents in the early part of the seventeenth century. Prynne came down particularly hard on specific claims of privilege made by the Commons under the spell of Coke. He showed that there was no warrant for Coke to serve in

Parliament while Sheriff of Buckingham; that there were no grounds for Sir Simon Steward's evasion of Star Chamber proceedings by a plea of privileged status. In the first case, Coke's practice ran contrary to custom and to the wording of the writs of summons; in the second case, the House voted itself judge of any offence done by its Members, "Upon Sir Edward Cookes assertion of it", against the evidence of parliamentary records. Prynne called Ferrers' Case

> the very first and onely Precedent I can yet discover, wherein the House of Commons assayed by their own sole authority (like a distinct Court, as Sir Edward Cooke styles it, without any ground, Record or antient Record to warrant it) to demand and enlarge any of their Members out of prison or out of execution.[69]

Prynne might extol the glories of the Petition of Right to students at Lincoln's Inn after the Restoration,[70] but in striking at Coke he was also wounding the case of Charles I's opponents. He seemed aware of this danger for, after citing other misrepresentations by Coke, he claimed the right to withhold further criticism:

> As for some other Commons late votes, presidents in the Parliaments of King James, King Charles the 1 and 2nd concerning priviledges of the Members and their Menial Servants, I conceiv it fitter silently to pretermit, than by any recital of them to expose them to the examination or censure of posterity.

He had said enough. So perhaps have we on Prynne and "reason". John Nalson, intrigued that Prynne who "writ as severely against the Sovereignty of Parliaments, as he had some times Violently for it" claimed to

> have heard a Gentleman his familiar averr, that he was so infinitely sensible both of the Folly and Mischief of those Youthful and Injudicious Essays of his Unfortunate Pen, which was rather the results of Prejudice and Revenge, than Law or Reason, that he heard Mr. Prinne say, That if the King had cut off his Head, when he only cropt his Ears, he had done no more than Justice, and done God and the Nation good service.[71]

We can take this "confession" with a pinch of salt – though one eighteenth-century writer indeed hailed it as "denoting a noble, generous and forgiving spirit"[72] – but Prynne *had* changed, that much was true. Nalson melodramatized it as an exchange of "Reason" for "Prejudice"; we might say that he had only swapped one prejudice (the sovereignty of the Commons) for another (the plea for the Lords). The British Library has recently acquired the papers of the regicide Henry Marten. We can see him in 1647 trying out various drafts of a response to Prynne's plea for the Lords. Apart from stock gibes at Prynne's Billingsgate language, Marten is not ready to take on Prynne in his history (and certainly not the revered Selden, who is also criticized); what he is driven to do is to invoke against these historical precedents conjured up by both men "right reason". The question should be not how long "wee have been ridde, but how justly".[73] It was a good point to make against Prynne in 1647: he was still playing the precedents game (for the Lords now, not the Commons) and could therefore be trumped by an appeal to Marten's "right reason". But this was a point that could not go on being levelled at Prynne in the 1650s and 1660s – when his greatest contribution to historical scholarship would be made – and when his case for the Lords rested not on the ability to cite a greater volume of precedents but on a sensitivity to the shift in historiography (which in one sense he only reflected, but in another which he also contributed to), which demanded more exacting standards of testimony. In that sense Prynne on the *Modus Tenendi Parliamenti* was not a world apart from Baxter on his 15-year-old girl voiding flint stones. Prynne knew why Coke, whom he called "the greatest Lawyer in the latter age", *could* not be the historian for the next one. Noy, Selden and Littleton had a "real" insight into historical records; Coke only "a borrowed, superficial" insight into them.[74] In the last analysis Prynne can't accept Coke because his kind of history (even if obviously this is not how Prynne himself puts it) fails the Lockeian tests of prudential maxims of testimony.

There are ways in which Baxter can be fitted into a progressive movement from puritanism to the Age of Reason (though not, as we saw, in the claims by his biographer F. J. Powicke, that he was shedding old prejudices against Popery and was newly discovering ecumenism). Prynne is more difficult altogether to fit into this pattern, although the recovery of his contribution to historical studies may represent a slight modification of the more familiar assumptions that historians have made about him. We know, however, the familiar assumptions about Muggleton: that he was the sworn enemy of "Reason". This was not only said of him then and later; it was said *by* him. "Reason", after all, was the False Seed, he taught his followers, as opposed to "Faith", the True Seed. Newtonian science would be the apotheosis of "Reason", and repugnant to all Muggletonians who continued to believe in their Heaven just a few miles up in the sky. But the 1870 anonymous advocate of Muggletonian faith made plausible, if selective, claims for it to possess the most "modern" of all Christian faiths – no witches, ghosts, Devil, Hell, patriarchs or priests. How do we resolve these contradictions, if that is what they are? An examination of what Muggleton wrote on witches may be illuminating here.

An interesting comparison can be made between two pamphlets with "Witch of Endor" on their title-page. One, written by Muggleton in 1669, is an attack on belief in witches, when such an attack was far from fashionable; the other is a defence of such beliefs in 1736 when opinion (and legislation) were running in the totally opposite direction. The first is anxious to show that witch-beliefs are the product of "Reason", and which are therefore bad; the other also says that they come from "Reason", but which are therefore good. The biblical text in contention is from the First Book of Samuel. Samuel had died, David was in a foreign land. The Amalekites were elated, Saul and his people were cast down. Saul, in his distress, faced the prospect of being routed by the enemy at Mount Gilbon. He visits the cunning woman at Endor. An evil spirit had troubled him since Samuel had appointed David to be king in his place. Saul, having lost the favour of Heaven, summoned up the powers of Hell. The Witch of Endor in her turn summoned up the form of Samuel, but heard no voice. Saul heard the voice, but did not see the form. From the outline of this story, very different inferences flowed.

The writer of 1736 addressed his pamphlet to those Commons Members who had brought in the bill to repeal the Jacobean statute against witchcraft. But witchcraft, he pointed out, had not been deemed "a Relict of Popery" during "the long Reign of Queen Elizabeth of glorious Memory". It was "easy and fashionable" in these days now "to act the Droll, in laughing at the Stories of Witches and Apparitions". But it was these jesters who themselves most contradicted the true tenets of "Reason": "it ought to be remembered, that our Reason should not always be an obedient Servant to a wanton Fancy. I never

yet could observe a Droll to be a close Reasoner." The writer began
with Shakespeare: "the same infinite Being, I likewise observed, that
permitted Julius Caesar's Appearance to Brutus at Philippi, as did
Samuel's to Saul at Endor", although he conceded that it was "probably, in a different Manner". The important thing was to defend
"Reason" against the superficial mocker: "neither to submit your
Reason to the Caprice and Humour of any Bel Esprit whatever, nor
suffer yourself to be argued or laughed out of your Religion, either by
the sly Deist, or noisy Free-Thinker". An examination of the text
showed the confusion that the witch was thrown into, when her
intended "Magic Tricks" were out-trumped by the *real* appearance of
Samuel. This should not occasion surprise: the writer quoted Baxter's
great friend, Sir Matthew Hale, coming down on the side of witchcraft at a trial on 10 March 1662. And there was Baxter's other friend,
Robert Boyle, who "did impartially know as much, if not more, of the
Powers of Nature, than any Man whatever: And yet his Knowledge
was not more extreme, than 'twas useful and serviceable to Religion".
Boyle's distinction was to recognize the limitations of men's knowledge: "who ever thought it unreasonable to disbelieve any certain
Truth, because our Faculties are found not sufficient to comprehend
it".[75] A more robust line was argued on the other side by Sir Robert
Filmer. He knew that "the History of the Woman of Endor, may seem
a strong evidence that the Devil covenanted with Witches", but he
applied to its standing the same critical analysis which had convinced
Prynne that the Commons' origins were novel. He refused the logic of
extending the reality of the encounter itself, to its status as proof "that
the Familiar Spirit entered upon Covenant, or had or would give
power to others to kill the person, or destroy the goods of others".[76]

Different glosses are then given on an encounter, which itself is not
disputed. But Muggleton's radicalism is to deny that the encounter
could ever take place at all, *except in the imagination of men*. Devils
and familiar spirits are always within men and women, not outside
them. The witches, like those on whom they prey, share the delusion
that God is "an infinite spirit, without any body or substance, as all
people almost do". Astrology, fasting, praying "unto an unknown
God" (who takes no notice of them) – all these are related to witchcraft as evidence of "wonderful things" that "may be accomplished
through the imagination of reason, when it hath set itself apart on
purpose to attain unto such things". The Quakers, "harkening to the

light within them", do procure "many strange visions and motional voices, but they being groundless and nonsensical they come to nothing". On the text at issue, it follows that it was "the fear of being destroyed by the Philistines" and the belief in the witch's powers that induced Saul to hallucinate. Samuel, he claimed, "began to speak in Saul's conscience". A guilty conscience creates terror and, by Saul's going to consult a witch, "Samuel is revived again in Saul's mind, and there Saul speaks fear, wrath, and terror". The mark of a true encounter, as that between God and John Reeve, is that plain words are spoken "as might be heard to the outward ear by the standers by"; of a false one, "that no standers by can hear this familiar spirit speak, but he or she that hath it". The false Prophets are "moved by this low voice within them to offer up their own children in sacrifices to their imaginary God, which they believe is an invisible Spirit without a body". For at the root of witchcraft belief is the "vain concept" of the immortality of the soul, as if spirits could be conjured up, separable from their bodily form. Or as if, says Muggleton, "speech could proceed from a shadow without substance". Muggleton confessed that he had once held such beliefs, "when I was zealous in religion according to the Puritan way", that is when he had a *literalist* understanding of Scripture. For how should one interpret Solomon's saying, "Then shall the dust return to the earth as it was, and the spirit shall return unto God who gave it" (Eccles. 12:7)? The meaning is traditionally taken to be that the body goes to dust, and the spirit returns to God but "the sayings of Solomon are no scripture, for Solomon was no scripture writer, for his writings were not written by the revelation of faith, but by the revelation of reason". Solomon is the perfect exemplar of "the wisdom of reason", nobody took "reason" to purer extremes, but "for all this he was ignorant of the revelation of faith and of spiritual and heavenly things, ignorant of the true God, and of the right Devil". The Book of Job is "no Scripture" either, but Job was a good and faithful man. The reported disputes between God and Satan were "nothing else but the motions of Job's heart passing through his troubled soul". The seed of Faith in him counselled patience; the seed of Reason in him prompted rebelliousness.[77]

The 1736 writer was in line with Baxter in 1691 in defending witchcraft as consonant with the rational theology of Robert Boyle; it was his opponents who were irrational in their drollery. Their opponents, though, in a tradition running from Scot to Webster and Filmer, on the contrary maintained that they were on the side of Reason in opposing such beliefs, and on the whole posterity has sided with them.[78] Such a view would seemingly put Muggleton on the side of the angels (if not the witches): in writing a 1669 repudiation of witch-craft beliefs he would be taking puritanism in a very dramatic way into the Age of Reason. Except, as we have seen, it is not in these terms that the debate is itself conducted. Muggleton doesn't say that witch-craft beliefs are irrational; it is their *rationality* that makes them rep-rehensible to him. Rationality comes in its purest form in Solomon, and he was wrong. One is reminded of how Muggleton had seen Moses as wrong when he "put the cart before the horse", and thought that God pre-existed matter. Muggleton doesn't have to explain the Witch of Endor as an allegory, but neither does he have to take Scrip-ture literally. He has a prophetic gift to distinguish between "priva-tive" and "positive" texts, and uses that gift to show how a belief in witchcraft is incompatible with a belief in the mortality of the soul. It was only in his zealous "Puritan" days, when literalism held him in thrall to the biblical text and when he believed in the immortality of the soul, that he gave credence to the Witch of Endor.

And so in 1669 Muggleton sees himself as post-puritan in opposing the reality of witchcraft, but emphatically not pre-Age-of-Reason. Is this a claim to be taken seriously? There is one historian who thinks that it should, and that is the late Edward Thompson. He had an almost lifelong conviction that William Blake should be understood against his background of Muggletonian beliefs. The recovery of the Muggletonian archive was to be a by-product of that search for proof of his hypothesis. Ironically the one certain finding it provided was that William and Catherine Blake never were Muggletonians, nor were any friends of their circle. The nearest to circumstantial evi-dence is the possibility, and it is no higher than that, that Blake's mother, Catherine Hermitage, might have been a Muggletonian. Thompson allows himself the indulgence of a vision of Blake's mother crooning a Muggletonian hymn to baby William, and then pulls himself to order by recognizing it for what it is, "a pleasant fic-tion".

Thompson's non-fictional case for continuing to make such a con-nection is in the end a more modest one. He sees Muggletonianism as one of the "vectors", as he calls it, of Blake's antinomian philosophy. He isolates four distinctive elements. First, there is the repudiation of the Moral Law. "The seed of faith is not under the law, but is above the law" is a clear, unambiguous antinomian principle asserted by Muggleton. This is not a plea for ungovernability; as we saw in Chapter 5, Muggleton favoured magistracy throughout his life (although only in the 1650s with the aspirations of Cromwellian rule did such advocacy carry apocalyptic overtones), and he was embarrassed by the Ranter associations of the movement, provoked by Reeve's brother and by Clarkson's murky antecedents. Nevertheless he is firm that the *Gospel* of Peace transcends the *Law* of Conflict. Secondly, there is the identification of "Reason" as the satanic principle, which entered the human race through the Fall and the seduction of Eve. Thirdly, there is the unusual symbolism of the Fall. The serpent copulates with Eve and begets Cain, whereas Abel and Seth (in whose generation the Devil had no part) were the offspring of the divine principle in which God had created Adam. At the moment of the Fall, two contrary seeds were therefore implanted: the offspring of Cain (Reason) and of Seth (Faith). Fourthly, God became Man Jesus on Earth, while Moses and Elias took care of things in Heaven. These are suggestive overlaps between Muggletonian beliefs and those of Blake, though they are not always easy to isolate from the general shared milieu of radical nonconformist thought. In one sense Thompson may even be making the case harder for himself than he needs to do. He repeatedly describes the "two Seeds" doctrine as "inexorably predestinarian" and, as such, abhorrent to Blake, when we have already seen that, while Muggletonianism was originally rooted in seventeenth-century Calvinist doctrines, there is a significant loosening quite early in the eighteenth century and by the nineteenth century Thomas Robinson is using the "two Seeds" principle in an emphatically *anti-predestinarian* way.

The wider purpose, however, of Thompson's study was to place Blake in a long "anti-hegemonic" artisan tradition against "The Beast"/"Satan's Kingdom"/"the Moral Law". Thompson believes that it offered a more powerful critique to the Establishment than that offered by Enlightenment "rationalism", or what Thompson called "the complacent doctrine of 'benevolence' of Goodwinian circles". In the battle between Tom Paine and Bishop Watson, Blake represented a third force: Blake says, "Paine has not attacked Christianity. Watson has defended Antichrist." Paine and the Bishop were both wrong: "The Bishop never saw the Everlasting Gospel any more than Tom

185

Paine." But Paine's was the venial sin, since he didn't attack the Ever-lasting Gospel (which he didn't understand), but the Moral Law of Antichrist. It was not from the "Newtonian" sciences opposed by both Blake and Muggletonians, or from a naturalistic psychology, that one could divine the "central antinomian affirmations of *Thou Shalt Love* or *Thou Shalt Forgive*". Thompson argues that "every realisation of these values (such as Blake's) is a plank in the floor upon which the future must walk".[79]

Perry Anderson is not convinced. He wonders if Thompson romanticized both Muggleton and Blake in making them planks for the future. Apart from a dip into the Gordon Riots as a boy, Blake's political activism was limited to his Chichester trial after a fracas in his garden with a soldier. Blake annotated Bishop Watson's attacks on Tom Paine with indignation, it is true, but it was Paine, not Blake, who took on the Bishop. If there is a Muggleton–Blake connection, suggests Anderson, it may be not with an activist tradition but with a prudential, keep-your-head-below-the-parapets one.[80]

Anderson is right, but so is Thompson. The Muggletonian who refused to get involved with peripheral matters like the American War of Independence is typical of one authentic strand in Muggletonianism, but the fact that he was a person who had previously been attracted to James Birch is a reminder of another authentic strand in the same movement. Before Birch, there was Reeve, there were Medgate and Buchanan, and after him the "Reevonians" in Victorian England who frightened the Frost brothers: all of them dedicated to a more dynamic reading of Revelation than that laid down by Muggleton. If Blake did believe that a New Jerusalem could be built in England's green and pleasant land we can't rule out as a possible "vector" at least one wing of the followers of Reeve and Muggleton.

The bigger question is whether we *should* imagine any of our seventeenth-century puritans to be building planks for the future to walk on? We know what C. H. George thought of that enterprise; his distaste provided the starting point for this book. William Prynne is an excellent witness he could have summoned to the Bar. Any attempt to enlist him in the ranks of modernity will not get very far, except, as we saw, in the one important area of historical research. In all other matters, Prynne belongs uncritically to his providentialist universe. He is a biblical literalist, who finds in the Old Testament the model for Christian magistracy. He wants "blind obedience" from the Christian subject, even if that's not what he himself gives Charles I (though only because of the latter's involvement in Catholic plots). But the King pays for his mistake with his life, and thereafter Prynne is a royalist (with a few blips on the way). What he is not is a "puritan revolutionary". Nor is he the friend of religious liberty; it is discipline that he wants. The man to administer that discipline is the magistrate, and there is no insistence (as with Hobbes, Muggleton, Roger Williams and Cromwell) that that discipline is strictly confined to externals, and should not touch the subject's inner beliefs. Special pleading by the clergy to have their powers recognized to discriminate between supplicants to communion (and *in extremis* to suspend the unworthy from the Sacrament) cut no ice with Prynne for two reasons. First, it wasn't the clergy's business; they shouldn't usurp the magistrate's role. Secondly, the Lord's Supper was an instrument of conversion; the sinner's absence from it was a renunciation of discipline rather than its enforcement. There wasn't, though, a third reason: scruples about tender consciences, cut off from comforts. The yardstick every time is discipline, not liberty. Nor was Prynne an egalitarian. The Lord of the Manor at Swainswick, William Prynne, Esquire, Utter Barrister of Lincoln's Inn, was a social as well as theological snob. The Elect's duty was to civilise the reprobate majority: inequality in both spheres rested not upon personal merit but upon capricious *and unchallengeable* Grace. This is more a feudal than a proto-capitalist ethic; it is no accident that even his "modern" historical scholarship is harnessed to "A plea for the Lords". But his heart would not be moved, as Baxter's was, by the plight of those who were the losers in a market economy. He was as apocalyptic in his history as most puritans were, but it was a conservative rendering (Foxe, Jewel) that he favoured – apart from his "Brightman" interlude in the 1640s. The headier millenarian brews – John of Leyden, Fifth Monarchy Men – once the *only* apocalyptic interests that historians recognized, were not for him, any more than they were for most of his contemporaries. They contradicted directly his political and social beliefs. His biblical literalism made him as credulous about witches as it made him suspicious of the new science. When C. H. George inveighed against historians who were "alchemists", converting the metal of seventeenth-century piety into the gold of rational modernity, he must have had just such a person as Prynne in mind.

But there were other puritans than Prynne in the seventeenth century, and they throw into doubt the assumption that C. H. George has said the last (wholly negative) word on the subject of this book. Richard Baxter, like Prynne, belongs to a providentialist universe, whose premises he also does not contest. But, unlike Prynne, what he does is to press rational enquiry *within that framework* to its very limits. It is his emphasis on rationalism that makes him appear at times to be more "modern" than he is. Baxter is no more a "revolutionary" than Prynne was. Like Prynne, he wants to rescue Protestant magistracy from its "French" connection. He was against toleration (like Prynne and other puritans) but he, much more than they, was in favour of narrowing the differences between the godly. The discipline that he wants is not a magistrate-run one, like Prynne's, but a cooperative venture between magistrate and pastor. The pastor must not be over-nice, like the Independents, about who should be admitted to the Sacrament; nor sloppily permissive, like the Erastians. How Baxter ran his Kidderminster parish in the 1650s is how Richard Cromwell could run a "Holy Commonwealth" in England: a believing magistracy plus a catechizing ministry. Because Baxter is a caring pastor, he cannot be indifferent to the victims of a market economy, which is why he ends his life as "the poor husbandman's advocate". Baxter is thus irredeemably seventeenth-century in his failure to champion such modern concepts as "revolution", "liberty" and "capitalism". Since he can, though, be linked with "millenarianism" and "witchcraft" – both perceived as "regressive", rather than "progressive", features – this is another puritan who can't simply be propelled into an "Age of Reason".

That is, until we address the nature of his interest in both. What we find is a very keen awareness in Baxter that millenarianism and witchcraft are the topics that particularly appeal to the ignorant and the credulous. As such, they provide the supreme challenge for a man like Baxter who wants to push rational enquiry to the limits. His enemy was the antinomian, and had been since the gigantic nose-bleed that took him out of the Civil War. It was in convalescence that the "light" struck him, which became his assault on antinomianism: his 1649 *Aphorismes of justification*. Antinomianism would be his prime target for the rest of his life. Once in 1690 he would refer to John Bunyan, "an unlearned Antinomian", as the type of an "honest, Godly man".[81] But this is an isolated compliment. In 1654 he had explained why he hated it so much. It was what was "naturally fastened in the hearts of the common profane multitudes", and even if the ignorant can't mouth it so plausibly as the learned, or get into fine distinctions about Free Grace, "yet have they the same tenets, and all men are naturally of the Antinomian Religion; and that the very work of preachers, (when Christ's death and the Promise of pardon and Life is once revealed), is principally the cure of naturall Antinomianism; and this is that we call the work of conversion".[82]

The ignorant were attracted to the irrational ("providences", witchcraft and millenarianism), and it was the duty of the pastor to combat antinomianism, above all therefore, in those areas, and to show how rational enquiry could throw light on the darkest of corners. It was as a believer in natural theology that Baxter collated "providences" with Poole, discussed ghosts and apparitions with More and Glanvill, and corresponded with Eliot and Increase Mather about witches and the millennium. He exposed the frauds and the cheats – Henry Jessey, Major Wilkie, Captain Venner – in order to preserve the truths that were damaged by these false associations. It was all very well corresponding with Thomas Beverley about nice points of difference over the way that they interpreted the Apocalypse; another thing altogether, when that same Beverley began flirting with the antinomian doctrines of Tobias Crisp.

Baxter's defence of witches and the Apocalypse, far from isolating him from later rationalism, therefore draws him closer to it. It is one fruit of his co-operation with Robert Boyle, the Royal Society, and their joint efforts to reconcile science with natural theology. The massive Baxter work, *A Christian directory* concludes with a remarkable response to the scientific stirrings of the age. There was a personal satisfaction to be derived from learning that was important, Baxter argued, but that was nothing compared to a richer impulse:

But another way is by exercising that learning and wisdom which he hath in reading and meditating in some excellent Books, and making discoveries of some mysterious excellencies in Arts and Sciences; which delight him more by the very acting than a bare conclusion of his own Learning in the general, would do: what delight had the inventers of the Sea-chart, and magnetick traction, and of Printing, and of Guns, in their inventions? What pleasure had Galileus in his Telescopes in finding out the irregularities and shady parts of the Moon, the Medicean Planets, the adjuncts of Saturn, the changes of Venus, the Stars of the *Via lactea* etc.[83]

Tawney had said: "so little do those who shoot the arrows of the spirit know where they will light".[84] Baxter thrillingly shot *his* arrow of the spirit in *A Christian directory* – the praise of collective action and the joys of scientific discovery – but it lighted on the pages of Tawney as just another affirmation of the Protestant Ethic.

Thompson rightly saw Muggletonianism as representative of the antinomian tradition in puritanism. Bunyan apart (once), Baxter had nothing good to say about antinomianism, but that tradition was more supple than he allowed for in his criticism of it. Muggleton was no Ranter, even if some of the earliest recruits to his movement were. He opposed Reason, but that did not mean that he was for ungovernability: he had a Pauline respect for magistracy. In the 1650s that respect took the form of a providentialist commitment to Cromwellian magistracy. He shed that commitment at the Restoration; more crucially, he also shed with it providentialism itself, when he denied God's "immediate notice". But that didn't lessen his resolve to render unto Caesar that which was Caesar's (he made comparisons here, to his own advantage, with the trouble-making Quakers). Conversely, there would be no rendering unto Caesar that which was God's: he believed (with Cromwell and Roger Williams) that the magistrate's job was confined to keeping the peace. Old Testament precedents for the magistrates as surrogates for a retributive God – lapped up by Prynne – cut no ice with a man who had freed himself from biblical literalism. Roger Williams had argued that the Old Testament was no "type" for the New; Muggleton similarly distinguished between "privative" and "positive" texts. By different routes, then, both men reached similar conclusions: the magistrate kept the peace and nothing else, and the subject honoured him for doing so. And both agreed (and Hobbes too) that the inner man could not be touched; liberty of the subject's conscience thus *complemented*, not contradicted, magisterial authority. The subject did not have to be harried into submission. Baxter had significantly defended the sanction of Hell as a "rational torment" (which went with his theology of conditional justification), but Muggleton banished an external Hell, along with a Devil, witches and ghosts, as bogeys that imposed unnecessary fears upon Christian worshippers. The days of worries about usury (or witches) belonged to his "puritan" past, confessed Muggleton in his posthumous memoirs. The mature Muggleton (and his followers) saw liberty of conscience and trade as natural complements to one another. Millenarianism was a false dream, and as a product of it, Muggleton had some entitlement to speak on the subject. It was not only that there *would be* no 1,000-year kingdom of Christ; there was not even the prospect of better things in the Last Days, which made even technical non-millenarians like Baxter, Foxe and Henry More, in their several ways, *optimistic* readers of the Apocalypse.

Puritans, we have seen, had no monopoly in the production of witch-hunters or scientists in their ranks. The assumption that they had, however, created the dilemma for later historians posed by the title of this concluding chapter: were puritans on the side of "Reason" if they were, like Baxter, for instance, *simultaneously* identified as being for witches *and* for science? This is a twentieth-century problem, not a seventeenth-century one. Both Baxter and Muggleton would have seen nothing paradoxical in claiming that an interest in *both* the new science and in the old witch-persecutions alike were the products of "Reason". They drew totally opposite conclusions from that judgement, of course. For Baxter, witchcraft and science were esoteric activities to be demystified by Reason; for Muggleton, they were both to be abhorred as the very products of Reason. That, in the nineteenth century, Mugggletonians would pat themselves on the back for denouncing spiritualism as a revised form of witchcraft, and would at the same time despise the 1851 Exhibition (that apotheosis of Victorian trust in science, progress and reason) as the certain forerunner of the Last Days, is wholly consonant with their seventeenth-century attitudes. But it poses the dilemma for the twentieth-century reader: Baxter is "sound" on science, "shaky" on witches; Muggleton is the other way round. Who then is the more "modern"?

But we should recognize, in this absurd formulation,[85] that it is our dilemma, not theirs; and it was just such a recognition that, as we saw, fuelled C. H. George's anger at the folly of relating puritanism to modern abstractions. *That does not mean, however, that their dilemmas and ours, when restored to their proper context, do not interconnect.* This book has worked if at least that sense has been conveyed. John Updike has given that interconnection literary expression in many of his novels, some of which have already been referred to here.

He, at least, has found nothing strange in turning to a Calvinist past to make sense of modern dilemmas, whether it is about swapping wives in New England or bombing Vietnam. The most direct representation of the central of these dilemmas (the subject of this concluding chapter) is to be found in his novel *Roger's version*.

There are two main antagonists in this novel. Dale Kohler is a scientist, and a committed Christian. He feels no tension between the two. His ambition is in fact to resolve such tensions for others. His research project is to prove God's existence by running the right data through the computer. Roger Lambert is also a Christian, but from a very different tradition. He is a historian whose Early Christian heroes are Marcion and Tertullian, because, on his own admission, they are seen by him as forerunners of Karl Barth's theological "severity". This was a severity that allowed no rational bridge, no Natural Law, between God and Man: "Barth had been right: *totaliter alter*. Only by placing God totally on the other side of the humanly understandable can any final safety for Him be secured."

Dale Kohler's God-by-computer is the logical end of that noble puritan quest (Baxter, Boyle) to discover rationalist order within a providentialist universe. Roger's version is no less noble, however, in its rejection of both providence and a rationalist order (Muggleton, Hobbes), and in its austere recognition that God takes no notice of His creatures. In Roger's version (which is also Barth's, which is also Updike's) "we are always in motion *toward* the God who flees, the *Deus absconditus*; He by his apparent absence is always with us". For Roger there is something, on the contrary, demeaning about a God who "lets himself be proven". Updike notes that "Tertullian, like Barth, took his stand on the only ground where he could: the flesh is man. 'All of him is flesh, and by nature ought to perish', Barth roundly wrote".[86] Muggleton linked credulity about witches (bodiless spirits) fundamentally to the erroneous belief in the immortality of the soul. Muggleton (like Hobbes) was a mortalist: probably he was even a mortalist before he was a Muggletonian.[87] Matter existed before God; the universe, in one nineteenth-century Muggletonian view, was too vast even for God to know; how could a man enjoy his wife if she didn't have a body?;[88] God *became* the Man Jesus: these were all "fleshly" truths to be pitted against the "spiritual" truth as conveyed here by Dale Kohler (and elsewhere by Baxter): "There's only one kind of God. God the Creator, Maker of Heaven and Earth. He made it, we now can see, in that first instant with such inevitable precision that a Swiss watch is just a bunch of little rocks by comparison." But Dale Kohler was wrong. There *was* another kind of God, and Updike quotes Barth on what response He demands from His followers: "There is no way from us to God – not even a *via negativa* – not even a *via dialectica* nor *paradoxa*. The god who stood at the end of some human way – even of this way – would not be God."[89] This is a God who is not to be reached by medieval schoolmen or by early-modern rational theologians; not to be reached by science and not by "wonders". This is a God who is not to be reached at all.

Notes

Chapter 1

1. T. Fuller, *The church history of Britain*, vol. vi, J. S. Brewer (ed.) (Oxford, 1845), pp. 86–7.
2. H. Parker, *A discourse concerning puritans* (London, 1641).
3. R. Samuel, "The discovery of puritanism, 1820–1914: a preliminary sketch", in *Revival and religion since 1700: essays for John Walsh*, J. Garnett & C. Mather (eds) (London, 1993), pp. 201–47.
4. *Ibid.*, p. 201.
5. C. H. George, "Puritanism as history and historiography", *Past and Present* 41, pp. 77–104, 1968.
6. C. H. George & K. George, *The Protestant mind of the English reformation, 1570–1640* (Princeton Univ., NJ, 1961).
7. M. Finlayson, *Historians, puritanism and the English revolution: the religious factor in English politics before and after the Interregnum* (Toronto, 1983).
8. J. C. Davis, "Against formality: one aspect of the English revolution", *Transactions of the Royal Historical Society*, sixth series, III, pp. 265–88, 1993.
9. *Ibid.*, p. 281 (note 75). As Davis's example shows, he is aware of the danger of replicating more "manic abstractionism": see also his footnote 2 on p. 266 to that effect. There is much to admire in his article: here (as he would agree) I am only pointing out that the new term doesn't in itself resolve the old problems.
10. F. Scott Fitzgerald, *The diamond as big as the Ritz and other stories* (London, 1964), p. 139.
11. (Doctor Williams's Library) *Baxter correspondence*, vol. iii, fol. 232.
12. B. Coward, *Oliver Cromwell* (London, 1991), p. 105.
13. M. Butler, *Theatre and crisis 1632–1642* (Cambridge, 1984), pp. 84–5.
14. (Bodleian Library) Tanner MSS 44, fol. 157.
15. W. Harper (ed.), *The life, diary and correspondence of Sir William Dugdale,*

(London, 1827), pp. 390–91.

16. A. P. Gordon, *The origins of the Muggletonians* (Liverpool Literary and Philosophical Society, 1869). When, a year later he gave a follow-up lecture *Ancient and modern Muggletonians* to the same body, he could draw upon the archive to which he had been allowed access in the interim.

17. F. J. Powicke, *A life of the Reverend Richard Baxter* (London, 1924), preface.

18. E. Hockliffe (ed.), *The diary of the Reverend Ralph Josselin*, Camden Society, third series, vol. 15, 1908; and the Introductions to A. Macfarlane, *The family life of Ralph Josselin: a seventeenth-century clergyman* (Cambridge, 1970) and to A. Macfarlane (ed.), *The diary of Ralph Josselin 1616–1683* (Oxford, 1976).

19. J. L. Malcolm, "A king in search of soldiers: Charles I in 1642", *Historical Journal* 21(2), pp. 252–3, 1978.

20. M. Phelan, "The Free Catholic Movement", *Baxter Notes and Studies* 2(2), pp. 20–21, 1994.

21. C. Hibbard, *Charles I and the Popish Plot* (Chapel Hill, 1983), pp. 6–8.

22. This was Edmund Bunny's adaptation of Robert Parsons, on which there is now an illuminating analysis: B. S. Gregory, "The 'true and zealous service of God': R. Parsons, Edmund Bunny and the first book of the Christian exercise", *Journal of Ecclesiastical History* 45, pp. 238–68, 1994.

23. On Baxter's ambivalence towards Grotius, see: W. Lamont, "Arminianism: the controversy that never was", in *Political discourse in early modern Britain*, N. Phillipson & Q. Skinner (eds) (Cambridge, 1993), pp. 45–66.

24. H. McLachlan, *Essays and addresses* (Manchester, 1950), pp. 290–310.

25. A. E. McGrath, *Reformation thought: an introduction* (Oxford, 1988), p. 227.

26. M. Weber, *The Protestant Ethic and the spirit of capitalism* (London, 1965), p. 53.

27. B. Franklin, *Autobiography and other writings* (Oxford, 1993), p. 81. The best critique of Weber on Franklin is: A. Owen Aldridge, "The alleged puritanism of Benjamin Franklin", in *Reappraising Benjamin Franklin*, J. A. Leo Lemay (ed.) (Newark, Delaware, 1993), pp. 362–71.

28. Christopher Hill, *The century of revolution* (Edinburgh, 1961), p. 94. In his *Intellectual origins of the English revolution* (Oxford, 1965), p. 91, he did refer to Bacon's "pious parents", but for a sceptical comment on this, see: T. K. Rabb, "Religion and the rise of modern science", in *The intellectual revolution of the seventeenth century*, C. Webster (ed.) (London, 1974), p. 268.

29. Christopher Hill, "William Perkins and the poor", in *Puritanism and revolution* (London, 1965), pp. 229–30.

30. E. P. Thompson, *Witness against the beast: William Blake and the moral law* (Cambridge, 1993), p. xxi.

31. D. Underdown, *Fire from heaven* (London, 1992), p. x.

32. S. T. Coleridge, *Complete works*, vol. v, W. Shedd (ed.) (New York, 1854), p. 348.
33. F. J. Powicke (ed.), *The Reverend Richard Baxter's last treatise* (Manchester, 1926), p. 48.
34. (British Library) Additional MSS 60206, no foliation.
35. W. Lamont, "The Left and its past: revisiting the 1650s", *History Workshop* 23, pp. 141–54, 1987.
36. A personal communication from Raphael Samuel.
37. P. Fussell, *Wartime* (Oxford, 1989), pp. 129–43.

Chapter 2

1. Documentation and further details are to be found in W. Lamont, *Marginal Prynne* (London, 1963), now reprinted as vol. I of W. Lamont, *Puritanism and the English Revolution* (Aldershot, 1991).

Chapter 3

1. Documentation and further details are to be found in Christopher Hill *et al.*, *The world of the Muggletonians* (London, 1983), pp. 111–61, and W. Lamont, "The Muggletonians 1652–1979: A 'vertical' approach", *Past and Present* 99, pp. 22–40, 1983.
2. One contemporary correspondent, with Muggletonian family links, had provided me with helpful material at one stage, but later dropped out when he felt that his eyesight was at risk from possible Muggletonian curses.
3. G. Borrow, *Lavengro* (London, 1961), p. 138.
4. I owe this allusion to the kindness of the editor of the Gladstone Diaries, Dr H. C. G. Matthew.
5. A personal communication from Mrs Hilary Clark. Mrs Jean Barsley (widow of Philip Noakes) and Mrs Carol Malone (his daughter) also provided a great deal of material. Miss E. Muggleton, who donated to the British Library her family copy of J. D. Aspland's commonplace book (now British Library Additional MS 61950), was also very helpful.

Chapter 4

1. Documentation and fuller details are to be found in W. Lamont, *Richard Baxter and the millennium* (London, 1979), now reprinted as vol. III of W. Lamont, *Puritanism and the English Revolution* (Aldershot, 1991).

Chapter 5

1. R. Baxter, *The true history of councils* (London, 1682), p. 82.

2. (Doctor Williams's Library) *Baxter correspondence*, vol. iii, fols. 272v–273.

3. W. Lamont, "The religion of Andrew Marvell: locating the 'bloody horse'", in *The political identity of Andrew Marvell*, C. Condren & A. D. Cousins (eds) (Aldershot, 1990), pp. 135–56.

4. (Doctor Williams's Library) *Baxter correspondence*, vol. iv, fol. 61v. Baxter was writing to his friend John Humfrey, on 23 July 1683, and these words are his answer to the Oxford Convocation's charge of sedition against him.

5. The point I argue at greater length in: "The two 'national churches' of 1691 and 1829", in *Religion, culture and society in early modern Britain: essays in honour of Patrick Collinson*, A. Fletcher & P. Roberts (eds) (Cambridge, 1994), pp. 335–52.

6. W. Prynne, *A vindication of four serious questions* (London, 1645), p. 7; W. Prynne, *A breviate of the prelates intollerable usurpations* (London, 1637), p. 123.

7. See Baxter's solidarity with Burges on this point in a letter to him of September 1659: (Doctor Williams's Library) *Baxter correspondence*, vol. iii, fol. 80.

8. C. Hibbard, *Charles I and the Popish Plot* (Chapel Hill, 1983), *passim*.

9. J. Ohlmeyer, *Civil War and Restoration in the three Stuart kingdoms: the career of Randal MacDonnell, Marquis of Antrim, 1609–1683* (Cambridge, 1993); J. Ohlmeyer, "Communications: the 'Antrim plot' of 1641 – a myth?", *The Historical Journal* 35, pp. 905–19, 1992; M. P. Maxwell, "The 'Antrim plot' of 1641 – a myth? A response" and J. Ohlmeyer, "The 'Antrim plot' of 1641: a rejoinder", *The Historical Journal* 37, pp. 421–30 and 431–8 respectively, 1994.

10. R. Mainwaring, *Religion and alegiance* (London, 1627); W. Dickinson, *The King's right* (London, 1619); R. Sibthorpe, *Apostolike obedience* (London, 1627).

11. W. Prynne, *A summary collection . . .* (London, 1656), p. 25.

12. W. Prynne, *Canterburies doome . . .* (London, 1646), p. 246.

13. W. Bradshaw, *English puritanisme* (London, 1605), p. 35.

14. W. Prynne, *A quench-coale . . .* (London, 1637).

15. W. Prynne, *Histriomastix . . .* (London, 1633), pp. 123–6, 467, 715; J. White, *Two sermons* (London, 1615), pp. 16–17, 36–7, 22.

16. D. Underdown, *Fire from heaven: life in an English town in the seventeenth century* (London, 1992).

17. G. Gillespie, *Male audis* (London, 1646), p. 37; see also his *Aarons rod blossoming* (London, 1646), p. 585.

18. (PRO) SP 16/534, fol. 148v.

19. H. Parker, *A discourse concerning puritans* (London, 1641), p. 7.

20. R. Baillie, *Letters and journals*, vol. i., D. Laing (ed.) (Edinburgh, 1841), pp. 308–9; P. Heylyn, *Cyprianus Anglicus* (London, 1668), pp. 464–5,

comments on Prynne's meeting with John Williams in December 1640.

21. W. Prynne, *A soveraign antidote* . . . (London, 1642), p. 5.

22. W. Prynne, *The soveraigne power of parliaments* . . ., vol. i (London, 1643), p. 103.

23. W. Prynne, *The Popish royall favourite* . . . (London, 1643), preface.

24. W. Prynne, *The soveraigne power of parliaments*, vol. iii, p. 2.

25. W. Prynne, *The Popish royall favourite*, preface.

26. James Howell, *The preheminence . . . of Parliament* . . . (London, 1643), p. 8; W. Prynne, *A modest apology against a pretended calumny* (London, 1643), p. 6.

27. (British Library) Sloane MSS 2035 B, fol. 12.

28. Prynne, *The Popish royall favourite*, pp. 48, 50, 56.

29. (British Library), Harleian MSS 980, fol. 468.

30. Prynne, *The Popish royall favourite*, p. 56.

31. (Anon.), *The fallacies of Mr. William Prynne* . . . (Oxford, 1644), p.8.

32. W. Prynne, *Canterburies doome*, dedicatory epistle.

33. W. Prynne, *The sword of Christian magistracy* . . . (London, 1647), p. 68.

34. *Ibid.*, pp. 5–6.

35. *Ibid.*, p. 109.

36. W. Prynne, *A true and perfect narrative* . . . (London, 1659), pp. 60–63; (British Library) Stowe MSS 755, fol. 14; P. du Moulin, *A vindication of the sincerity of the Protestant religion* (London, 1671), p. 64.

37. J. Goodwin, *Right and might well met* (London, 1649), pp. 4, 8, 9.

38. (Anon.), *The resolution of His Excellency the Lord General Fairfax and his Generall Councell of officers* (London, 1648), p. 3.

39. (Anon.), *Mr Prinns charge against the King* (London, 1648), no pagination.

40. (Anon.), *Mr. William Prynne his defence of stage-plays* (London, 1649), p. 3.

41. W. Prynne, *Prynne the member reconciled to Prynne the barrester* . . . (London, 1649), dedicatory epistle.

42. W. Prynne, *A briefe memento to the present unparliamentary junto* . . . (London, 1649), pp. 3, 5, 10, 14, 12.

43. *Mercurius Pragmaticus*, vol. 18, 11–18 January 1649.

44. *Mercurius Elencticus*, vol. 58, 24 December 1648–2 January 1649.

45. Historical Manuscripts Commission, (HMC) *Ormonde report*, vol. ii, pp. 86–7.

46. (Bodleian Library) Tanner MSS 57, fol. 497.

47. Dorothy Margaret Stuart, "Milton and Prynne: some new light on the secret history of the Commonwealth", *New Statesman and Nation* (28 February 1931), pp. 15–16.

48. W. Prynne, *A new discovery of free-state tyranny* . . . (London, 1655), pp. 66–70, 73, 75.

49. *Calendar Clarendon State Papers*, vol. iv, pp. 591, 592, 593, 603, 606, 615.

50. M. Coate (ed.), *The letter-book of John Viscount Mordaunt 1658–60*, Camden Society, third series, vol. 69, 1945, p. 126.

51. *Calendar State Papers Domestic, Charles II 1660–1661*, p. 564.

52. *Bath Council minutes*, vol. II, fol. 68; R. E. M. Peach, *History of Swains-wick* (Bath, 1890), pp. 43–5.

53. A. Wood, *The life and times . . .*, vol. i, A. Clark (ed.) (Oxford, 1891), p. 481.

54. A. Grey, *Debates of the House of Commons, from the year 1667 to the year 1694* (London, 1769), p. 118.

55. J. Murch, *William Prynne* (Bath, 1878), pp. 31–2.

56. W. Prynne, *The second part of the signal loyalty and devotion of God's true saints . . .* (London, 1660), dedicatory epistle; W. Prynne, *Letter and proposals to our gracious lord and sovereign King Charles* (London, 1660), *passim*.

57. H. Jessey, *The lords loud call to England* (London, 1660), p. 32.

58. *Commons Journals*, vol. viii, pp. 282, 291.

59. W. Prynne, *Summary reasons, humbly tendred to the most honourable House of Peeres . . .* (London, 1661).

60. *Commons Journals*, vol. viii, pp. 299, 302; *Mercurius Publicus*, vol. 28, 11–18 July 1661.

61. *Mercurius Publicus*, vol. 28, 11–18 July 1661; (British Library) Additional MSS 38490, fol. 80; *Calendar State Papers Venetian, Charles II*, vol. 32, p. 26.

62. HMC, *12th Report*, vol. ix, pp. 50–51.

63. Lord Shaftesbury, *A letter from a person of quality* (London, 1675), pp. 1–2.

64. J. Milward, *Diary*, C. Robbins (ed.) (Cambridge, 1939), p. 293.

65. W. Cobbett (ed.), *Parliamentary history of England*, vol. iv (London, 1808), p. 293; *Commons Journals*, vol. viii, p. 563.

66. Milward, *Diary*, p. lxvii.

67. *Commons Journals*, vol. viii, p. 394.

68. HMC, *12th Report*, vol. ix, pp. 50–51.

69. W. Prynne, *Brevia parliamentaria rediviva . . .* (London, 1661), p. 515.

70. *Mercurius Publicus*, vol. 28, 11–18 July 1661.

71. HMC, *5th Report*, p. 170.

72. R. Baxter, *Against the revolt to a foreign jurisdiction* (London, 1691), p. 318.

73. W. Prynne, *Aurum reginae* (London, 1668), dedicatory epistle.

74. W. Prynne, *The first tome of an exact chronological vindication . . . of our kings supreme ecclesiastical jurisdiction . . .*, vol. iv (London, 1666), pp. 1, 2, 7, 77. Lincoln's Inn Library has the unique copy of this volume, originally intended as an introduction to the whole.

75. (Doctor Williams's Library) *Baxter correspondence*, vol. vi, fols. 72–75v.

76. (Doctor Williams's Library) *Baxter treatises*, vol. i, fols. 132v, 199v.

77. e.g. *ibid.*, fol. 266; (Doctor Williams's Library) *Baxter treatises*, vol. iv, fols. 288, 289v.

78. W. Prynne, *Romes master-piece . . .* (London, 1644), p. 33.

79. Prynne, *The Popish royall favourite*, p. 35.

80. R. Baxter, *The Grotian religion discovered* (London, 1658), pp. 4, 105, 106, 108.

81. Cf. R. Baxter, *A key for Catholicks* (London, 1659), p. 355 and (London, 1674), p. 416.

82. *Ibid.*, p. 319: the reference is to Edward Sexby's 1657 apology for tyrannicide, *Killing no murder*.

83. *Ibid.*, p. 323.

84. R. Baxter, *A holy commonwealth*, W. Lamont (ed.) (Cambridge, 1994), pp. 251–2.

85. (Doctor Williams's Library) *Baxter correspondence*, vol. vi, fol. 37.

86. R. B. Schlatter, *Richard Baxter and puritan politics* (Rutgers, NJ, 1957), p. 148; cf. Baxter, *A holy commonwealth*, pp. 18–21.

87. Schlatter, *Richard Baxter*, p. 148; Baxter, *A holy commonwealth*, p. 114.

88. Schlatter, *Richard Baxter*, p. 149; Baxter, *A holy commonwealth*, pp. 215–17.

89. Schlatter, *Richard Baxter*, p. 149; Baxter, *A holy commonwealth*, p. 96, where he quotes both works by Edward Gee: *A vindication of the oath of allegiance* (London, 1650) and *The divine right and originall of the civil magistrate from God* (London, 1658).

90. Schlatter, *Richard Baxter*, p. 150; Baxter, *A holy commonwealth*, pp. 38–9.

91. Schlatter, *Richard Baxter*, pp. 150, 151, 155; Baxter, *A holy commonwealth*, p. 219.

92. Baxter, *Against the revolt*, pp. 32–3, 78, 360.

93. *Ibid.*, p. 102.

94. R. Baxter, *A paraphrase on the New Testament* (London, 1684), *passim*. Among the offended Protestants: H. More, *Paralipomena prophetica . . .* (London, 1685), preface; J. Owen, *A brief and impartial account of the nature of the protestant religion* (London, 1682), pp. 27–8.

95. (Doctor Williams's Library) *Baxter treatises*, vol. vii, fol. 45; R. Baxter, *A reply to Mr. Thomas Beverleys answer . . .* (London, 1691), p. 12.

96. E.g. (among many such statements in 1691): (Doctor Williams's Library) *Baxter treatises*, vol. vii, fol. 300v – "That Christs Kingdome was but in its Infancy till he visibly ruled by the sword, by Christian Princes".

97. Cf. Baxter, *A holy commonwealth*, p. 210: "How sad a blow was it to England that Edward the Sixth was so soon taken away".

98. Baxter, *Against the revolt*, p. 87.

99. In his manuscript of 1691, *A political primer for Nationall Churches*, he attacks, not just James II, but "the designe of K. Charles I and II" to bring in "Popery": (Doctor Williams's Library) *Baxter treatises*, vol. vi, fol. 299v.

100. The details are in: W. Lamont, *Puritanism and the English revolution*, vol. III, *Richard Baxter and the millennium* (Aldershot, 1991), pp. 76–123.

101. Prynne, *Romes master-piece*, p. 34.

102. J. Reeve & L. Muggleton, *A transcendent spiritual treatise . . .* (London, 1652), p. 46.

103. L. Muggleton, *The neck of the Quakers broken* (London, 1676), pp. 64–5.

104. L. Muggleton & J. Reeve, *A stream from the tree of life* (London, 1758), p. 62.
105. Muggleton, *The neck of the Quakers broken*, p. 89.
106. L. Muggleton, *The acts of the witnesses of the spirit* (London, 1699), p. 163.
107. (British Library) Additional MSS 60171, fol. 432.
108. (British Library) Additional MSS 60170, no foliation.
109. (British Library) Additional MSS 60171, fol. 888.
110. *Ibid.*, fol. 819.
111. *Ibid.*, fol. 610.
112. *Ibid.*, fol. 671.
113. *Ibid.*, fol. 677.
114. *Ibid.*, fol. 745.
115. (British Library) Additional MSS 60190, fol. 207.
116. (British Library) Additional MSS 60198, fol. 6.
117. (British Library) Additional MSS 60173, no foliation.
118. (British Library) Additional MSS 60206, no foliation.
119. (British Library) Additional MSS 60171, fol. 750.
120. *Ibid.*, fol. 367.
121. *Ibid.*, fols. 421–3.
122. (British Library) Additional MSS 60168, no foliation.
123. *Ibid.*
124. I have been allowed access to a letter from Mrs F. Lee to Mrs F. Noakes of 9 February 1933 on this topic (from Mrs Jean Barsley's family papers).
125. (British Library) Additional MSS 60168, no foliation.
126. C. Leslie, *The snake in the grass* (London, 1696), preface.
127. L. Muggleton & J. Reeve, *A divine looking glass* (London, 1656), pp. 73, 76, 77.
128. *Ibid.*, dedicatory epistle, pp. 79, 81, 82.
129. (British Library) Additional MSS 60168, no foliation.
130. (British Library) Additional MSS 60206, no foliation.

Chapter 6

1. W. K. Jordan, *The development of religious toleration in England*, [4 vols] (London, 1932–40).
2. A. S. P. Woodhouse (ed.), *Puritanism and liberty* (London, 1950).
3. W. Haller, *Liberty and reformation in the puritan revolution* (New York, 1955); W. Haller (ed.), *Tracts on liberty in the puritan revolution 1638–1647* (New York, 1934); W. Haller, *The rise of puritanism* (New York, 1938).
4. (British Library) Additional MSS 60170, no foliation.
5. W. Walwyn *et al.*, *A manifestation* . . . (London, 1649), in *The writings of*

William Walwyn, J. R. McMichael & B. Taft (eds) (Athens, Ga., 1989), p. 341.

6. W. Walwyn, *The compassionate Samaritane* (London, 1644) in *ibid.*, p. 102.

7. B. Worden, "Toleration and the Cromwellian Protectorate", in *Studies in Church history*, vol. 21, W. J. Sheils (ed.) (London, 1984), p. 199.

8. F. Kermode, "The Fairie Queene, I and IV", in his *Renaissance essays* (London, 1971), pp. 42–4, 47–8; F. Raab, *The English face of Machiavelli* (London, 1964).

9. Haller, *The rise of puritanism*, p. 219.

10. R. Williams, *The bloudy tenent of persecution* (London, 1644), p. 224.

11. (British Library) Additional MSS 37682, fol. 74v.

12. W. Prynne, *A short demurrer . . .* (London, 1656), p. 201.

13. W. Prynne, *The antipathie . . .*, vol. ii (London, 1641), p. 310.

14. J. Milton, *Of reformation touching church discipline* (London, 1641).

15. Prynne, *The antipathie*, vol. ii, pp. 505–7.

16. (Anon.), *William Prynne . . . a memorable new year's gift . . . now re-published . . .* (London, 1727), pp. xiv–xv.

17. (PRO) SP 16/503, fol. 35.

18. W. Prynne, *Twelve considerable serious questions touching church government . . .* (London, 1644), p. 7.

19. J. Goodwin, *Innocencies triumph* (London, 1644), p. 11.

20. W. Prynne, *A full reply to certaine brief observations . . .* (London, 1644), pp. 8–9.

21. Prynne, *A vindication of foure serious questions*, p. 45; W. Prynne, *Independency examined . . .* (London, 1644), pp. 8–9; W. Prynne, *A catalogue of such testimonies . . .* (London, 1637), p. 23.

22. Prynne, *A vindication of foure serious questions*, pp. 57–8.

23. (British Library) E305/13: *Ordinances of Lords and Commons . . . 20th October 1645*.

24. W. Prynne, *Suspention suspended . . .* (London, 1646), pp. 3, 40.

25. H. Burton, *A vindication of churches commonly called independent . . .* (London, 1644), p. 1.

26. W. Dell, *Right reformation* (London, 1646), p. 7.

27. Prynne, *The sword of Christian magistracy*, p. 106.

28. Burton, *A vindication*, p. 13.

29. H. Burton, *Vindiciae veritatis* (London, 1645), p. 6.

30. J. Ley, *The new querie* (London, 1645), p. 65; G. Gillespie, *A sermon . . .* (London, 1645), p. 33.

31. R. Baillie, *Letters and journals*, vol. ii, D. Laing (ed.) (Edinburgh, 1841–2), p. 279.

32. *Ibid.*, p. 315.

33. H. Burton, *Conformities deformity . . .* (London, 1646), p. 6.

34. HMC, *13th Report*, vol. i, p. 300.

35. Burton, *Conformities deformity*, pp. 19, 21: he was referring to H. Parker,

The Trojan horse of the Presbyteriall government unbowelled (London, 1646).

36. Jordan, *The development of religious toleration*, vol. ii, p. 547 notes that "Erastianism was a sword which could be wielded to cut both ways" – for repression no less than for toleration – but treats the Erastians as part of a group, "The Laymen and the Moderates" (Bacon, Cotton and Selden) favourable to toleration. This is to misconstrue the role, not only of Prynne, but of Coleman, Fiennes, Henry Parker, Lightfoot, Cartwright and Hussey, who rather saw discipline in the late 1640s as too important a task merely to be left to the clergy.

37. A. Palmer, *A scripture-rule to the Lords table* (London, 1654), pp. 5, 21, 40.

38. (Doctor Williams's Library) *Baxter treatises*, vol. vi, fol. 203.

39. R. Baxter, *Christian concord* (London, 1653), p. 69.

40. J. Morrow, *Coleridge's political thought* (New York, 1990), p. 151.

41. (Folger Library) Pointer MS, vol. xvii, no foliation.

42. Baxter, *A holy commonwealth, passim.*

43. W. Prynne, *An appendix to a seasonable vindication of free-admission* . . . (London, 1657), pp. 2, 9.

44. W. Prynne, *A legal resolution of two important queries* . . . (London, 1656), p. 17.

45. M. James, "The political importance of the tithes controversy in the English Revolution, 1640–60", *History* XXVI, p. 6, 1941: she is quoting a contemporary pamphlet of 1654, Robert Culmer's *Lawlesse tithe robbers discovered.*

46. W. Prynne, *A gospel plea* . . . (London, 1653), p. 3; W. Prynne, *Ten considerable questions concerning tithes* . . . (London, 1659), *passim.*

47. Baxter, *A holy commonwealth*, pp. 23, 27, 26, 32, 34, 35.

48. H. Boersma, *A hot pepper corn* (Zoetermeer, 1993), pp. 322–30.

49. Baxter, *Against the revolt*, p. 53.

50. R. Baxter, *Catholick theologie*, vol. ii (London, 1675), p. 283.

51. (Doctor Williams's Library) *Baxter treatises*, vol. vi, fol. 287.

52. (Doctor Williams's Library) Thomas Jolly MS, fol. 8.

53. *Ibid.*, fol. 65.

54. J. Owen, *The doctrine of the saint's perseverance* (London, 1654), p. 352.

55. McMichael & Taft, *The writings of William Walwyn*, p. 82.

56. Baxter, *Catholick theologie*, vol. iii, pp. 107–16.

57. Coleridge, *Complete works*, vol. v, p. 200.

58. R. Baxter, *Confession of his faith* . . . (London, 1655), pp. 123–4.

59. R. Baxter, *The saints everlasting rest* (London, 1650), pp. 338, 271.

60. *Noakes papers*: no foliation (private papers belonging to Mrs Jean Barsley, formerly Noakes).

61. Muggleton & Reeve, *A divine looking glass*, (London, 1656), pp. 199, 202.

62. Muggleton & Reeve, *A stream from the tree of life*, (London, 1758), p. 56.

63. (British Library) Additional MSS 60171, fols. 420, 428, 458.

64. (British Library) Additional MSS 60190, fols. 177–9, 186.

65. (British Library) Additional MSS 60171, fol. 926.

66. (British Library) Additional MSS 60206, fol. 283v.

67. (British Library) Additional MSS 60170, no foliation.

68. Owen, *The doctrine*, p. 380.

69. J. Owen, *Righteous zeal encouraged by divine protection* (London, 1649), pp. 163–4; J. Owen, *A peace-offering* (London, 1667), p. 37; (Doctor Williams's Library) *Baxter correspondence*, vol. ii, fol. 273.

70. J. Owen, *The chamber of imagery . . .* (London, 1682), p. 572; J. Owen, *Animadversions on a treatise intituled fiat lux* (London, 1662), p. 253; J. Owen, *Indulgence and toleration considered* (London, 1667), pp. 11–12; J. Owen, *An enquiry into the original, nature, institution, power, order and communion of evangelical churches . . .* (London, 1681), p. 117; J. Owen, *A peace-offering*, p. 28.

71. D. Cawdrey, *Independencie a great schism* (London, 1657), pp. 13, 217.

72. J. Owen, *A defence of Mr. John Cotton . . .* (Oxford, 1658), p. 65.

73. Cawdrey, *Independencie a great schism*, p. 14.

74. J. Owen, *Evidences of the faith of God's elect* (London, 1695), p. 69.

75. J. Owen, *On indwelling sin* (London, 1668), p. 270.

76. Owen, *An enquiry*, p. 116.

77. Owen, *Righteous zeal*, p. 196.

78. *Ibid.*, p. 203.

79. W. Prynne, *God, no imposter nor deluder* (London, 1629), pp. 16–17.

80. Woodhouse, *Puritanism and liberty*, p. 271.

81. P. Miller, *Roger Williams* (New York, 1962), pp. 224–6.

82. A. Woolrych, "Oliver Cromwell and the people of God", *Cromwelliana*, P. Gaunt (ed.), pp. 3–4, 1992.

83. Baxter, *A holy commonwealth*, p. xvii.

84. T. Hobbes, *Leviathan*, R. Tuck (ed.) (Cambridge, 1991), pp. 479–80.

85. McMichael & Taft, *The writings of William Walwyn*, p. 57.

86. R. Tuck, "The civil religion of Thomas Hobbes", in *Political discourse in early modern Britain*, N. Phillipson & Q. Skinner (eds) (Cambridge, 1993), pp. 120–38.

87. McMichael & Taft, *The writings of William Walwyn*, pp. 57, 329, 379.

88. S. Parker, *A defence and continuation of the ecclesiastical politie* (London 1671), pp. 45, 142; Owen, *A peace-offering*, p. 37.

89. W. Lamont & S. Oldfield (eds), *Politics, religion and literature in the seventeenth century* (London, 1975), pp. 205–9.

90. F. Crews, "Mr Updike's planet", *New York Review of Books,* 19, pp. 7–14, 1986.

91. J. Updike, "On not being a dove", in his *Self-consciousness: memoirs* (London, 1989), pp. 107–55. Updike here acknowledged the connection between Protestant theology and his "Hawk" stand on Vietnam (whereas his wife's Unitarianism and "protest" politics seem to us a more natural fit). Why one *should* seem natural, and the other not, is however questioned in my essay, "The two 'national churches' of 1691 and 1829", pp. 335–52,

and of course in Chapter 5 of this book.

92. G. Orwell, "Politics versus literature", in his *Collected essays* (London, 1961), p. 402; D. Wootton, "A perpetual object of hate to all theologians", *London Review of Books* 17(8), p. 13, 1995; J. Updike, *Couples* (London, 1968), p. 481.

93. The best commentary on Cromwell's religion is B. Worden, "Oliver Cromwell and the sin of Achan", in *History, society and the churches*, D. Beales & G. Best (eds) (Cambridge, 1985), pp. 125–46. But now to be supplemented with J. C. Davis, "Cromwell's religion", in *Oliver Cromwell and the English revolution*, J. Morrill (ed.) (London, 1990), pp. 181–208.

94. W. Lamont, "Oliver Cromwell and English Calvinism", *Cromwelliana*, P. Gaunt (ed.), pp. 2, 6, 1994.

95. (British Library) Additional MSS 60206, no foliation.

96. (British Library) Additional MSS 60198, fol. 6.

97. (British Library) Additional MSS 61093, no foliation.

98. (British Library) Additional MSS 60173, no foliation.

99. R. Tuck, "The civil religion of Thomas Hobbes", pp. 137–8.

Chapter 7

1. Weber, *The Protestant Ethic*, p. 91.

2. H. Lehmann, "The rise of capitalism: Weber versus Sombart", in *Weber's Protestant Ethic: origins, evidence, contexts*, H. Lehmann & G. Roth (eds) (Cambridge, 1993), p. 205.

3. M. Prestwich (ed.), *International Calvinism 1541–1715* (Oxford, 1985).

4. A. Macfarlane, "The cradle of capitalism: the case of England" and Peter Burke, "Republics of merchants in early modern Europe", in *Europe and the rise of capitalism*, J. Baechler *et al.* (eds) (Oxford, 1988), pp. 185–203 and p. 230 respectively.

5. J. Updike, *Self-consciousness* (London, 1989), p. 174.

6. D. Underdown, *Fire from heaven* (London, 1992); K. Wrightson & D. Levine, *Poverty and piety in an English village: Terling 1525–1700* (London, 1979).

7. Macfarlane, *Witchcraft in Tudor and Stuart England* (London, 1970), pp. 205–6.

8. P. Collinson, "Cranbrook and the Fletchers: popular and unpopular religion in the Kentish Weald", in his *Godly People* (London, 1983), pp. 399–428; N. Tyacke, "Popular puritan mentality in late Elizabethan England", in *The English Commonwealth 1547–1640*, P. Clark *et al.* (eds) (Leicester, 1979); M. Spufford, "Can we count the godly?", *Journal of Ecclesiastical History* 36, pp. 428–38, 1985.

9. Collinson, *The religion of Protestants* (Oxford, 1982), p. 240.

10. G. Roth, "Weber the would-be Englishman: anglophilia and family his-

tory", in *Weber's Protestant Ethic*, pp. 83–122.

11. *Ibid* ., p. 391.
12. R. Baxter, *A Christian directory* (London, 1673), p. 862.
13. R. Baxter, *Chapters from a Christian directory*, J. Tawney (ed.) (London, 1925).
14. K. von Greyerz, "Biographical evidence on predestination, covenant, and special providence", in *Weber's Protestant Ethic*, p. 273; C. L. Cohen, *God's caress* (Oxford, 1986), pp. 115–17.
15. H. Trevor-Roper, *Catholics, Anglicans and Puritans* (London, 1987), pp. 201–4.
16. Baxter, *A Christian directory*, p. 197.
17. Baxter, *Catholick theologie*, vol. 1, pt. 2, p. 93; vol. 2, p. 199.
18. Baxter, *A Christian directory*, pp. 197, 200, 274, 294, 295, 297, 304, 317, 318, 333, 356, 357, 358, 360, 482.
19. Christopher Hill, *The world turned upside down* (London, 1972), pp. 266.
20. Baxter, *A Christian directory*, p. 722; Baxter, *A holy commonwealth*, pp. 251–2.
21. Baxter, *A Christian directory*, pp. 725, 727, 804, 823, 825.
22. *Ibid.*, pp. 803, 830, 831.
23. E. Duffy, "The godly and the multitude in Stuart England", *The Seventeenth Century* 1(1), pp. 32, 38–40, 1986.
24. Baxter, *A holy commonwealth*, pp. 10–12.
25. M. Walzer, "Puritanism as a revolutionary ideology", *History and Theory* 3, pp. 63–5, 1963–4.
26. Baxter, *A holy commonwealth*, pp. 129–34.
27. *Ibid.*, pp. 167–71.
28. *Ibid.*, pp. 251–2.
29. R. H. Tawney, *Religion and the rise of capitalism* (London, 1926), pp. 191–204.
30. W. Lamont, "Arminianism: the controversy that never was", in *Political discourse in early modern Britain*, N. Phillipson & Q. Skinner (eds) (Cambridge, 1993), pp. 56–8.
31. Baxter, *A Christian directory*, p. 813.
32. Powicke, *The Reverend Richard Baxter's last treatise*, pp. 20, 21, 22, 38, 42, 43, 46, 48, 51, 52, 53.
33. See particularly those cited in footnote 21 above.
34. (Doctor Williams's Library) *Baxter treatises*, vol. ii, fol. 172v.
35. (Doctor Williams's Library) *Baxter treatises*, vol. vi, fol. 302.
36. R. Baxter, *The glorious kingdom of Christ* (London, 1691), p. 6.
37. J. Humfrey, *Union pursued* (London, 1691), pp. 12–13; (Doctor Williams's Library) *Baxter treatises*, vol. vi, fol. 297.
38. The works are well matched in more than the detail of their proposals. They breathe the same air of optimism, as Powicke grasped in his preface to *The Reverend Richard Baxter's last treatise*: "it reveals the old man of 76 as cherishing the same fire in his heart as the man of 43". The odd man out is

the man of 58 who wrote *A Christian directory*; whereas, for Weber and Tawney, *he* is the authentic Baxter.

39. R. Baxter, *Of national churches* (London, 1691), pp. 49–70.

40. J. Henretta, "The Protestant Ethic and the reality of capitalism in colonial America", in *Weber's Protestant Ethic*, pp. 329–33.

41. (Doctor Williams's Library) *Baxter treatises*, vii, fol. 7.

42. (Doctor Williams's Library) *Baxter treatises*, vi, fol. 301.

43. Powicke, *The Reverend Richard Baxter's last treatise*, p. 56.

44. D. Reid, "The decline of Saint Monday 1766–1876", *Past and Present* 71, p. 94, 1976.

45. R. Baxter, *A treatise of self-denial* (London, 1675), pp. 332–3.

46. (Doctor Williams's Library) *Baxter correspondence*, vol. iv, fol. 183.

47. (Doctor Williams's Library) *Baxter correspondence*, vol. iii, fol. 288.

48. S. Shaw, *The true Christian test* (London, 1682), pp. 322, 351, 305, 307.

49. (British Library) Additional MSS 5944, fol. 187.

50. Prynne, *Canterburies doome*, dedicatory epistle.

51. (Bodleian Library) Laud Misc. MSS 760, fol. 1. On Laud's sensitivity on this matter, see: Heylyn, *Cyprianus Anglicus*, p. 43.

52. Prynne, *Ten considerable questions*, p. 1.

53. W. Prynne, *A plea for Sir George Booth* (London, 1660), no pagination.

54. Sir Richard Baker, *Theatrum triumphans* (London, 1670), p. 25.

55. D. L., *Israels condition and cause pleaded* (London, 1656), p. 70.

56. (Anon.), *To the supream authority of England, Scotland, and Ireland* (London, 1659), single sheet.

57. W. Prynne, *Anti-arminianisme* (London, 1630), p. 123.

58. Prynne, *A gospel plea*, p. 2.

59. M. James, "The political importance of the tithes controversy in the English Revolution, 1646–60", *History* XXVI, p. 13, 1941.

60. (Anon.), *A proclamation* (London, 1658). For Prynne's unrepentant pride in this tactic, see his *A new discovery of some Romish emissaries* (London, 1656), p. 51.

61. J. N. Figgis, "Erastus and Erastianism", *Journal of Theological Studies* ii, especially pp. 65–88, 1900.

62. John Eliot in New England was not *obliged* to give to poorer neighbouring ministers if there were calls on his purse for converting the native Indians, which Baxter put first among 12 good causes for charity: Baxter, *A Christian directory*, pp. 861, 862, 864. Like Prynne's, Baxter's is a significant statement of priorities.

63. B. Reay, "The Muggletonians: an introductory survey", in *The world of the Muggletonians*, Christopher Hill *et al.* (eds) (London, 1983), pp. 46–53.

64. (British Library) Additional MSS 60171, fol. 952.

65. T. Tomkinson, *The Muggletonians principles prevailing* (London, 1695), p. 6.

66. (British Library) Additional MSS 60171, fol. 801.

67. (British Library) Additional MSS 60171, fol. 337.

68. (British Library) Additional MSS 60171, fols. 796–7.

69. M. H. Mackinnon, "The longevity of the thesis: a critique of the critics", in *Weber's Protestant Ethic*, p. 240.

70. A. Woolrych, "Oliver Cromwell and the people of God", pp. 3–4.

71. N. Jones, *God and the money lenders* (Oxford, 1989), pp. 203–4.

72. C. Russell, *Parliaments and English politics* (Oxford, 1979), p. 30.

73. (British Library) Additional MSS 60171, fol. 1043.

74. Muggleton, *The acts of the witnesses of the spirits* (London, 1699), p. 9.

75. (British Library) Additional MSS 60171, fol. 346.

76. (British Library) Additional MSS 60171, fol. 1052–3.

77. (British Library) Additional MSS 61093, fol. 93.

78. S. Parker, *A discourse of ecclesiastical politie* (London, 1670). Peter Burke concludes from his research on North Italy and the Netherlands that "the most efficient economies in early modern Europe were those where the culture and the regime hindered entrepreneurs least": Burke, "Republics of merchants in early modern Europe", p. 291. This is what Parker didn't want to hear.

79. And John Wesley too? For a similar non-Weberian interpretation of another great Protestant divine, see: J. Walsh, "John Wesley and the community of goods", in *Protestant evangelicalism: Britain, Ireland, Germany and America c.1750–c.1950*, K. Robbins (ed.) (Oxford, 1990), pp. 25–50.

Chapter 8

1. L. Festinger *et al.*, *When prophecy fails* (New York, 1956).

2. On all these, the classic study is J. Harrison, *The Second Coming* (London, 1979).

3. L. Gordon, *Shared lives* (London, 1994), p. 18.

4. S. Bercovitch, *The puritan origins of the American self* (New Haven, Conn., 1975); S. Bercovitch, *The American Jeremiad* (Madison, Wis., 1978); S. Bercovitch, *The millennium in America* (New York, 1980).

5. A. Heimert & A. Delbanco (eds), *The puritans in America* (Cambridge, Mass., 1985), p. 91.

6. T. Bozeman, *To live ancient lives* (Chapel Hill, 1988), pp. 82–119 is a trenchant critique of Perry Miller, *Errand into the wilderness* (New York, 1956). F. Bremer, "To live exemplary lives: puritans and puritan commentaries as lofty lights", *The Seventeenth Century* VII(1), pp. 27–39, 1992 qualifies Bozeman to some extent, without in any way reasserting Miller.

7. S. H. Moore, "Popery, purity and Providence: deciphering the New England experiment", in *Religion, culture and society*, A. Fletcher & P. Roberts (eds) (Cambridge, 1994), pp. 257–89.

8. S. Fender, *Sea changes* (Cambridge, 1992), pp. 149–52.

9. K. Kupperman, *Providence Island 1630–1641: the other puritan colony* (Cambridge, 1993), pp. 229, 354. W. Hunt, *The puritan moment* (Cam-

bridge, Mass., 1983), p. 265 similarly sidelines New England, and relates Cromwell's Caribbean expedition in 1656 to the Providence Island aspirations of the 1630s.

10. B. Worden, "Oliver Cromwell and the sin of Achan", pp. 125–45.
11. Heimert & Delbanco, *The puritans in America*, pp. 321–2.
12. (British Library) Additional MSS 60171, fol. 723.
13. (Doctor Williams's Library) *Baxter treatises*, vol. ii, fol. 18v.
14. M. Sylvester (ed.), *Reliquiae Baxterianae,* vol. ii (London, 1696), p. 294.
15. (Doctor Williams's Library) *Baxter treatises*, vol. vii, fols. 3, 3v, 4v, 7.
16. (Doctor Williams's Library) *Baxter treatises*, vol. vi, fol. 301.
17. P. Burke, "The rise of literal-mindedness (an essay)", *Common Knowledge* 2, pp. 108–21, 1993.
18. J. S. Coolidge, *The Pauline renaissance in England* (Oxford, 1970).
19. Galileo, "Letter to the Grand Duchess Christina", in *Discoveries and opinions of Galileo*, S. Drake (ed.) (New York, 1957), pp. 175–216.
20. P. Collinson, *The religion of Protestants* (Oxford, 1982): for the title of his Ford Lectures, he hijacked William Chillingworth's 1638 pamphlet title.
21. N. Cohn, *The pursuit of the millennium* (London, 1957).
22. M. Reeves, "History and eschatology: medieval and early Protestant thought in some English and Scottish writings", *Medievalia et Humanistica*, new series, 4, pp. 99–123, 1973.
23. P. Collinson, *The birthpangs of Protestant England* (London, 1988), p. 12; B. Capp, *The world of John Taylor the water-poet* (Oxford, 1994), p. 17.
24. Cohn, *The pursuit of the millennium*.
25. M. Walzer, *The revolution of the saints* (London, 1966).
26. Samuel Pepys, *Diary*, vol. ii, R. Latham & W. Matthews (eds) (London, 1970), pp. 7, 10, 11.
27. B. Capp, *The Fifth Monarchy Men* (London, 1972), pp. 46–9.
28. F. Kermode, "Spenser and the allegorists", in his *Renaissance essays* (London, 1971), pp. 12–32.
29. D. H. Lawrence, *Apocalypse* (London, 1981), pp. 102, 10, 11, 63, 4.
30. L. Muggleton, *A true interpretation of all the chief texts . . . of the whole book of the Revelation of St John* (London, 1665), p. 51.
31. Lawrence, *Apocalypse*, p. 101.
32. J. Mee, *Dangerous enthusiasm* (Oxford, 1992), p. 12.
33. Muggleton, *A true interpretation*, p. 51.
34. (British Library) Additional MSS 60190, fol. 72.
35. Thompson, *Witness against the beast*, pp. 77–81 and 96–101.
36. (British Library) Additional MSS 60168, no foliation.
37. *Ibid.*
38. (British Library) Additional MSS 60171, fol. 137; Noakes papers, no foliation.
39. (British Library) Additional MSS 60168, no foliation.
40. Muggleton & Reeve, *A divine looking glass*, p. 54.
41. M. Hopkins, *The discovery of witches* (London, 1647).
42. (British Library) Additional MSS 60171, fol. 932.

43. Mee, *Dangerous enthusiasm*, p. 11.
44. Lawrence, *Apocalypse*, p. 3.
45. Muggleton & Reeve, *A divine looking glass*, p. 44.
46. Muggleton, *The answer to William Penn, Quaker* (London, 1753), p. 68.
47. Lawrence, *Apocalypse*, pp. 11, 29.
48. Muggleton, *A true interpretation*, p. 268.
49. Muggleton, *The answer to William Penn, Quaker*, p. 79.
50. Muggleton & Reeve, *A divine looking glass*, p. 205.
51. *Ibid.*, p. 210.
52. *Ibid.*, p. 216.
53. *Ibid.*, p. 246.
54. Muggleton, *A true interpretation*, p. 119.
55. Mee, *Dangerous enthusiasm*, p. 11.
56. Noakes papers, no foliation.
57. (Doctor Williams's Library) *Baxter treatises*, vol. iii, fols. 302–9.
58. Baxter, *The saints everlasting rest*, p. 246.
59. (Doctor Williams's Library) *Baxter treatises*, vol. iii, fol. 303v.
60. Baxter, *The Quakers catechism* (London, 1655), dedicatory epistle; J. Nayler, *An answer to a book called the Quakers catechism* (London, 1655), p. 13.
61. R. Baxter, *A key for Catholicks* (London, 1659), p. 301.
62. Baillie, *Letters and journals*, vol. ii, p. 313.
63. P. J. Olsen, "Was John Foxe a millenarian?" *Journal of Ecclesiastical History* 45, pp. 600–24, 1994; Reeves, "History and eschatology", p. 108.
64. R. Baxter, *A reply to Mr Thomas Beverleys answer* (London, 1691), p. 12.
65. (Doctor Williams's Library) *Baxter treatises*, vol. vii, fol. 45.
66. (Doctor Williams's Library) *Baxter treatises*, vol. ii, fols. 132v–133.
67. (Doctor Williams's Library) *Baxter treatises*, vol. vii, fol. 295v.
68. (Doctor Williams's Library) *Baxter correspondence*, vol. v, fols. 239–40 (Beverley likened Baxter to a father); (Doctor Williams's Library) *Baxter treatises*, vol. vii, fol. 7 (Mather urges Baxter to publish views which he did not wholly endorse).
69. (Doctor Williams's Library) *Baxter correspondence*, vol. ii, fols. 11–12v.
70. Baxter, *The glorious kingdom of Christ*, p. 10.
71. Baxter, *Against the revolt*, p. 102.
72. (Doctor Williams's Library) *Baxter treatises*, vol. vii, fols. 249v, 254, 277.
73. "J. B.", *Kedarminster-Stuff* (London, 1681), p. 16.
74. (Doctor Williams's Library) *Baxter treatises*, vol. ii, fol. 103v.
75. B. W. Ball, *A great expectation* (Leiden, 1975), p. 110.
76. Prynne, *A quench-coale*, pp. 318–19.
77. Prynne, *A catalogue of such testimonies*, pp. 18, 20, 22.
78. W. Prynne, *The unbishoping of Timothy and Titus* (London, 1636), p. 142.
79. W. Prynne, *A looking-glasse for all lordly prelates* (London, 1636), dedicatory epistle, pp. 49, 62, 64.
80. (Bodleian Library) Tanner MSS 69, fol. 1.

81. W. Prynne, *Anti-arminianisme* (London, 1630), p. 81.

82. Prynne, *The antipathie*, vol. i, pp. 132–3.

83. Prynne, *Anti-arminianisme*, p. 97; W. Prynne, *The antipathie*, vol. i, p. 149.

84. *Ibid.*, vol. i, p. 152; W. Prynne, *A breviate of the life of William Laud* (London, 1644), p. 11.

85. *Calendar State Papers Domestic, Charles I, 1640–1641*, p. 312.

86. For which, see (Bodleian Library) Cherry MSS 2, fols. 143–63.

87. Baillie, *Letters and journals*, vol. i, p. 274.

88. Prynne, *The antipathie*, vol. i, p. 334.

89. T. Brightman, *The revelation of the Revelation* (Amsterdam, 1615), p. 507.

90. "Reverend Mr. Brightmans judgment" appended to: A. Dent, *The ruine of Rome* (London, 1656), pp. 14–15.

91. (Anon.), *Brightmans predictions and prophesies . . . written 46 yeares since: concerning the three churches of Germanie, England and Scotland* (London, 1641), pp. 2–3.

92. B. Hubbard, *Sermo Saecularis* (London, 1648), p. 28.

93. R. Vines, *A treatise of the institution, right administration, and receiving of the Sacrament of the Lords Supper* (London, 1656), p. 242; J. Ball, *An answer to two treatises* (London, 1642), pp. 12, 18–21; J. Canne, *A necessity of separation* (London, 1654), p. 33.

94. T. Edwards, *Gangraena*, vol. iii (London, 1646), dedicatory epistle.

95. H. Knollys, *A glimpse of Sions glory* (London, 1641), p. 32.

96. Fuller, *The church history of Britain*, vol. v, p. 383; T. Case, *The quarrell of the covenant* (London, 1643), p. 47; J. Pocklington, *Altare Christianum* (London, 1637), p. 35; P. Heylyn, *A brief and modeste answer* (London, 1637), pp. 4–5.

97. E. Symmons, *Scripture vindicated* (Oxford, 1645), preface.

98. (Anon.), *The second part of Vox Populi* (London, 1642), no pagination.

99. (Anon.), *Scripture and reason pleaded for defensive armes . . . by divers reverend and learned divines* (London, 1643), p. 66.

100. N. Holmes, *The new world or the new reformed church* (London, 1641), p. 72; J. Symonds, *A sermon* (London, 1641), no pagination. Cf. Brightman, *The revelation of the Revelation*, pp. 889–909.

101. T. Case, *The second sermon* (London, 1641), p. 47.

102. Prynne, *The popish royall favourite*, dedicatory epistle.

103. Prynne, *A vindication of foure serious questions*, dedicatory epistle.

104. For evidence see: HMC, *9th Report*, vol. ii, p. 499; W. Walwyn, *A helpe to the right understanding of a discourse concerning independency* (London, 1645), pp. 5–6; W. Prynne, *A true and perfect narrative* (London, 1659), p. 46; W. Prynne, *A seasonable vindication* (London, 1660), p. 89.

105. Prynne, *A vindication of foure serious questions*, p. 54.

106. *Ibid.*, dedicatory epistle.

107. W. Prynne, *Four serious questions* (London, 1645), no pagination.

108. H. Palmer, *A full answer to a printed paper* (London, 1645), p. 5.

109. (Doctor Williams's Library) *Baxter correspondence*, vol. iii, fol. 115.

110. Baxter, *The glorious kingdom of Christ*, pp. 12, 16.

111. J. G. A. Pocock, "Time, history and eschatology in the thought of Thomas Hobbes", in *The diversity of history*, J. H. Elliott & H. G. Koenigsberger (eds) (London, 1970), p. 180.

112. M. Stocker, *Apocalyptic Marvell: the Second Coming in seventeenth-century poetry* (Sussex, 1986); M. Stocker & T. Raylor, "A new Marvell manuscript: Cromwellian patronage and politics", *English Literary Renaissance* 20, pp. 106–162, 1990.

113. B. Worden (ed.), *A voyce from the watch tower*, Camden Society, fourth series, vol. 21, 1978.

114. A. Macfarlane (ed.), *The diary of Ralph Josselin 1616–1683* (Oxford, 1976), pp. xix–xxii.

115. M. Forey, "Francis Bacon and the Apocalypse" (University of Sussex Work-in-Progress Seminar, 27 October 1994): her published study is eagerly awaited.

116. E. Gosse, *Father and son* (London, 1959), pp. 56–8.

117. Lawrence, *Apocalypse*, p. 63.

Chapter 9

1. G. R. Cragg, *From puritanism to the age of reason* (London, 1950).

2. B. Rosenthal, *Salem story* (Cambridge, 1993), p. 216.

3. N. Keeble & G. Nuttall (eds), *Calendar of the correspondence of Richard Baxter*,vol. ii (Oxford, 1991), p.307.

4. C. Hansen, *Witchcraft at Salem* (New York, 1969), p. 118.

5. P. Miller, *The New England mind: from colony to province* (Boston, 1953), p. 191.

6. Hansen, *Witchcraft at Salem*, p. 143.

7. M. Hopkins, *The discovery of witches* (London, 1647), p. 10. The *exceptionality* of the witch-finding movement of 1645 in Essex is well brought out in: A. Macfarlane, *Witchcraft in Tudor and Stuart England* (London, 1970), pp. 135–42. He is more ready to accept the witch-finders' *post facto* defence of their motives at face value, however, than the present writer, which does not mean that one has then to subscribe to the view that Hopkins and his colleague, John Stearne, were simply "black-hearted villains leading on an innocent populace" (p. 140). These polarities seem unhelpful.

8. J. Sharpe, "Witchcraft in seventeenth-century Yorkshire" (Borthwick Paper no. 81, University of York, 1992), p. 22.

9. This comment on the different ways that English puritans felt about witches compared with their Scottish counterparts is quoted as part of the evidence for English superciliousness about Scottish backwardness: D. Hirst, "The English Republic and the meaning of Britain", *Journal of Modern History*

66, p. 474, 1994.

10. Rosenthal, *Salem story*, p. 209 shows how tenacious is the belief that Salem witches were burned at the stake.

11. The assumption that puritans went in for whipping beggars had an early challenge in a well-researched local study: A. L. Beier, "Poor relief in Warwickshire 1630–1660", *Past and Present* 35, pp. 77–100, 1961.

12. M. Walzer, *The revolution of the saints* (London, 1966), p. 300 calls Calvinism "an agent of modernization, an ideology of the transition period". When historians hear the phrase "the transition period", it is time to reach for their revolvers. His critique of Marxist historiography is to be found in his "Puritanism as a revolutionary ideology", *History and Theory* 3, pp. 63–5, 1963–4.

13. *Ibid.*, p. 116. One letter to Peter Martyr in 1559 is enough to convince Walzer that Jewel was homesick for Zurich.

14. D. Ward, *The life of Henry More* (London, 1710), pp. 134–7, 166, 181.

15. S. T. Coleridge, *Notes on English divines*, vol. i, D. Coleridge (ed.) (London, 1853), p. 250.

16. B. Worden, *A voyce from the watch tower*.

17. A. Macfarlane, *The diary of Ralph Josselin*, pp. xx–xxii on its predecessors.

18. Powicke, *A life of the Reverend Richard Baxter*, pp. 258–61.

19. T. Huff, *The rise of early modern science: Islam, China and the West* (Cambridge, 1993); W. Eamon, *Science and the secrets of Nature* (Princeton Univ., NJ, 1994).

20. S. Shapin, *A social history of truth* (Chicago, 1994), pp. 201, 212, 191. Boyle, as much as Baxter, was alert to the apocalyptic implications of the "new science": M. Oster, "Millenarianism and the new science: the case of Robert Boyle", in *Samuel Hartlib and universal reformation: studies in intellectual communication*, M. Greengrass *et al.* (eds) (Cambridge, 1994), pp. 137–48. Oster (p. 148) sensibly argues that Boyle's interest did not go so far as Baxter's belief in a future millennium, but equally sensibly makes the point that Baxter's own concession of the *probability* (though, note, even here not the *certainty*) of some such future rule is confined to the prison manuscripts which he kept *in secret* (see Chapter 8).

21. R. Baxter, *The certainty of the worlds of spirits* (London, 1691), pp. 18, 63.

22. Lamont, The two "national churches" of 1691 and 1829, pp. 342–4.

23. Keeble & Nuttall (eds), *Calendar of the correspondence of Richard Baxter*, vol. i, pp. 227, 317.

24. *Ibid.*, vol. ii, p. 307.

25. *Ibid.*, vol. ii, pp. 7, 40, 43, 44, 45.

26. R. Baxter, *Plain scripture proof* (London, 1653), p. 148.

27. Baxter, *Catholick theologie*, vol. 1, pt. i, pp. 76–7.

28. (Doctor Williams's Library) *Baxter correspondence*, vol. v, fols. 217–217v.

29. Baxter, *Catholick theologie*, vol. 1, pt. 3, pp. 107–16.

30. T. Edwards, *Baxterianism barefaced* (London, 1699), p. 408.

31. On Catholic fideism see: L. I. Bredvold, *The intellectual milieu of John*

Dryden (Ann Arbor, Mich., 1956), pp. 73–129.

32. J. Cope, *Joseph Glanvill: Anglican apologist* (St Louis, 1956), pp. 7, 9, 13, 15, 50, 51, 62.

33. (Doctor Williams's Library) *Baxter correspondence*, vol. vi, fols. 123–5.

34. K. Thomas, *Religion and the decline of magic* (London, 1971), pp. 110–11.

35. (Doctor Williams's Library) *Baxter correspondence*, vol. iv, fol. 255.

36. (Doctor Williams's Library) *Baxter correspondence*, vol. i, fol. 217v.

37. R. Baxter, *The successive visibility of the Church* (London, 1660), pp. 164–5.

38. On which see: Thomas, *Religion and the decline of magic*, p. 111; C. G. Whiting, *Studies in English puritanism* (London, 1931), pp. 547–51; B. W. Ball, *A great expectation* (London, 1975), pp. 111–14.

39. R. Baxter, *The life of faith* (London, 1670), p. 142.

40. R. Baxter, *A key for Catholicks* (London, 1659), pp. 184–5.

41. Baxter, *The certainty of the worlds of spirits*, p. 43.

42. (British Library) Egerton MSS 2570, fol. 88v.

43. Baxter, *The certainty of the worlds of spirits*, pp. 41–2.

44. *Ibid.*, pp. 60, 182, 178, 250, 251.

45. Shapin, *A social history of truth*, p. 333.

46. J. Glanvill, *Sadducismus triumphans* (London, 1666), p. 55.

47. Quoted in Shapin, *A social history of truth*, p. 411.

48. Quoted in Huff, *The rise of early modern science*, p. 357.

49. C. Webster, *The Great Instauration, science, medicine and reform 1626–1660* (London, 1975).

50. J. Martin, *Francis Bacon, the state, and the reform of natural philosophy* (Cambridge, 1992), p. 175.

51. M. Hunter, *Science and society in Restoration England* (Cambridge, 1981), p. 26.

52. (Doctor Williams's Library) *Baxter correspondence*, vol. iv, fol. 43.

53. A. Clark (ed.), *The life and times of Anthony Wood*, vol. ii (Oxford, 1891), pp. 110–11.

54. J. Milward, *Diary*, C. Robbins (ed.) (Cambridge, 1938), pp. 288–9.

55. J. G. A. Pocock, *The ancient constitution and the feudal law* (Cambridge, 1951), p. 167, on Prynne: "in essentials a survivor from the age of Coke".

56. W. Prynne, *Mount-Orgueil* (London, 1641), no pagination.

57. Sir Robert Filmer, *The freeholders grand inquest touching our Soveraigne Lord the King and his Parliament* (London, 1648), pp. 4, 5, 13.

58. On which, see the full discussion in M. Mendle, *Dangerous positions* (Alabama, 1985).

59. Filmer, *The freeholders grand inquest*, pp. 18–19, 30, 48.

60. W. Prynne, *The soveraigne powers of Parliaments*, vol. i (London, 1643), p. 43.

61. W. Prynne, *A plea for the Lords* (London, 1648), dedicatory epistle.

62. W. Prynne, *Irenarches Redivivus* (London, 1648), pp. 28–9, 42–4.

63. W. Prynne, *The first part of a brief register* (London, 1659), pp. 422, 440, 446.

64. W. Holdsworth, *A history of English law*, vol. v (London, 1955), p. 407.

65. W. Prynne, *Brief animadversions* (London, 1669), p. 7.

66. W. Prynne, *Aurum reginae* (London, 1668), dedicatory epistle.

67. W. Prynne, *The fourth part of a brief register* (London, 1664), pp. 604–6, 625, 640.

68. W. Cobbett (ed.), *Parliamentary history of England*, vol. iv (London, 1808), p. 163.

69. Prynne, *The fourth part of a brief register*, pp. 696, 840–50.

70. (British Library) Stowe MSS 302, fols. 48v–49.

71. J. Nalson, *An impartial collection of the great affairs of state*, vol. i (London, 1682), p. 798.

72. W. Prynne, *A memorable New-Years gift* (London, 1727), p. xxvi.

73. (British Library) Additional MSS 71532, fol. 5v; Additional MSS 71534, fol. 14.

74. W. Prynne, *The Levellers levelled to the very ground* (London, 1648), p. 20; W. Prynne, *The second part of a short demurrer* (London, 1656), p. 142.

75. "Pisteuo-Daimon", *The witch of Endor* (London, 1736), pp. iv, 3, 41, xix, 98–100.

76. R. Filmer, *Collection of tracts* (London, 1684), pp. 337–8.

77. L. Muggleton, *A true interpretation of the witch of Endor* (London, 1669), pp. 5, 12, 13, 15, 26, 64, 68, 70.

78. R. Scot, *The discoverie of witchcraft* (London, 1584); J. Webster, *The displaying of supposed witchcraft* (London, 1677).

79. Thompson, *Witness against the beast*, pp. 91, 9, 228.

80. P. Anderson, "Diary", *London Review of Books*, 21 October 1993, pp. 24–5.

81. R. Baxter, *The scripture-gospel defended*, vol. ii (London, 1690), p. 49.

82. R. Baxter, *Richard Baxter's confutation of a dissertation for the justification of infidels* (London, 1654), p. 288.

83. Baxter, *A Christian directory*, vol. iv, p. 214.

84. Tawney, *Religion and the rise of capitalism*, p. 205.

85. This absurdity has been wittily exposed in C. Condren, *The language of politics in seventeenth-century England* (London, 1994): see particularly his devastating attack on modern historians for their confusion of "resistance" with "rebellion" (pp. 115–31) and his argument that seventeenth-century "radicalism" is in the eye of the beholder (pp. 140–68).

86. J. Updike, *Roger's version* (London, 1986), pp. 32, 152.

87. At least that was what Muggleton said about the evolution of his beliefs in his posthumous memoirs, *The acts of the witnesses of the spirits*, p. 25: "for I believed the Soul was Mortal many Years before, which Belief yielded me much Peace of Mind, and was in Hope God would never raise me again".

88. (British Library) Additional MSS 60168, no foliation. Lawrence Clarkson in his *A parodoxical dialogue betwixt Faith and Reason* of 1660 asked: "for what delight could a man have with his wife, if she had no person?"

89. Updike, *Roger's version*, pp. 11, 41.

Guide to further reading

Chapters 1–4: Puritans

W. Lamont, *Puritanism and the English Revolution* (Aldershot, 1991) in three volumes – i, *Marginal Prynne*; vol. ii, *Godly rule*; vol. iii, *Richard Baxter and the millennium* – contains fuller references to William Prynne and Richard Baxter.

On Muggleton, see: C. Hill *et al.*, *The world of the Muggletonians* (London, 1983); W. Lamont, "The Muggletonians: a 'vertical' approach", *Past and Present* **99**, pp. 22–40, 1983 and the debate between W. Lamont & C. Hill, "The Muggletonians", *Past and Present* **104**, pp. 153–63, 1984.

The best starting point for students of puritanism is P. Collinson's brief *English puritanism*, Historical Association General Series **106**, 1983. For students bewildered by technical theological terms, there is the invaluable Appendix II, "Terminology", in *Tudor puritanism*, M. M. Knappen (Chicago, 1939), pp. 487–93. Knappen as a textbook, however, has been superseded by the definitive work on Elizabethan puritanism: P. Collinson, *The Elizabethan puritan movement* (London, 1967). Other important Collinson contributions are: his collection of essays, *Godly people* (London, 1983) and his *The religion of Protestants* (Oxford, 1982). P. Lake, *Anglicans and puritans?* (London, 1988) is another excellent introduction.

The early Stuart church 1603–1642, K. Fincham (ed.) (London, 1993) is a collection of essays in the valuable "Problems in focus" series which summarize well many of the current findings on puritanism. "William Laud deserves to rank among the greatest archbishops of Canterbury since the Reformation" is the opening sentence of Nicholas Tyacke's essay in that volume ("William Laud", pp. 51–70). We can almost anticipate: "Discuss". It is certainly not the puritan perspective on Laud offered in this book, and is none the worse for that.

Anthony Milton, *The Laudians and the Church of Rome c. 1625–1640* (unpublished PhD thesis University of Cambridge, 1989), examines the substance behind puritan fears of a "popish" take-over: the publication of this important work is eagerly awaited. Meanwhile two excellent works have recently thrown light on this phobia: C. Hibbard, *Charles I and the Popish Plot* (Chapel Hill, 1983) and J. Ohlmeyer, *Civil War and Restoration in the three Stuart kingdoms: the career of Randal MacDonnell, Marquis of Antrim, 1609–1683* (Cambridge, 1993); the latter's debate with M. P. Maxwell can be followed in *The Historical Journal* **35**, pp. 905–19, 1992 and 37, pp. 421–38, 1994.

Christopher Hill, *The English Bible and the seventeenth-century Revolution* (London, 1993) is only the most recent of many distinguished works by a master historian on the nature of puritanism. He is criticized, along with almost everybody else who has ever written about puritanism, in C. H. George's stimulating article, "Puritanism as history and historiography", *Past and Present* **41**, pp. 77–104, 1968. A more searching, but not unsympathetic, critique of Hill's methodology is to be found in: W. Dray, "Causes, individuals and ideas in Christopher Hill's interpretation of the English Revolution", in *Court, county and culture*, B. Y. Kunze & D. D. Brautigan (eds) (Rochester, 1992), pp. 21–40.

Finally, the historians can learn much from literary scholars about the nature of puritanism, and no work has seemed to me more compelling recently in that context than: J. Stachniewski, *The persecutory imagination: English puritanism and the literature of religious despair* (Oxford, 1991).

Chapter 5: Puritanism and revolution

Michael Walzer, in his *The revolution of the saints* (London, 1966), p. x, made clear that his case for linking puritanism with revolution rested not upon the fringe groups, where it would be easy to do so, and they have in any case now been comprehensively handled in Christopher Hill's *The world turned upside down* (London, 1972), but with "the Puritan mainstream, the true English Calvinists". The argument in Chapter 5 is that this is over-ambitious for reasons argued there, but it is still an exciting introduction to the topic for students, and should be read in conjunction with his article, "Puritanism as a revolutionary ideology", *History and Theory* **3** pp. 59–90, 1963–4.

We know more about the nature of the English Revolution than when Walzer nailed his theses at – Geneva? – and works particularly significant are: J. Morrill, *The nature of the English Revolution* (London, 1993); C. Russell, *The causes of the English Civil War* (Oxford, 1990); A. Fletcher, *The outbreak of the English Civil War* (London, 1981); A. Hughes, *The causes of the English Civil War* (London, 1991). Much has been written on the incarnation of revolutionary puritanism – Oliver Cromwell – but not as yet a definitive full-length biography. B. Coward's *Oliver Cromwell* (London, 1991) is a good, brief, introductory biography.

Best of the recent research is to be found in the essays edited by J. Morrill, *Oliver Cromwell and the English Revolution* (London, 1990). Cromwell as Hitler was always a loony idea, put to rest in an important article by A. Woolrych, "The Cromwellian Protectorate: a military dictatorship?", *History* 75, pp. 207–31, 1990.

Some of the strange stereotypes favoured by different generations are to be found in: R. C. Richardson (ed.), *Images of Cromwell* (Manchester, 1993). The outstanding essay in this collection is by T. Barnard, "Irish images of Cromwell", pp. 180–206, which are not as straightforward as one might suppose. Christopher Hill, *God's Englishman* (London, 1970) is less a biography than a series of essays on Cromwell, of which his views on "Providence" are particularly acute.

Other excellent works on "Providence" are: B. Worden, "Providence and politics in Cromwellian England", *Past and Present* 109, pp. 55–99, 1985; B. Worden, "Oliver Cromwell and the sin of Achan", in *History, society and the churches*, D. Beales & G. Best (eds) (Cambridge, 1983), pp. 125–46; B. Donagan, "Providence, chance and explanation: some paradoxical aspects of puritan views of causation", *Journal of Religious History* 11, pp. 385–403, 1981; J. C. Davis, "Against formality: one aspect of the English Revolution", *Transactions of the Royal Historical Society*, sixth series, III, pp. 265–88, 1993; A. Walsham, "'The Fatal Vesper': providentialism and anti-popery in late Jacobean England", *Past and Present* 144, pp. 36–87, 1994.

Chapter 6: Puritanism and liberty

"Toleration is a Victorian subject: a monument to Victorian liberalism": thus begins Blair Worden's essay, "Toleration and the Cromwellian Protectorate", in *Studies in Church History*, vol. 21, W. Sheils (ed.) (London, 1984), pp. 199–233. The failure of an older group of historians to recognize that insight vitiates some of their conclusions: for example, W. K. Jordan, *The development of religious toleration in England*, [4 vols] (London, 1932–1940); W. Haller, *Liberty and reformation in the Puritan Revolution* (New York, 1955); W. Haller (ed.), *Tracts on liberty in the Puritan Revolution, 1638–1647* (New York, 1934). The best recent survey, which builds upon Worden's point with subtlety, is: J. C. Davis, "Religion and the struggle for freedom in the English Revolution", *The Historical Journal* 35, pp. 507–30, 1992.

It is good to have now the definitive edition of William Walwyn's writings, as he was one puritan for whom liberty was unarguably central to his thought: *The writings of William Walwyn*, J. R. McMichael & B. Taft (eds) (Athens, Ga., 1989).

Hobbes and liberty would once have seemed an odd coupling, by contrast, but not now: Q. Skinner, "Thomas Hobbes and the proper signification of liberty", *Transactions of the Royal Historical Society*, fifth series, **40**, pp. 121–52, 1990; R. Tuck, "The civil religion of Thomas Hobbes", in *Political discourse in early modern Britain*, N. Phillipson & Q. Skinner (eds) (Cambridge, 1993), pp. 120–38.

See W. Lamont, "Arminianism: the controversy that never was", *ibid.*, pp. 45–66 on the relationship between Arminianism and liberty: a theme also explored in H. Trevor-Roper, *Catholics, Anglicans and Puritans* (London, 1987).

The dangers of bandying such words as "liberty" about, without sensitivity to their seventeenth-century uses, is discussed in a general way in: C. Condren, *The language of politics in seventeenth-century England* (London, 1994); and in a specific way which relates to the theme of this chapter in: *Freedom and the English Revolution*, R. C. Richardson & G. M. Ridden (eds) (Manchester, 1986), especially pp. 1–21.

Chapter 7: Puritanism and capitalism

We must begin with Max Weber, *The Protestant Ethic and the spirit of capitalism* (London, 1904–5), and we now have a first-class volume which lists the controversies and offers up-to-date reappraisals of Weber: *Weber's Protestant Ethic: origins, evidence, contexts*, H. Lehmann & G. Roth (eds) (Cambridge, 1993).

Not much on puritanism but much on capitalism in: *Europe and the rise of capitalism*, J. Baechler *et al.* (eds) (Oxford, 1988). Not much on capitalism but much on puritanism in: *International Calvinism*, M. Prestwich (ed.) (Oxford, 1985). R. H. Tawney, *Religion and the rise of capitalism* (London, 1926) has much on both in a sympathetic, but critical, adaptation of Weber's thesis to England. His hunches about changing views on usury have been vindicated, according to Norman Jones, *God and the money-lenders: usury and law in early modern England* (Oxford, 1989), although the confidence of his claim that, as early as the beginning of the seventeenth century, economics was divorced from religion, inspires unease.

Malcolm Kitch, *Capitalism and the Reformation* (London, 1967), with its nice blend of primary and secondary sources, gives the students an opportunity to weigh up Norman Jones's thesis for themselves. The Protestant Ethic is seen rampant and triumphant in Dorchester (D. Underdown, *Fire from heaven* (London, 1992)), and in Terling (K. Wrightson, *Poverty and piety in an English village* (London, 1979)); but it works less effectively as an explanation in studies of individuals (R. C. Latham, "Roger Lowe, shopkeeper and nonconformist", *History* (June 1941), pp. 19–35; P. S. Seaver, "The puritan work ethic revisited", *Journal of British Studies* **19**, pp. 35–53, 1980) or of counties (A. L. Beier, "Poor relief in Warwickshire 1630–1660", *Past and Present* **35** (December 1966), pp. 77–100) or by other commentators

(Patrick Collinson, "Cranbrook and the Fletchers: popular and unpopular religion in the Kentish Weald", in his *Godly People* (London, 1983), pp. 399–428).

Eamon Duffy, "The godly and the multitude in Stuart England", *The Seventeenth Century* i, pp. 31–55, 1986, provides the most impressive rebuttal of the thesis that the godly were hostile to the poor. R. B. Schlatter, *The social ideas of religious leaders 1660–1688* (New York, 1971) is in a better position than Weber or Tawney to show how one of the godly (Baxter) was anything but hostile to the poor, since unlike them he could refer to the Baxter pamphlet, *The poor husbandman's advocate* published posthumously in 1926. He correctly calls it "one of the few important works of social criticism written by a divine of the period", but then devalues its importance by following Tawney's lead, and taking the political passivity of Baxter's *A Christian directory* at face value. Why he should not have done so, is argued in Chapter 7.

Chapter 8: Puritanism and millenarianism

The millennial vision that inspires reformers is well captured in J. Spence's *The gate of heavenly peace: the Chinese and their revolution, 1895–1980* (London, 1982). The epigraph he chooses for this volume on Chinese revolutionary intellectuals is actually from Milton's *Areopagitica*, in which the puritan revolutionary looks forward to a millennium beginning in five months' time; five *weeks*, if people put their minds to it.

The way in which millenarianism inspired revolutionary fervour is recorded in detail in the classic work by Norman Cohn, *The pursuit of the millennium* (London, 1957). But, since Cohn, there have been historians who have emphasized the ways in which millenarianism could bolster authority as well as subvert it: K. Firth, *The apocalyptic tradition in Reformation Britain* (Oxford, 1979); Christopher Hill, *Antichrist in seventeenth-century England* (Oxford, 1971); B. W. Ball, *A great expectation* (Leiden, 1975); P. Christianson, *Reformers and Babylon* (Toronto, 1978) and his "From expectation to militance: reformers and Babylon in the first two years of the Long Parliament", *Journal of Ecclesiastical History* 24, pp. 225–44, 1973.

The influence of Joachim has been recognized in two volumes: M. Reeves, *The influence of prophecy in the later Middle Ages: a study in Joachimism* (Oxford, 1969); *Prophecy and millenarianism: essays in honour of Marjorie Reeves*, A. Williams (ed.) (London, 1980). The influence of Foxe was argued by Haller in: W. Haller, "John Foxe and the puritan revolution", in *The Seventeenth Century*, R. F. Jones (ed.) (Stanford, 1951); and in his *Foxe's Book of Martyrs and the Elect Nation* (London, 1963). Palle Olsen has asked "Was John Foxe a millenarian?", *Journal of Ecclesiastical History* 45, pp. 610–24, 1994, and has answered "No, but . . .". Which is the conclusion that

Marjorie Reeves, expert on Joachimism, came to when she studied how much of seventeenth-century puritan revolutionary thought drew on earlier antecedents: "History and eschatology: medieval and early Protestant thought in some English and Scottish writings", *Medievalia et Humanistica*, new series, 4, pp. 99–123, 1973.

From Foxe – to Brightman – to the millennial "errand into the wilderness" is the thesis developed in Avihu Zakai, *Exile and kingdom: history and apocalypse in the puritan migration to America* (Cambridge, 1992). This millennial interpretation of the migration is also to be found in: P. Miller, *Errand into the wilderness* (New York, 1956); S. Bercovitch, *The American jeremiad* (Wisconsin, 1978); W. McLoughin, *Revivals, awakenings and reform: an essay on religion and social change in America* (Chicago, 1978). But it has been convincingly challenged in: T. Bozeman, *To live ancient lives* (North Carolina, 1988); D. Cressy, *Coming over* (Cambridge, 1987); S. Fender, *Sea changes* (Cambridge, 1992); S. Hardman Moore, "Popery, purity and providence: deciphering the New England experiment", in *Religion, culture and society in early modern Britain*, A. Fletcher & P. Roberts (eds) (Cambridge, 1994), pp. 257–89.

That the "New England experiment" meant less to English puritanism than the "Providence Island experiment" is the thesis argued well by Karen Kupperman, *Providence Island 1630–1641: the other puritan colony* (Cambridge, 1993). E. P. Thompson's posthumous *Witness against the beast* (Cambridge, 1993) is a worthy last work from a great historian.

Chapter 9: Puritanism and reason (witches and science)

Keith Thomas, *Religion and the decline of magic* (London, 1971) remains the best introduction to the student of the complex interconnections between "Reason", science and witchcraft. Alan Macfarlane, *Witchcraft in Tudor and Stuart England* (London, 1970) draws on the evidence of Assize and Quarter Sessions records to show us what Essex Man in the sixteenth and seventeenth century thought about witches. Both of these were pioneering works, yet the feeling persists that they underplayed the gender issue. See (for England) C. Larner, *Witchcraft and religion: the politics of popular belief* (Oxford, 1984) and (for America) C. Karlsen, *The Devil in the shape of a woman* (New York, 1987). There is a very good article addressed to that theme: C. Holmes, "Women: witnesses and witches", *Past and Present* **140** (August 1993), pp. 45–78. And see also his "Popular culture: witches, magistrates and divines in early modern England", in *Understanding popular culture: Europe from the Middle Ages to the 19th century*, S. Kaplan (ed.) (Berlin, 1984), pp. 85–111.

Jim Sharpe also has raised the gender issue in an interesting form: "Witchcraft and women in seventeenth-century England: some Northern evidence", *Continuity and change* 6 (2), pp. 179–99, 1991 and *Witchcraft in seventeenth-century Yorkshire: accusations and countermeasures* (Borthwick Paper, University of York, 81, 1992), pp. 1–28. Two good essays on James I's change of mind about witches are: S. Clark, "King James's daemonologie", in *The damned art*, S. Anglo (ed.) (London, 1977), pp. 156–81, and C. Larner, "James VI and I and witchcraft", in *The Reign of James VI and I*, A. G. R. Smith (ed.) (London, 1973), pp. 74–90. Stuart Clark, "Inversion, misrule and the meaning of witchcraft", *Past and Present* 87 (May 1980), pp. 98–127 is a brilliant essay on the conceptual significance of witchcraft.

Bernard Rosenthal, *Salem story* (Cambridge, 1993) is a cool and persuasive study of the witch trials of 1692. Among the vast literature on the subject particularly to be commended are: J. Demos, *Entertaining Satan* (Oxford, 1982); P. Boyer & S. Nissenbaum, *Salem possessed* (Harvard, 1974) and (with some reservations) C. Hansen, *Witchcraft at Salem* (New York, 1978).

In 1938, R. K. Merton formulated a link between puritanism and science: his work was reprinted, with the author's updated preface, as *Science, technology and society in seventeenth-century England* (New York, 1970). The ensuing controversies are usefully documented in: *Puritanism and the rise of modern science: the Merton Thesis*, I. B. Cohen (ed.) (Rutgers, 1990). Christopher Hill, *Intellectual origins of the English Revolution* (Oxford, 1965) developed the Merton Thesis, and raised an interesting controversy with Hugh Kearney and others, mainly in the journal *Past and Present*. That debate is now helpfully collated in one volume, *The intellectual revolution of the seventeenth century* (London, 1974), C. Webster (ed.).

Charles Webster's personal contribution to the debate was a significant one: *The Great Instauration: science, medicine and reform 1626–1660* (London, 1975). Despite the dates in the title, the bulk of the book and the thrust of the argument centres on the 1650s "Baconian" attempt to remodel society.

Hugh Kearney, *Origins of the scientific revolution* (London, 1964) deftly weaves primary and secondary extracts to form a useful quarry for the student. The geographical range of *The scientific revolution in national context*, R. Porter & M. Teich (eds) (Cambridge, 1992) makes this volume useful.

There have been a number of good books recently on the rise of science (others are to be found in the bibliographies of these works): M. Hunter, *Science and society in Restoration England* (Cambridge, 1981); T. E. Huff, *The rise of early modern science: Islam, China and the West* (Cambridge, 1993); W. Eamon, *Science and the secrets of nature* (Princeton Univ., NJ, 1994); S. Shapin, *A social history of truth* (Chicago, 1994).

Arthur Koestler, *The Sleepwalkers* (London, 1959) is an idiosyncratic but stimulating statement of the correlation between scientific discovery and *"unreason"*, a proposition that Baxter would have rejected because of his respect for "reason", and Muggleton because of his disregard for "science".

Index